3/93 W1015

69483

338.7 F
Ferguson, Charles H.
Computer wars

NO LONGER OWNED
BY
HOLDREGE PUBLIC LIBRARY

D0122500

Holdrege Public Library
Holdrege, Nebr. 68949

GAYLORD M

ALSO BY CHARLES R. MORRIS

The Coming Global Boom

Iron Destinies, Lost Opportunities:
The Arms Race Between the U.S.A. and the U.S.S.R.,
1945–1987

A Time of Passion: America, 1960–1980

The Cost of Good Intentions:
New York City and the Liberal Experiment

COMPUTER WARS

COMPUTER WARS

How the West Can Win in a Post-IBM World

CHARLES H. FERGUSON

AND

CHARLES R. MORRIS

TIMES T BOOKS

RANDOM HOUSE

Holdrege Public Library
Holdrege, Nebr. 68949

For Carl Kaysen and Beverly De Shiro

Copyright © 1993 by Charles H. Ferguson and Charles R. Morris

All rights reserved under International and Pan-American Copyright Conventions. Published in the United States by Times Books, a division of Random House, Inc., New York, and simultaneously in Canada by Random House of Canada Limited, Toronto.

ISBN: 0-8129-2156-9

Book design by Naomi Osnos and M. Kristen Bearse

Manufactured in the United States of America

9 8 7 6 5 4 3 2

First Edition

ACKNOWLEDGMENTS

Authors invariably impose on friends, family, and colleagues. Many people contributed in many different ways to the book's completion. We should like to thank Mary Ann McGrail, Andrew Kerr, Feisal Nanji, Chris Waldman, Liz Givoni, Melanie McArthur, Denise Brouillette, Ann Faulk, Beverly Morris, and Kathleen Morris. Charles Ferguson would also like to thank Charlotte Ferguson, Laura Dinwiddie Kritchfield, Marc Gorenstein, Joe Farrell, Suzanne Scotchmer, John Seely Brown, Susan Haviland, Paul Ricci, Roger Levien, Rocky Nevin, John Missouris, Chris and Lisa Suits, and many friends at MIT, Harvard, and Xerox PARC. McKinsey & Company kindly permitted us the use of their extensive computer industry data base. We are extremely appreciative of the many men and women, including many past and present executives of IBM, who took time out from their busy schedules to submit to lengthy and sometimes repeated interviews. Finally, our thanks to Peter Osnos, Paul Golob, Naomi Osnos, Della Smith, and Nancy Inglis at Times Books and to our agent, Tim Seldes.

69483

CONTENTS

Part III · Prospects and Opportunities

INTRODUCTION

IBM's chairman, John F. Akers, finally had a temper tantrum. Akers is a *Fortune* magazine cover photographer's ideal of what an American chief executive should look like—steel-gray hair, piercing blue eyes, firm jaw, tall, lean, calm, direct. But here was Akers at an April 1992 seminar for top managers, "goddamn mad." IBM, he thundered, was losing shares in all its markets, with no upturn in sight. The company's "tension level is not high enough," Akers accused. If IBM's managers and their people "can't change fast enough . . . good-bye."

Firing people at IBM used to be unheard of. But IBM had cut its work force by almost fifty thousand people in five years, with no visible result. In 1991, for the first time in IBM's history, its sales, at $62 billion, were lower than in the previous year. In the twelve months before Akers exploded, the company had lost $500 million. IBM's market share was down in virtually every product line. A stockholder who bought IBM in 1987, the stock's last peak, would have lost almost 7 percent a year on his investment, *after* taking into account his 5 percent annual dividend.

IBM is no ordinary American company. It is the Bluest of the Blue Chips, the best company in the world in the world's most important industry. The electronics and computer industry is not only the world's biggest but also the one on which almost all other technological progress depends. Whether a business is making cars or television sets or medical equipment, or trying to run the best banks or hotels, its use of computer technology is more and more the difference between winning and losing. As long as IBM was their top company, Americans never had to worry about their standing in computer technology. IBM *was* computer technology. It was not just the flagship of American high technology industry; it was almost the entire navy. In the 1970s, IBM's computer sales were bigger than those of all other computer companies in the world combined. Even now, IBM's share of the world market in computers is about the same as Japan's.

The decline and fall of IBM is therefore a major event. And despite Akers's new fighting mood, there is a serious possibility that IBM is finished as a force in the industry. Bill Gates, the software tycoon whom everybody in the industry loves to hate, denies having said in an unguarded moment that IBM "will fold in seven years." But Gates may be right. IBM is now an also-ran in almost every major computer technology introduced since 1980. That is alarming enough; that it took Akers, who has been CEO for seven years, until 1992 to recognize it is even more alarming. IBM has a lead position only in traditional mainframes and minicomputers, which together with related software, services, and equipment account for more than two thirds of IBM's sales and much more than 100 percent of its profits. Traditional big computers are not going to disappear overnight, but they are old technology, and the realm in which they hold sway is steadily shrinking. The brontosaurus moved deeper into the swamps when the mammals took over the forest, but one day it ran out of swamps.

At a time when America is locked in a battle for technological supremacy with Japan, the collapse of IBM is a major event. Stagnation at General Motors meant the loss of leadership in the automobile industry to Japan. IBM's demise could be even more serious. The two cases are not strictly parallel, however. General Motors slipped in all aspects of its business—technology, design, production, management. IBM's problems can be pinned much more directly on its management; during its fifteen-year slide, it possessed much of the world's best computer technology, it invested massively, and in key computer components, its manufacturing and process technologies matched any in the world. But IBM's managers were very late to understand the fundamental changes afoot in the industry, changes they had often initiated, and IBM quickly slipped from being market leader to an also-ran in a broad range of products. Akers is betting that a reorganization of IBM into smaller companies will help, but it is already very late.

This is not an alarmist book. We are both business consultants and writers. One of us (Ferguson) has been deeply involved in this debate for more than a decade—as the author of numerous articles, as a member of government and industry study commissions, and as a person who has testified before the U.S. Congress—and has been a leading spokesman for a pessimistic view: that the great Japanese advantage in manufacturing and process technology will inevitably result in their seizing world leadership in computer technology. The other of us (Morris) has argued in a book and articles that innovative computer design and software from newer American companies, such as the ones that have sprung up in California's Silicon Valley, will determine the industry's future.

We now believe that neither the pessimistic nor the optimistic argument is the correct one. We believe that American technological leadership can survive the demise of IBM. It is becoming clear that the Japanese manufacturing advantage by itself has not been, and will not be, sufficient to dominate the computer industry—Japanese competitors were far from the major factor in IBM's decline. But it is also clear that the great software and design skills of the smaller American firms are by themselves too fragile a base on which to build a Western resurgence. But we strongly believe that Western, and particularly American, firms are in a strong position to recover the technology initiative *if* they apply the correct strategies.

It is hard to exaggerate how important it is for America to prevail in, or at least not lose, the computer wars. Computers and electronics are not normal industries. In the first place, they are very large. Global computer industry sales are more than $200 billion annually; sales for the total global electronics industry are in excess of $800 billion, making it the largest in the world. American computer industry employment is more than 400,000. But far more important than the gross size of the computer industry is its fundamental role in national competitiveness. Leadership in almost all major industries—manufacturing, financial services, medical diagnostics, even entertainment—now depends to a great degree on a country's prowess in computers and electronics. The next generation of consumer electronic products, such as digital televisions, will have powerful computers inside them. Slippage in computers means slippage everywhere.

The decline of IBM is thus a critical event in America's drive to improve its national competitiveness. Understanding what happened to IBM not only provides important insights into the fundamental forces driving the industry in the 1990s but also points the way to winning strategies for American companies in this crucial decade. Part I of this book, then, is the story of IBM's rise to dominance in its industry and its dramatically accelerating decline. We have tried to tell the story from a point of view inside IBM. IBM executives are extremely intelligent; we think it is crucial to understand what they thought they were doing as their company drifted away from the path of success. Our prime source of material, therefore, was extended interviews with dozens of senior IBM executives, many of them now retired but some still with the company. Most of them were angry—they were acutely aware of their company's decline—and were not only willing but often eager to talk to us. With few exceptions, for obvious reasons, they did not want their names used in the text, and we have respected that wish.

Since most of our sources are anonymous, we have taken extra precautions to ensure that our information is correct.

Where there was conflict between interviews we reviewed them with the interviewees to see if we could reconcile the versions. (In a company of IBM's size, there is an inevitable *Rashomon* quality to the narratives of any major episode; the information gaps between middle and top managers can be quite wide, usually to the detriment of both.) When we completed our interviewing, we prepared a detailed chronology of the events we planned to cover in the book and furnished it to IBM's senior management, who corrected a number of chronological details, but withheld comment on its main body.

Winning the computer wars without IBM is our focus in Part II. To place the IBM story in broader context, we first survey the key technological trends that will dominate the 1990s and the emerging competition between three main groups of contenders: the traditional Western computer companies, primarily IBM and DEC; the Japanese integrated electronics firms, like Fujitsu, Hitachi, Toshiba, and NEC; and the Third Force, the quick-footed American start-ups, like those that dot California's Silicon Valley, many of which have prospered in an era of hyperrapid change. We outline the nature of the strategic struggle, analyze the characteristic strategies of the three main contenders, and lay out the essential rules for strategic success in the 1990s.

In Part III, we draw the policy implications from the first two parts of the book, in particular for the major new opportunities that may now be emerging for Western firms in areas like consumer electronics. We analyze the impact that government policy has had on the computer industry both in the United States and abroad, look at the prospects and problems facing the major computer companies, and outline a realistic program for the American government that could help shape the outcome of this decade's computer wars.

PART I

The Fall of IBM

1

Coloring the World Blue

When IBM announced the System/360 series of computers in 1964, *Fortune* magazine called it a "$5,000,000,000 gamble . . . possibly the 'riskiest business judgment of modern times.' " The name "360" came from the 360 degrees in a circle, because IBM intended the 360 to take over the *entire* world of computing—business, science, defense, everything. It was the kind of daring, "bet the company" gamble that few companies had the guts, the vision, or the resources to make. But it was not the first time IBM had rolled the dice so boldly, and it was characteristic of the style that had made IBM the world's outstanding company—the most admired, and most feared, in any industry.

The modern IBM, the company that emerged at the end of World War II as the world's leading business punch-card company, was very much the creation of Thomas J. Watson, Sr., universally recognized as one of the world's greatest sales and marketing geniuses. It was Watson who focused a small scales and measuring device company on solving business accounting problems, changed its name to International Business Machines, and piloted it to Fortune 500 status, able to hold its own in its chosen arena with much more powerful and technologically grounded giants like General Electric and Remington Rand. The secret of Watson's success, a principle that was ground into the very bones of IBM's salesmen, was that IBM would sell machines by solving problems; IBM would win if its accounting machines truly helped its customers' businesses run better. IBM's understanding of its clients, its commitment to customer support, the dedication to quality, the fanatical devotion to deadlines and delivery schedules, were legendary.

IBM was regarded as a technology lightweight at the end of the war, even though it had dipped a toe into electronic computing and had collaborated with Harvard University to build the Mark I, a giant electromechanical calculator—or a "robot brain," as the press called it—to assist in wartime code-breaking. In 1947 Watson had his engineers build the Selective Sequence Electronic Calculator, a 120-foot-long Rube Goldberg monster that stood in a huge glass enclosure in the IBM lobby in New York City, available to any scientist for free. But the world's leading computer company was Rand, and the name of its big machines, UNIVAC, became a household word when Edward R. Murrow's 1952 election night newscast used a UNIVAC to forecast the winner in the Eisenhower-Stevenson presidential race, with the big computer's whirring tape drives and blinking console looming behind Murrow like an alien presence on the CBS set.

As American business boomed at the end of the war, IBM's customers began demanding faster and bigger calculating machines to keep pace with the headlong expansion of their sales and territories. IBM was already selling electronic business calculators by the end of the 1940s—desk-sized machines that used vacuum tubes to do arithmetic and could compute a payroll ten times faster than the punch-card readers could feed in the data. In 1952 the company produced a vacuum-tube-based scientific computer, the 701; two years later, facing a chorus of demand from its punch-card customers, it introduced the 702, an electronic computer specifically designed to replace accounting department punch-card machines. As Tom Watson, Jr., took control of the company in the mid-1950s, he consciously set out to push IBM into the newest electronic technologies. He recruited Emanuel Piore, head of the Office of Naval Research, as chief scientist, and increased research spending from about 15 percent of net income in the 1940s to 35 percent in the 1950s and to 50 percent by the 1960s and 1970s. By the 1960s, IBM's computer R&D budget was bigger than the federal government's.

The seminal event in postwar electronics was the invention of the first useful solid-state semiconductor electrical device at Bell Labs in 1948. The inventors, William Shockley, Walter Brattain, and John Bardeen, shared the 1956 Nobel Prize for their achievement. Their new device, which they called a transistor, was an electronic switch that took advantage of the fact that certain "semiconducting" crystals, such as silicon, sometimes conducted electricity and sometimes blocked it. By embedding impurities in a tiny fragment of semiconductor crystal, they found they could alter quite precisely how the crystal shifted between its conductive and insulating states in response to electrical currents. The transistor was therefore the simplest electrical switching device imaginable, with no moving parts; very small arrays of on-off switches are an ideal way to represent the 1s and 0s that are the language of a digital computer. It took a decade for companies to learn how to manufacture high-quality transistors in quantity; but once they were available, their small size, great durability, low rate of power consumption, and low rate of heat output quickly made them the technology of choice over vacuum tubes.

It was but a small step from the solid-state transistor to the integrated circuit—a single piece of silicon with two or more solid-state devices embedded in it and connected with wires made of thin layers of metal. Jack Kilby at Texas Instruments and Robert Noyce at Fairchild Semiconductor both independently invented the integrated circuit in 1959. The theoretical limits on the size of solid-state devices are vanishingly small, so as manufacturing technologies improved, integrated circuits could get more and more complex, squeezing enormous numbers of devices onto a single microchip of silicon. The smaller the devices, the less power they required, the less heat they produced, the lower the cost per device, and the faster and more powerful computers became. Noyce's and Kilby's first integrated circuits had only two devices on them, but within just a couple of years, even simple integrated circuits could reduce the size of a computer by 150 times. By 1970, state-of-the-art memory chips had 1,000 transistors; by 1980, the newest chips had 64,000 transistors; by 1992, 16 million transistors. A 1970 memory chip cost less than $10; a 1992 chip still cost less than $10.

IBM's entry into transistorized computing was smoothed by two massive 1950s contracts to provide computers for the SAGE and BMEWS early warning systems against Russian air and missile attacks. Defense computing made up a full half of IBM's computer revenues throughout the 1950s, and still funded 35 percent of its research in 1960. IBM's first fully transistorized computer, the 709, was built for the BMEWS project in 1958 and rolled out in a commercial version in 1960. High-speed ferrite core memories, magnetic tape drives, and flexible designs that could handle both business and scientific data requirements—all developed with government contracts—were recycled almost immediately into business products.

Other companies also won major defense contracts, but were typically much slower to adapt their products commercially. Rand's UNIVACs, for example, had to be painstakingly assembled on the customer's site, while IBM computers came in sleek, attractive casings, were easily installed, and were designed to perform operations that its customers really needed. The 650, a small business computer, sold more than a thousand units in the 1950s, becoming the world's first mass-produced computer. The 1401 became the industrial world's medium-sized mainframe standard at the end of the decade. The powerful 700 series dominated the high end of the market. Every new machine outsold the wildest marketing forecasts. The company's sales, which were only $40 million before the war, passed the billion-dollar mark in 1957. The CBS 1956 election night newscast pointedly used an IBM computer.

BETTING THE COMPANY

The decision to plunge ahead with the System/360 (later 360/ 370) mainframe computers was even more daring than the decision to go into electronic computing in the first place. The 1400 series of machines were hardly obsolete, and along with older IBM equipment, enjoyed the lion's share of installed back offices. But the fundamental objective of the System/360 was to replace virtually *all* other computers, including all the thousands of lease-paying IBM machines happily ticking away on customer sites (IBM equipment was almost always rented). As the 360 project leader, Vin Learson, wrote to a foot-dragging colleague, "Corporate policy . . . is that by 1967 the 1401 [IBM's then-current flagship] will be dead as a Dodo. Let's stop fighting this."

IBM's leading position was by no means beyond assault when it gambled on the 360. It had pioneered most of the business computer technology on the market, but now other companies—Philco, GE, RCA, Rand, Control Data—had learned from IBM's success. They were steadily chipping away at IBM's market share—cherry-picking opportunities where an IBM solution was becoming dated and vulnerable to newer products. The very breadth of IBM's success presented a daunting challenge—having created such a large and diverse new market, the dilemma was how to stay on top across the board.

The 360 decision was also forced by a drastic shift in the relative value of hardware and software in the short decade of commercial electronic computing. Only about 8 percent of the value of the earliest systems was accounted for by software. By the early 1960s, the software component was up to 40 percent of delivered value. Software development was becoming a major capital item for both IBM and its customers, and as systems proliferated, it was getting out of control. Customer reluctance to learn new software or rewrite their applications for each new generation of technology was looming as a major obstacle to continued market growth. To IBM, it was a crisis. Multiple machine designs and skyrocketing software costs pointed to an explosion of development expenses, since every important software product had to be redesigned for each class of machine.

The revolutionary new principle of the System/360 was *compatibility*, at a single stroke cutting through both the software problem and the breadth-of-market conundrum. Customers would be able to buy a range of computers, from a small $2,500/month machine up to an $115,000/month behemoth, a thousand times more powerful. But all the machines would run on the same software; better yet, IBM could emulate the 1400 software on the 360, so customers could, for the most part, transfer their 1400 programs directly to the 360. With the same software, the full range of machines would have the same "look" to the outside world, and so could plug into any of the full range of IBM memory units, printers, disk drives, and all the other peripheral equipment that supported a big computer operation. Before the 360, whenever a customer's operations outgrew its computer, the whole installation had to be ripped out, and a new system had to be put in almost from scratch—new equipment, new software, often new file designs. With the System/360, the installation could expand gracefully to meet the customer's needs—adding a faster processor here, more memory there, better software, upgraded printers, whatever. It was a much better deal for the customer, and also for IBM—as Watson put it, "Once a customer entered the circle of 360 users, we knew we could keep him there for a very long time."

It was a brilliant vision, but a huge gamble; the investment was so enormous that a botched product could have sunk the company, and for a very shaky time in 1965, it wasn't obvious that IBM would pull it off. IBM hired sixty thousand new employees, sank $750 million into engineering development, and opened five major new factories at a cost of $4.5 billion. The technical challenges were stupendous, and worse, were layered one on top of the other. The 360 was the first computer to use a hybrid integrated circuit—a way station to full integration—as a base technology. But no one had ever manufactured integrated circuits on the scale and at the quality level the 360 demanded. There was no recourse but for IBM,

which had always bought almost all its electronic components, to create its own integrated circuit factories—at three
times the cost of any previous computer factory—and create
brand-new process technologies for the manufacture of integrated circuits on a mass scale.

Every peripheral component in the IBM product line had
to be redesigned to assure the target compatibility throughout
the series. More important, the software for the 360 series had
to be consistent up and down the entire line. But that required
millions of lines of code, the largest software program that
had ever been written, and all under terrible time pressures.
The cost overruns were appalling. At one point, when $600
million of inventory had been "lost," seemingly unfathom-
able metallurgical problems were shutting down the integrated circuit factories, and the huge software project was
hopelessly bollixed, Watson admitted being close to panic,
beset by fears that he had destroyed his father's company.

But the 360 pulled through. Not all the products were
delivered on time, and the early versions underperformed
specifications. Some of the software problems, despite a half
billion dollars sunk into programming, bedeviled the system
for years to come. But customers didn't mind waiting a bit.
There was enormous loyalty to IBM and great confidence that
it was a company that delivered on its promises. Even more
important was the recognition that the 360/370 series was the
right answer to a new era of pervasive high-performance computing. Once the kinks were out of the system and all the new
factories were humming, IBM couldn't fill orders fast'enough.
The 360/370 series completely redefined the concept of modern business computing, and just as Watson predicted, once
customers adopted the 360 concept, IBM owned them.

For twenty years thereafter, IBM's dominance of the industry was almost total. The formidable competitors of the
1950s and early 1960s—Burroughs, UNIVAC, NCR, Control
Data, and RCA/Honeywell—were now just the "BUNCH." A
new, and ignominious, sobriquet entered computer jargon—
the "PCM," or Plug-Compatible Manufacturer. With no
chance of taking on IBM frontally, competitors were reduced
to manufacturing clone products, mostly peripheral devices

and other equipment that could fit inside the 360/370 system architecture—like small animals darting in and out to snatch pieces of the lion's kill. By 1970, IBM's sales had soared to $7 billion, and kept growing, by more than 15 percent a year, every year, making it the largest and most profitable industrial company in history, with a grip on its industry that exceeded even that of Standard Oil or U.S. Steel in the turn-of-the-century heyday of unrestrained capitalist expansion.

IBM's success drew forth two new hostile forces, both more powerful than any single competitor. The first was its own home government, the second was the government of Japan.

UNITED STATES VS. **IBM**

Ramsey Clark, the attorney general of the United States during the last waning days of the Johnson administration, on January 17, 1969, signed a complaint charging IBM with unlawful monopolization of the computer industry and requested that the federal courts dismember the company. It was not the first time Justice Department's trustbusters had looked upon IBM's success with a jaundiced eye. When IBM's heavy investment in basic research began to pay dividends in the 1950s, the Justice Department initiated an action that forced IBM to license all of its patents, at a "reasonable" price to all comers, including the technology-hungry Japanese.

The 1969 suit had been expected for a long time, and IBM had already begun to unbundle the pricing of its systems, making it easier for other companies to sell compatible devices and software. But IBM's overall reaction to the case was arrogantly imperious. Fundamental antitrust theory, after all, in the words of Judge Learned Hand, held that a company was not to be penalized for its "superior skill, foresight, and industry." Surely, the courts, if not the Antitrust Division of the Justice Department, would quickly recognize that IBM had earned its market share simply by being better than everyone else.

In the event, the action dragged on for thirteen years. The government's case was meretricious from the outset, shot through with contradictions and misconceptions. It took six years even to bring the case to trial, during which time the government repeatedly changed its theory of the case to keep pace with the dramatic changes in the industry and the constant turnover of Justice Department lawyers. The government's action brought forth a long series of private antitrust complaints. With the exception of a suit brought by Control Data before the antitrust action, which was settled out of court, IBM fought and won every one, twice on directed verdict—that is, without having to present a defense.

When the antitrust action finally came to trial, it was assigned to a federal judge, David M. Edelstein, whose behavior was frequently bizarre—at one point, he ordered depositions (previous sworn oral statements of witnesses) to be read aloud to an empty bench for seventy days. The case cost hundreds of millions of dollars, possibly as much as a billion, and spawned an entire industry of IBM-case lawyers and expert witnesses. As Frank Cary once put it, he told his legal staff to spend whatever was necessary, "and they still went over budget." IBM's chief expert witness, Professor Frank Fisher of MIT, named his new yacht *The Section 3* in honor of the key section of the antitrust statute.

An extensive review of the IBM case was an early priority of the Reagan administration Justice Department. The suit was dropped in June 1982 with a curt four-sentence appraisal by the solicitor general that the case was "without merit."

The government's action did great damage to the company. By the mid-1970s, the easy confidence of IBM executives that they would prevail on the merits had long since dissipated. The case had become a devouring monster, and the company was beginning to scrutinize every decision for how it might play in a hostile courtroom. Many of IBM's actions in the 1970s and 1980s, particularly its supine attitude toward small suppliers of PC components and software, can be explained as the reflexes ingrained by a decade in the courtroom's harsh glare. One of the more serious consequences of the antitrust case is that, in the anti-IBM atmosphere prevailing in the government, the United States typically refused to help against a much less principled assault being mounted by Japan.

JAPAN VS. IBM

IBM first established a presence in Japan in 1925 and reentered during the Occupation, so that as much as the postwar Japanese government might have liked, it could not banish IBM from its shores. By bargaining over import and manufacturing licenses, however, it gained extremely favorable royalty arrangements on the IBM patents and made them available to the entire Japanese industry. The American government took a generally benign view of such activities—it was happy to build up Japan as a democratic Asian power and equally happy to see someone cutting IBM down to size.

Japan's hardware manufacturing skills developed rapidly, and by the mid-1970s, Japanese research and production capabilities in certain semiconductor technologies were the equal of America's. But Japan had—and still has—a great weakness in software. Japanese companies could make good reproductions of IBM mainframes, but could not duplicate the IBM operating system, the extremely complex software that gave IBM computers their unique "look" to the outside world. Without the operating system, Japan's companies would be limited to making peripherals or other plug-ins for IBM environments and could not offer full substitutability for IBM systems.

The solution was massive, government-supported Japanese theft and industrial espionage against IBM. Throughout the 1970s, new IBM software, like the MVS operating system, which had taken years to develop, would show up in Japanese products almost immediately after its introduction. Japanese companies managed to fend off IBM's attempts to purchase their products, even through third parties, so IBM could not demonstrate the thefts. Fujitsu, the primary offender, has never sold mainframe operating system software in the United States, to avoid the reach of the federal courts and rules of discovery. Finally, in the early 1980s John Opel, IBM's chairman, refused to sell any further products or technology to Fujitsu unless they turned over their system software for inspection. When Fujitsu finally did so, the theft was obvious. A prolonged, multistage arbitration proceeding eventually awarded IBM $833 million in damages.

The climactic event in the history of Japanese thievery from IBM came in 1982. Bob O. Evans, who was director of IBM's advanced technology programs, received a telephone call in 1981 from a friend, Max Paley, a West Coast computer consultant and former IBM executive, asking what the "Adirondack Notebooks" were. The notebooks were an ultra-secret, eighteen-volume set of operating and software specifications for the next generation of IBM mainframes. Paley had been approached by Hitachi executives, who said they had half of the volumes, claimed to know precisely where the others were located, and hoped to hire Paley to obtain the notebooks and a Clark board, a key module in IBM's highest performance computers. (A trace on the stolen notebooks eventually disclosed that they had been removed and copied after an an IBM executive had left them for safekeeping in a Tokyo hotel safe. The hotel manager's brother was a Fujitsu employee. Fujitsu, in legendary "Japan, Inc." style, shared them with Hitachi, its bitter rival.) IBM, Paley, and the FBI mounted an elaborate sting operation that trapped Hitachi and Mitsubishi offering more than $600,000 in bribes to Paley, and suggesting an impressively large network of informers within IBM. In Evans's view, at least, the FBI terminated the operation prematurely for fear of losing their prey, but at the cost of not entrapping Fujitsu, who had stayed circumspectly on the fringes of the negotiations.

The initial reaction of the Japanese government and computer companies was outraged denial. There were demonstrations outside of IBM's Japanese headquarters and angry speeches in the Diet. IBM, however, finally got court approval to turn over three hundred hours of incriminating videotapes to the Japanese, bringing the protests to a shocked and embarrassed halt. Hitachi meekly agreed to pay IBM damages of $250 million and to allow IBM to inspect its new products for a period of five years. Incredibly, the Japanese government managed to swallow its embarrassment sufficiently to introduce a law into the Diet in 1984 to legalize software theft from foreigners—it was withdrawn only when IBM finally roused the American government to protest.

DOMINATING INFORMATION TECHNOLOGY

Reprehensible though it was, Japan's campaign to undercut IBM's dominant position in global computing demonstrated a much more sophisticated understanding of the industry than the American government's antitrust action.

Dominance in electronics is emphatically not the same as control. Standard Oil's dominance of the world petroleum industry at the turn of the century was based on its actual control of physical facilities—oil wells, pipelines, tankers, even barrel-stave forests. Computers and electronics are not that kind of industry. In the twenty years from the time IBM first established its leadership position in business computing, the price of processing power dropped by more than 100 times—processing power that cost $1 in the mid-1950s cost less than a penny in the 1970s. The price of computer memory dropped by more than 500 times, and the storage capacity of standard devices increased thousands of times. To maintain its lead position, IBM had to stay in front of an extremely fast-moving technology curve. The ratio of price to performance for the IBM 360 was about 50 percent superior to that of almost all competing machines. Instead of raising prices, in traditional monopolist style, IBM typically forced widespread price-cutting throughout the industry, always following up its initial offerings with a steady stream of new technology break-throughs, such as faster memories, faster processors, and more extensive time-sharing capability. IBM's leadership was based not on controlling a technology, but on exploiting it better than anyone else.

By the mid-1970s, there were more than a hundred substantial companies competing in computers, most of which had not even existed when the 360 was announced. The 360's objective of compatibility over a broad product line—the ability to mix and match peripheral devices such as the central processor, memory, and input and output devices (like terminal keyboards, printers, and display screens)—required that the system be relatively "open." As long as a peripheral device conformed to specific electronic communication rules, it could be plugged in and work as a part of a seamless system. Openness and compatibility were opportunities for quick-moving companies that could offer products and software that were better and cheaper than IBM's own. Memorex and Storage Technology sold IBM-compatible memory equipment; Four Phase and Systems Engineering sold terminals; Texas Instruments, Intel, Ampex, and many other companies provided semiconductor components; Cullinane, Shared Medical Systems, and many others sold software. Data General, Prime, and Wyse created new classes of smaller, special-purpose computers that would work within an IBM computing environment. By the middle of the 1970s, Amdahl, part-owned by Fujitsu, but the creation of Gene Amdahl, one of the 360's key designers, was producing IBM mainframe clones, completely look-alike machines that matched, or some customers said, exceeded, IBM's performance point for point.

Clearly, IBM did not control the computer industry in any classic sense, and as competitors proliferated, and governments forced broader and broader licensing, its overall market share inevitably declined. But, paradoxically, IBM's sales and profitability continued to bound ahead, and its dominance over the industry became, if anything, even more pervasive. By the end of the 1970s, 70 percent of the world's computer installations were still centered around IBM equipment, and IBM's share of world computer profits was even higher.

The secret of IBM's dominance, as IBM itself understood better than anyone, was that it had created, and owned, a pervasive industry *architecture*. All the competitors were playing by IBM's rules—making devices, writing software, manufacturing clones, running time-share centers—all within a computing environment that IBM defined and that only IBM had completely mastered. The confidence of IBM customers was so great, their commitment to the 360/370 architecture so deep, that no competitor had a chance of replacing it. It would mean throwing out too much investment built up over too long a time.

The consequence was that no one could beat IBM to market with a new product line. If a competitor tried to invade its space *ahead* of IBM, it could never be sure that IBM's next operating system release would be compatible with its product, especially if the product was one IBM wanted for itself. Competitors had no choice but to reverse-engineer IBM products only *after* they became available, and therefore were condemned always to be second to market. And by the time competitive plug-compatible products became available, IBM was usually already moving on to the next product generation. That explains the desperation of the Japanese to steal information in advance of its release.

IBM's "lock" on the mainframe industry was never complete and was under constant challenge from almost every quarter. The astonishing pace of technological advancement in electronics demanded continual leapfrogging innovation to stay apace. The loyalty of IBM's customer base depended on a deeply engrained confidence that, on average, IBM technology would always be the best, that its price/performance would always be at the top, that the industry-shaking innovations would always come from IBM first. It was an extraordinarily demanding game, and IBM played it brilliantly for more than twenty years, an accomplishment that ranks as one of the signal industrial achievements in all of business history. It was easy to poke fun at Big Blue—the stiff uprightness, the formalities of the blue suits and white shirts, the flat inflections of computerspeak. But IBMers knew, and they knew the rest of the world knew, that IBM was truly the best at what it did, outdistancing its competition to a degree that perhaps no company ever had.

So it is the more surprising that IBM's top management missed the straws swirling in the wind in the 1970s and 1980s that computing was undergoing fundamental change, that the 360/370—indeed, the whole mainframe principle—was heading for a dead end. But one of the most important of those straws had been floated by IBM itself, who had already, by 1982, made the personal computer the product of the decade.

2

GUERRILLA WARFARE

Revolutions have a way of beginning inauspiciously. In Albuquerque late in February 1975, at the run-down headquarters of a shoestring company called MITS, twenty-two-year-old Paul Allen, red-eyed from eight straight weeks of working round the clock, entered a paper-tape instruction telling an awkward little machine called the Altair to add 2 + 2. The machine correctly answered "4." Allen and his friend Bill Gates, who had not yet turned twenty, had managed to write a version of BASIC, a widely used computer programming language, that would fit inside a microprocessor.

The microprocessor had been invented just four years before at a start-up company called Intel whose main product was semiconductor memories. A young Intel engineer, Ted Hoff, was working on a contract to build a hand-held calculator for a Japanese company called Busicom. His assignment was to build a series of integrated circuits to perform each of the calculator's functions. Hoff had the insight that he could use Intel's memory technology to store the calculator's operations in the form of software instructions. Then, instead of building hard-wired circuits for each operation, he could put enough general-purpose logic circuits on a silicon chip to perform whatever operations the software instructed them to. As Intel well understood, a general-purpose processor executing instructions from memory was a pretty good definition of a computer. It was quite a primitive computer, to be sure, but in truth, a computer-on-a-chip nonetheless. Before Intel could brag about its invention, however, they first had to persuade Busicom to accept the microprocessor as a substitute for the hard-wired circuits it was expecting; then they struck a deal to refund the $60,000 Busicom had paid for the design in return for letting Intel keep the rights to its new chip. Busicom's chip has been called one of the epochal milestones of American technology, on a par with the light bulb, the telephone, and the airplane. The radical decentralization of computing power that drove the technological upheavals of the 1980s was made possible by the microprocessor.

But in 1975 Intel itself thought its microprocessors were too limited to be useful as anything but specialized controllers, say, for traffic light systems. By proving that BASIC could run on a microprocessor—the "coolest" program he ever wrote, said Gates, who wrote the actual code—Gates and Allen showed that Intel's new invention could serve as the brain for a truly serious computer. (Their feat was a substantial intellectual accomplishment, an extremely compact and elegant piece of programming.) Few people today would recognize the Altair as a computer; it had no screen, no keyboard, and no disk drive. It was assembled from a kit that sold through the mail for only $397; it was a microwave-oven-sized box with rows of switches on the front. Only proficient "hackers" could use it, painstakingly writing and loading their own programs. But it was nonetheless a real computer, and one that would be the hacker's very own. The following spring, on April Fool's Day, twenty-one-year-old Steve Jobs and twenty-six-year-old Steve Wozniak—who had written his own version of BASIC for another microprocessor from MOS Technologies, a Motorola spinoff—incorporated the Apple Computer Company. Their Apple I was just a circuit board, but it was as powerful as the Altair and could plug into a television set display; a computer revolution was suddenly in full swing.

The personal computer revolution hit so fast, so forcefully, and so unexpectedly because it was an odd combination of social and technological upheaval. An important stage-setting technical step was the Digital Equipment Corporation's new line of small mainframes introduced in the late 1960s—to the company's chagrin, in the era of the miniskirt, it was dubbed the "minicomputer." Secondary schools and colleges could afford to buy, or rent time-sharing space on, DEC's minicomputers, and they vaguely understood that "computer literacy" would be important in future decades. A number of the better secondary schools began to offer their brightest kids elective courses in BASIC.

There was a peculiar "click" between the circuitry of a computer and the circuitry inside the heads of a very large number of teenagers, almost all of them male. Computers became an obsession, for games, for code-breaking, for sending messages, for anything. Gates and Allen and the other young pioneers of the new industry were all typical—bright, intense, remote young people utterly seduced by the lure of the blinking consoles. (At one point, Gates's parents had declared computers off-limits for a year and a half, so he would pay attention to his other studies.) Contention for time-sharing slots on school machines was fierce, and for the truly obsessed, extraordinarily frustrating. For these young hackers, the personal computer was a sunburst of salvation—a computer *all their own*, on which they could hack to their hearts' content. The 1970s hackers, in fact, are the source of a vast number of the information technologies in which the United States currently leads the world. If introducing BASIC into high school curricula were the result of a conscious industrial policy, it would have to be one of the most successful in history.

Once the concept of the personal computer was in the air, technologies quickly multiplied to make it more accessible. The awkward paper tape system that Allen used to load BASIC into the Altair that day in Albuquerque was actually an unusual luxury. The first Altair kits were programmed by flipping the on-off switches in the front of the machine; loading BASIC would have required some thirty thousand sequential switch settings. But a company called Shugart Associates commercialized the disk drive, allowing a whole program to be stored and loaded from a floppy disk. (Two lineal descendants of Shugart, Seagate Technologies and Conner Peripherals, still make most of the world's personal computer disk drives.)

Gary Kildall, who was doing contract programming for Intel, understood the importance of the disk drive before it was even commercially available and wrote the first general-purpose operating system, called CP/M, specifically for disk-drive computers. An operating system is software that directs the overall operations of a computer—the way it loads data, the interaction between the processor and the memory, the way it interprets keystrokes—and it provides handles and hooks that make it much easier for programmers to develop special-purpose "application" programs, like word processors. Kildall's operating system and convenient floppy disk storage vastly increased the flexibility and power of these new machines.

Personal computers caught the attention of business with the publication of Visicalc, the first spreadsheet. It was designed by Dan Bricklin, who'd quit programming to attend Harvard Business School and wanted a tool to speed up his finance homework. A programmer friend, Bob Frankston, coded Visicalc to run on the Apple II, the first of Jobs and Wozniak's products that we would recognize today as a real computer. The Apple II had a display screen, disk drive, and keyboard, and came bundled with its own operating system and additional software programs for storing addresses, keeping a diary, doing word processing, or playing games. But it was Visicalc that made the Apple II a runaway success: it freed businessmen, accountants, and financial planners from the tyranny of pencil-and-paper spreadsheets, where a single mistake often meant hours of tedious erasures and recalculations. It was the hottest office product in years. Apple's initial public stock offering in 1980, at $100 million, was one of the largest in Wall Street history, Personal computers were now a market that IBM could no longer afford to ignore.

IBM ENTERS THE FRAY

IBM's entering the personal computer market was like an American carrier fleet sailing into a Third World port. By comparison with IBM's main businesses, personal computing was still scruffy and disorganized, a business peopled by nerds, wonks, and fast-talking salesmen, hardly yet an industry. IBM was more a global empire than a company. Its employees could recognize each other passing on the street in a strange country. If they were lost or in trouble abroad, their IBM badges were more useful than an American passport. IBM's managers were tougher, smarter, more clearheaded than anyone else. They looked alike, thought alike, fought alike, and were proud of it. IBM was extremely aware of the differences between itself and other computer companies. It was completely self-sufficient. It did its own science, invented its own technology, and could make every screw in every one of its products if it chose to. When other computer companies clustered together along Route 128 in Massachusetts or in California's Silicon Valley, IBM stayed self-consciously apart in its Armonk, New York, headquarters, underscoring its supreme indifference to moods and fads.

The sheer efficiency of IBM was the stuff of legend. It was completely self-contained. In primitive countries with rudimentary telephone systems, IBM calls came through instantly, loud and clear, through its own global communication system. It had at least three internal universities, which ran MIT-caliber courses for technologists and Harvard Business School–caliber programs for managers. The top scientists and the top management thinkers in the world were on staff, or were on the internal faculties, or were consultants. No other company in the world could afford programs like the IBM Fellows. Fellows were awarded a high salary for life and an office budget to work on whatever they pleased.

Despite IBM's size, there was none of the slack, perk-ridden, golf-clubby, old-boy atmosphere that characterized other big American companies in the 1970s. Executives were tall, frosty, and forcefully articulate. Both Watsons fostered a deliberately contentious management style; shouting at meetings was not only not discouraged, it was expected. There was no room for the easily intimidated. But any employee at any level could appeal any decision over his supervisor's head, all the way to the chairman. IBM's work ethic was grueling, but except at the very top, salaries were not high. People worked there, and clamored to get in—99 applicants were turned down for every hire—because it allowed them, forced them, to be their very best in the company that was better at what it did than any other company in the world.

IBM officially focused on personal computing in the mid-1970s. Low-end computing was very much a personal project of Frank Cary, IBM's chairman. Cary had led the company into minicomputers in the late 1960s; he was convinced that, while IBM had no peers in the mainframe world, the greatest future growth would always be in the low end. At times, Cary was almost alone in his advocacy of personal computing. Senior managers, by and large, were distinctly unenthusiastic; making personal computers simply did not fit the IBM way of doing business. Personal computers were sold through dealers, like a retail product; quality standards were low; software was amateurish; the multiplicity of products and the rapid product cycles seemed chaotic—all too quick-moving and faddish, a battle for commandos, not carriers. But Cary was convinced that as mainframe sales inevitably flattened out, moving down to the personal market was the only way IBM could keep to its accustomed 15 percent annual growth path.

IBM was no stranger to small computers. In the late 1960s, it had designed a number of small processor boards, and used one of them to build what was probably the world's first personal computer, the SCAMP, which now sits in the Smithsonian Institution. The SCAMP was followed in the mid-1970s with the 5100, a desktop computer designed for science labs; it had a small display screen, could be programmed in BASIC and FORTRAN, and included statistical and mathematical software. There were a variety of 5100 follow-ons, none of them particularly successful. IBM also made the Displaywriter, a free-standing word processor, arguably a personal computer, which used a floppy disk drive, an IBM invention.

Cary also started a series of projects focusing on video disks for home entertainment and business education, none of them successful.

By 1980, however, as personal computers proliferated, it was obvious that IBM was missing a major opportunity. MITS, the maker of the Altair, was out of business, but Apple was prospering, Tandy was having difficulty keeping up with orders for the "tabletop" computer it sold through Radio Shack, and a host of new "microcomputer" companies, such as Atari, Commodore, and Osborne, were springing into life. The total number of actual personal computers sold was still under 200,000, but the business potential was obviously large. Cary decided it was time for an all-out push and picked an IBM veteran, Bill Lowe, head of the laboratory at Boca Raton, the home of the 5100, to come up with an IBM product within a year, by August 1981. Lowe was not absolved from normal IBM processes, as is sometimes alleged; but anyone who tried to slow him down would have to justify the action to Cary himself, which was as close to carte blanche as anyone ever got at IBM. A few months after Lowe got the project off the ground, he was, in inimitable IBM fashion, transferred to Minnesota. Lowe himself picked Don Estridge as his replacement in Boca Raton, and it was Estridge who actually put together the team that created the IBM PC.

The PC almost immediately became just one more of IBM's long string of dazzling success stories—in this case, all the more impressive because it proved that IBM was *not* the slave to its own culture that everyone supposed. Estridge assembled a group of mavericks from throughout the company—they called themselves the "wild ducks"—and announced that for the first time in IBM's history, a product would be built almost entirely with parts from outside suppliers. IBM's own plants could bid on parts, but would be subject to the same cost and time requirements as anyone else. Even more heretically, the PC would not be subject to normal IBM quality-control procedures. The rigorousness of IBM's product testing was legendary—and necessary—since mainframes typically ran twenty-four hours a day almost every day of the year. Normal product testing cycles alone, Estridge argued, would take more time than he had available, and, anyway, personal computers would never be used as brutally as main-frames.

The Boca Raton team started combing the world for parts to assemble their computer, all under a thick veil of secrecy—IBM was even more paranoid than usual about premature product leaks. The overall project was code-named "Chess," while the PC itself was "Acorn." The intention was to create an excellent, state-of-the-art product, but *not* a technical breakthrough. By buying only parts that had proved them-selves by several years' performance on the open market Estridge could finesse two tough issues: he could demonstrate the reliability and quality of the parts without extra testing *and* the wisdom of using outsiders. Tandon supplied the disk drives, Zenith the power supplies, SCI Systems made the cir-cuit boards, and Japan's Epson made the first printers. One procurement argument that Estridge regretted winning was his choice of a keyboard arrangement different from the well-established IBM Selectric standard, a source of much cus-tomer annoyance until it was changed with the release of the PC-AT in 1984.

Although it was not apparent at the time, the two most critical decisions for the future of the industry were the choice of a microprocessor and the PC's basic software. Both were made with little controversy. Most personal computers had an 8-bit architecture, which severely limited their processing ability. ("Eight bits" refers to the number of 1s and 0s the computer could process in a single package or "word." Mod-ern PCs are mostly 32-bit machines.) IBM decided early that it would launch with a 16-bit chip and chose Intel's 8088 microprocessor, a more capable version of the 8080 chip that powered the original Altair. The 8088 had been around for several years, and there were a variety of other microproces-sors available, including several from Motorola and Intel's own 8086, with far superior capabilities.

Boca Raton's technical staff favored the Motorola chips, as did Gates, who was scornful of the 8088. But the PC design team had used a predecessor chip, the Intel 8085, in one of the versions of the 5100 computer and were familiar with the

Intel architecture. Intel also had an advantage from the standpoint of software availability, which, the PC team well understood, would be a major factor in the sales of its machine. Gates's original microprocessor BASIC, once it became available on a floppy disk, had been widely circulated within the hacker community, pulling the Intel architecture along with it. Kildall's CP/M operating system had made the Intel architecture a popular choice for software writers. And once IBM settled on Intel as the obvious choice, the 8088, for all its limitations, was the best fit with the peripheral chips the Boca Raton team was designing into the PC.

Gordon Moore, cofounder and chairman of Intel, recalls that, in Intel's view, IBM's choice of the 8088 was viewed as "a small design win." Intel's major business at the time was selling memory chips; IBM paid only about $9 a chip for the 8088, or, as Moore put it, "about the same as the solder on a PC circuit board." For both companies, understandably, it was just not a big deal.

The decision on an operating system was equally uncontroversial, but became one of the most famous in the short history of the industry. It made Gates and Allen billionaires and created a sorcerer's apprentice in Microsoft that grew to become one of IBM's most formidable adversaries. Gates was originally contacted by the PC team to supply programming languages. They wanted BASIC, FORTRAN, and COBOL, which Gates was eager to provide. A new company called Peachtree would supply a list of applications programs, such as spreadsheets; IBM also commissioned a word processing package called Easy Writer, which allegedly was written by a hacker serving prison time for illegally breaking into telephone long-distance lines. The operating system, they assumed, would be Kildall's CP/M, which had become the standard for Intel-based computers.

There are many versions of what happened between Kildall and IBM. The standard story is that when the IBM team made a scheduled visit to Kildall's company, Digital Research, he was off flying his plane. (Kildall insists he was on a business trip.) Kildall's wife refused to sign IBM's imposing nondisclosure agreement, so the IBM team left without stating their business. For whatever reason, Kildall apparently took his time getting back to IBM when he returned, and blew one of the business opportunities of the century. IBM decided they couldn't work with Digital Research, and suddenly desperate and running out of time, told Gates he would have to supply an operating system too. After a brief negotiation, they agreed that Gates would own the system and that they would pay him on a royalty basis, instead of with a lump sum. (Because of the still-pending antitrust action, IBM was wary of owning operating system software for fear of suits from software writers.)

At first, Gates and Allen appreciated the opportunity little better than Kildall and agonized for some time before accepting the challenge. Fortunately, Gates knew of a company, Seattle Computing, that had developed an alternative to CP/M, called QDOS, for "Quick and Dirty Operating System," that would look like CP/M to outside software developers. Gates bought licensing rights for $25,000, without disclosing his customer, and later bought exclusive rights for $50,000. (Some years later, Seattle Computer sued and won a $1 million judgment.) The Microsoft team worked feverishly improving their new "MS-DOS," and when the summer of 1981 rolled around all the required software was ready for the scheduled PC introduction.

The machine that was be officially launched in October 1981 was an outstanding product, if no technological marvel. It had one floppy disk drive and 64K (64 kilobytes, or thousands of bytes) of RAM, or permanent "random access" memory—the effective limit on the size of a program it could run at any one time. It came with a monochrome television-resolution screen, but one much larger and easier to read than Apple's, and the 8088 processor. It had been intelligently designed for growth, with expansion slots for connecting add-on devices and increasing the RAM by adding circuit boards inside the machine to boost memory to 640K—even Bill Gates couldn't imagine anyone ever using more than that—and with the internal circuitry to handle an eventual upgrade to more advanced processors. IBM had made an uneasy peace with Kildall, so customers had a choice of three operating systems:

MS-DOS, the cheapest; a new version of CP/M; and a third, UCSD P-system, which was both slow and expensive.

The PC sold for $1,595, not including the price of software, a printer, and cabling, which at retail prices brought the total package to about $3,000. For comparison, a typical business IBM-compatible PC today would come with 4.5 megabytes (millions of bytes) of RAM—the minimum for effective operation of the current best-selling Windows/DOS operating system—some 100 megabytes of hard drive memory storage, two different-sized disk drives, a built-in modem, a color high-resolution screen, would run on an 80486 32-bit chip many times more powerful than the 8088, and would cost less than the original PC. Almost everyone vastly underestimated how rapidly users' appetite for computer power would grow once it became conveniently available.

MACHINE OF THE YEAR

Estridge's team broke the IBM mold in marketing their machine as much as they did in building it. In contrast to Apple, their target market was businesses, rather than schools and homes. But instead of selling through the normal IBM marketing channels, they subcontracted sales to Computerland, a chain of computer retail stores, and Sears Business Centers. IBM would provide service and technical support, but Computerland and Sears were expected to, and did, get up to speed in short order to provide on-site technical service themselves. The stroke of genius was the selection of a Charlie Chaplin look-alike, the Tramp, for the advertising campaign, emphasizing how easy any businessman would find the PC to use. For all the everyman image of the Tramp, the ad campaign stayed quite explicitly focused on the usefulness of the PC in business—the Tramp was usually a harassed small businessman.

The day after the press conference announcing the PC right on schedule in August 1981, Apple ran a full-page ad welcoming IBM to *its* industry. They might have been less cheeky had they guessed what a smash hit the PC would be;

two years later, Apple itself almost folded. For at least the first eighteen months of the PC's existence, the tidal wave of orders hopelessly outran IBM's ability to pump out new machines. Actual sales consistently ran five to eight times higher than forecasts made only months before. PC revenues for the last four months of 1981 were more than $40 million, and since volumes were much higher than expected, so were profits. In 1984, its third full year of life, PC revenues were $4 billion. Had it been a free-standing business, the PC division would have been the seventy-fourth largest industrial company in the country; with ten thousand employees, it was the third largest computer manufacturer, behind only the rest of IBM and DEC; and its sales had grown faster than any company's in history.

The PC created a host of new industries. At the Comdex computer trade show in November 1981, only three months after the PC's announcement, a company called Tecmar introduced no less than twenty-six new peripheral products for the PC, from a speech synthesizer for the blind to an electric appliance controller. Mitchell Kapor's new company, Lotus, wrote a spreadsheet specially for the DOS-based PC. Since Lotus, unlike Visicalc, was customized to the 8088's circuitry, it ran much faster on the PC than Visicalc. The bigger screen on the PC as compared to the Apple was also ideal for a spreadsheet user. A "Lotus model" became almost a generic term for a business spreadsheet, like Scotch tape. Visicalc disappeared, and Kapor became a multimillionaire, as MS-DOS and the PC became the business computer standard. Hundreds of third-party software writers poured out new PC programs; a series of the Tramp ads showed him staggering under a precariously balanced stack of software packages. By 1983, there were several dozen weekly or monthly publications devoted exclusively to the PC.

The crowning laurel came at the end of 1982, when *Time* magazine picked the IBM PC for its "Man of the Year" cover story. In the words of *Time*'s editors, "There are some occasions when the most significant force in a year's news is not a single individual, but a process. . . . *Time*'s Man of the Year for 1982, the greatest influence for good and evil, is not a man at all. It is a machine: the computer. . . . The creamy white PC (for personal computer) introduced in August 1981, has set a standard of excellence for the industry. . . . IBM had built the Cadillac of the 1982 class."

Estridge and the Boca Raton PC team deserved all the kudos. Taking a business from zero to $4 billion in three years is astonishing enough; doing it while breaking so dramatically from the prevailing IBM business methods makes it even more remarkable. The IBM PC was also the first deliberately "open" computer architecture, a fundamental insight that shaped the future of personal computing. From the very start, Boca Raton recognized that the best way to make the PC the industry standard was to publish all its technical specifications and make it easy for third parties to build add-on devices or write PC software applications, a principle that took Apple years to understand. And from the very outset the PC team decided not to bundle IBM software with their computer. "Nobody was confident that they could predict everything the public wanted," one executive recalled. The greater the software availability for the PC, the more machines they would sell.

By 1984, to all appearances, IBM owned the personal computer market. The blowout success of the original PC was followed by another great success with the PC-XT, with a color monitor and a hard disk drive capable of storing 10 megabytes of data. A famous Apple Super Bowl ad campaign portrayed its new Macintosh competing against an IBM PC that dominated the world in Orwellian *1984*, Big Brother style.

IBM was never to be so powerful or feared again.

3

THE ROOTS OF DECLINE

IBM's after-tax profits in 1984, the year the PC hit full stride, were just short of $7 billion, a stunning 15 percent of sales. No other company before or since has ever earned as much, and IBM's rate of return was never so high again. The year 1984 was a turning point, and the yellow canary in the mine was the PC. A string of botched new PC products damaged IBM's reputation for quality and marketing judgment and tarnished the old sheen of invincibility. But the rot was much deeper than in PCs and had begun many years before; IBM's other markets were simply much slower to react. By the mid-1980s, IBM was living on past capital to a dangerous degree, although the slippage in its position was still almost imperceptible. By the time the company awoke to the seriousness of its position, it was already plunging headlong toward the huge losses of 1991.

The hairline cracks that were crisscrossing IBM's edifice in the mid-1980s had nothing to do with technology. The company's scientific research and technology development capabilities were still unparalleled. Indeed, over the previous fifteen years, billions of dollars had been lavished on an array of dazzling new computer technologies. But there had been almost no success in forging them into a coherent IBM approach to a new generation of computing. Instead, they were dribbling away into a swamp of failed initiatives, half-finished prototypes, and interdivisional rivalries. Ominously, large cadres of the very best technical staff had been quietly leaving IBM for years. The decline, in fact, set in following the retirement of Tom Watson, Jr., after a heart attack in 1970.

Project F/S

Frank Cary, a hearty, bluff marketing executive whom insiders generally credit as being the strongest and best of Watson's successors, took over as IBM's chief executive officer in 1972, after a brief interregnum by Vin Learson, the key manager of the System/360 project. John Opel moved up to president.

For executives of Cary and Opel's vintage, the System/360 was the defining episode in IBM's history. The decision to proceed with the 360 combined sweeping strategic insight with a technical boldness so staggering that it bordered on the reckless. Conventional managerial wisdom, whether in the military or in high technology, is to attack on only one salient at a time. The 360 flouted all those rules. Nobody had attempted to create a modular family of computers before. The concept of a family of computers with a mixed and matched catalog of peripheral equipment was brand-new. The 360's partial integrated circuits were a major advance. IBM's decision to manufacture its own electronic circuits was a first for the company. Writing software that could run on so many different machines was a first, as was emulating the software from previous generations of machines. The time schedules were much too short, and far too many people were working along far too many parallel lines. No conventionally prudent manager would have let the project get off the ground, much less bet the company's entire future on its success.

Cary took over during a time of unusual pessimism at

Armonk. The 370, the successor to the 360, had been rolled out just as the United States and most of the rest of the world slipped into a major recession. IBM sales flattened out, and for the first time in anyone's memory, a major new product fell far short of marketing forecasts. A high-level planning group, the Summer Task Force, worked under Opel's direction through much of 1971 trying to sort out the implications of the 370's apparent failure.

The task force drew an alarming picture of the direction of the industry. They assumed that IBM would adhere to its normal five-year mainframe generational cycle and roll out a successor to the 370, a hypothetical "380," by about 1975, incorporating the same trend rate of power improvement over the 370 as the 370 had over the 360. But staff projections showed that the cost, and presumably therefore also the sales price, of computing power would fall very rapidly over the next five years. When the task force factored those cost/price assumptions into the most optimistic sales and profit margin forecasts for their 380, the result showed that IBM revenues and profits would *fall* sharply.

The work of the Summer Task Force convinced Cary and Opel that they were facing a crisis as severe as the one that had prompted the development of the 360 a decade before. And the solution seemed obvious. If adhering to the current technological trend line meant falling sales and profits, IBM had to redefine the shape of the trend line. They decided to vault over the normal "380" development cycle into a brand-new generation of technology with a project called F/S, for "Future Systems," under Opel's direct supervision.

The overall director of F/S was Bob Evans, who had distinguished himself as one of the lead managers on the System/360 and was the head of the powerful corporatewide development organization. Evans was universally recognized as brilliant, but he was cantankerous in the extreme—"Bob could sometimes make Hitler seem like a mildly unpleasant fellow," one former IBM executive joked. He also had a tendency toward indiscriminate advocacy. "Bob would have twenty-five new ideas a minute," said another executive, "and he'd throw them at you all at once. At least one of them would always be pure gold, but a lot of the rest would be just bad, and he didn't always bother to sort them out"—a dangerous attribute in a project as ambitious as F/S. Evans somewhat defensively insists that even he had misgivings from the very beginning about the reach of F/S, but insists that Opel controlled the project's direction.

IBM was already too big and too rich for any single project to pose a bet-the-company risk. But F/S was about as close as you could get. It had all the hallmarks of the 360 project, but it was even more ambitious and less practical. Its goal was to redefine the direction of computing technology so computers could become much more ubiquitous tools—in effect, if falling costs and prices meant that traditional markets could not support IBM's accustomed rate of revenue growth, IBM would change the shape of the markets. That required at least two major efforts: the first was aimed at radically increasing the power of hardware; and the second was to make software much easier for business clients to use. The goal was to deliver products in five years.

F/S was absurdly ambitious; much of the effort was focused on technologies that are advanced even today. There was a major effort on multiprocessing, for example—having several, or many, processors work on a problem simultaneously—and thin film disk storage, although neither was introduced by IBM until the late 1980s. Wafer-scale integration was another key focus, although it is still mostly a laboratory technology even in the 1990s. In standard technology, multiple identical semiconductors are fabricated on a wafer of silicon, then cut into individual chips. In theory, one could fabricate many different interconnected semiconductors on a single wafer, producing the smallest and fastest subsystems imaginable, or even an entire wafer-scale computer. IBM actually fabricated wafer-scale memory system prototypes during F/S, but never got close to real products.

One of the major software efforts concentrated on "object-oriented" programming, which even now is on the leading edge of software innovation. The idea is that, instead of writing new code for each new program, code can be created in tiny chunks, or objects, that each accomplish some discrete, small operation. If the objects are self-contained, that is, un-affected by how they are linked to other objects, much of the tedium would disappear from writing software: one could just string together the necessary objects from an object encyclo-pedia. Twenty years ago F/S not only set out to create object-oriented programs but also tried to wire the objects right into the circuitry of a computer. Some of the object-oriented tech-nology actually did show up in a successful 1980s line of minicomputers, the System 38 (now the AS400), which is known for its ease of use. But the scope of the F/S effort and the time schedule were utterly unrealistic.

Almost as soon as F/S got under way, its main justification disappeared. The recession ended and 370 sales boomed, van-quishing all of IBM's competitors and utterly panicking the Japanese. It also became clear that the cost of computing power was not going to fall nearly as fast as forecast. But F/S charged ahead anyway, and the conventional wisdom—try only one breakthrough at a time—that had been flouted with the System/360 proved itself with a vengeance. Before it was finally killed in 1976, F/S flailed away expensively and hope-lessly on multiple fronts, with surprisingly little to show for all the effort.

A circuit packaging technology that greatly increased 370 performance was probably the most important result of F/S. (It was one of the technologies Hitachi was trying to steal in the 1982 sting.) But poor results from F/S also blackened the reputation of good technologies. CMOS (Complementary Metal Oxide Silicon) semiconductor technology, for example, is a type of design that has very low power requirements and is particularly suitable for microprocessors. F/S included a major CMOS project, but IBM lost interest in the technology when the F/S results were poor. A decade later, IBM's com-petitive performance in microprocessors was badly handi-capped by its inexperience with CMOS designs.

The enormous diversion of effort slowed development across the company. Almost all the mainframe division's ma-chine designers were tied up in F/S for the first half of the decade. The next iteration of the 360/370 architecture, the 3080, did not appear until 1980 and incorporated approxi-

mately the same technology as was projected for the hypothetical 380, which normally would have appeared about
1975. A whole 370 development cycle, that is, was missed,
handing a major catch-up opportunity to the Japanese.

F/S was IBM's own quiet Vietnam. The confidence of top
management was badly shaken—at one point, during the
project's last years, Cary confessed to an associate that he
wasn't sleeping at nights and even feared for his job. But the
effects ran very deep and affected a whole generation of managers. For all of its overreaching, the principle behind F/S
represented everything that had made IBM great. When
threatened with adversity, the old IBM did not pull back, it
leaped forward. When products were profitable and well established, like the System/360, the old IBM didn't rest on its
laurels, it blew them away with new products that were even
better, more cost-effective, more useful, and ultimately more
profitable. The old IBM never shrank from cannibalizing its
own; it went after them with the same aggressiveness, enthusiasm, even exuberance, that it took on the competition.

But the aftermath of F/S brought subtle, but profound,
changes in management attitudes at IBM. Armonk never lost
its appetite for big, expensive projects. But F/S was the last
time a centrally driven technology initiative ever challenged
an existing profitable product line. The mainframe division
felt badly used by F/S, and with good reason—the cost of
missing the mid-1970s development cycle has been estimated
in the billions of dollars. But from then on the 370 architecture was sacrosanct, even as it grew old and creaky through
the 1980s and 1990s. In the 1960s, the 1401's managers also
fought bitterly against the 360—division executives are measured on sales and will always defend their most successful
architectures and products. But the old IBM had the discipline and esprit to inspire, or flog, managers to transcend
their narrow self-interests. In the new, post-F/S IBM, power
slowly shifted to the stakeholders in existing methods and
products.

Self-protectiveness was made easier by a rapid decentralization of the company's development programs to the divisions in the early 1970s, partly to stay a jump ahead of the

government's antitrust enforcers, and partly in reaction to F/S's failures. Decentralization meant a gradual loss of the overall system and architectural compatibility that had been the great achievement of the System/360. The cost might have been worth it if the divisions had reacted faster and been more entrepreneurial than the old IBM; but with the single exception of Boca Raton's early years with the PC, that was not the case. Decentralization sprang from uncertainty, not conviction; while responsibility was nominally pushed down to the divisions, the old centralized management apparatus stayed in place. But instead of driving a strategy, top managers began to administer process. Coordinative, consultative, and deliberative machinery proliferated, and a slow process of politicization crept over the company. The newer fast-track executives were good at presentations, quick to sniff out majority sentiment, skilled at stitching together consensus. Armonk became dead weight, spinners of grand but harmless visions, rule-makers and administrators, not leaders. Fearful of challenging entrenched marketing baronies, they piled political and bureaucratic baggage on promising new technologies, muffling their impact, blunting their effectiveness.

Most corrosive of all, the old IBM candor died with F/S. Top management, particularly Opel, reacted defensively as F/S headed toward a debacle. The IBM culture that Watson had built was a harsh one, but it encouraged dissent and open controversy. But because of the heavy investment of face by the top management, F/S took years to kill, although its wrongheadedness was obvious almost from the very outset. "For the first time, during F/S, outspoken criticism became politically dangerous," recalls a former top executive. It got much worse when Opel became CEO in 1980, and even worse under Akers. For the first time, IBM had room at the top for placeholders and sycophants.

It took many years for IBM to succumb to its own bureaucracy. Cary could still rouse the organization to produce the PC in 1980—although, significantly, the PC did not challenge any existing product stakeholders. For all the affection and respect that IBM executives still hold for him, Frank Cary's tenure marked a distinct downturn in the company's fortunes.

It is sad, perhaps, that F/S was the first significant event of his tenure. Cary and Opel, of course, were also preoccupied by exogenous and uncontrollable events, such as the mindless punishment inflicted by the American government's legal apparatus and the coordinated assault by the Japanese government and computer companies. But the egregious overreaching and undisciplined execution of F/S, and even more important, the failure to control its toxic aftereffects, must be laid at their feet.

No one can measure the cost of the loss of managerial effectiveness at IBM, but its effects can be felt in the tortured journey of one of the most important technologies in the recent history of computing, known as RISC, which IBM once had all to itself.

THE BIRTH OF RISC

RISC, standing for "Reduced Instruction Set Computing," is a major element in the American advantage in computer design and innovation compared to other countries. RISC is a new way of thinking about computers that, without any advances in manufacturing and process technologies, produces machines that run two to four times faster than conventional designs. The first commercially successful RISC computer was Sun Microsystem's SPARCstation, introduced in late 1986. IBM's 1986 RT PC workstation was also a RISC machine, but it was so poorly executed that it made almost no impact on the market.

Microprocessors utterly confounded conventional notions of computer processing speeds; RISC microprocessors push those speeds to their outer limits. Processing speed is usually measured in millions of instructions per second, or mips. A top-of-the-line IBM 370 mainframe ran at about 8 to 10 mips in the early 1980s. An IBM PC with an Intel 386 microprocessor could hit 2.5 to 3 mips in 1986. Sun's first SPARC RISC microprocessor, also introduced in 1986, ran at 10 mips, with a much simpler design than Intel's. The SPARC was followed by a flood of new RISC designs from MIPS, Hewlett-

Packard, IBM itself, Intel, DEC, and many others, with speeds roughly doubling every year. (Since widely established conventional microprocessors, like Intel's, are mostly old designs, the newer RISC chips typically have much more than the canonical two to four times speed advantage.) Current top RISC designs run in the 100 to 200 mips range (there is much gamesmanship, or "mipsmanship" in the detailed speed claims) and are closing in on supercomputer records. Chips costing only hundreds of dollars with processing capabilities in the *billions* of instructions per second are just over the horizon, radically reshaping the geography and economics of high-performance computing.

RISC was invented by John Cocke, a senior scientist at IBM's Yorktown Heights Research Center. Cocke is one of the great figures in the recent history of computing technology. In an age when computer scientists often jump from company to company chasing publicity and stock options like sports-hero free agents, Cocke's loyalty to IBM is as remarkable as his fecundity as a researcher, which is legendary. For example, Intel recently introduced "clock-doubling," a technology that greatly speeds microprocessors. "Cocke gave them that," an IBM executive told us. "He thought of it at a cocktail party. We shouldn't let him out without bodyguards to take notes. Ten minutes of small talk with Cocke can be worth billions of dollars."

Every computer's circuitry is optimized to carry out some list of fundamental operations like "ADD." Adding two numbers may involve up to a dozen or so discrete steps (for instance, moving the first digit to the ADD register, moving the second digit to the second ADD register, and so forth). The basic collection of available fundamental operations and the detailed logic steps attached to each make up a computer's "instruction set." Complex computer operations are carried out by programming sequences of instructions from the available instruction set. Each type of computer or microprocessor has its own unique instruction set, and it will execute any standard computer operation by a unique sequence of its own native instructions.

One of the important breakthroughs of the IBM 360 was

to store the 360 instruction set in silicon right in the central processor; a stored processor instruction set is called micro-code. The common microcode in all 360 models made it possible for software to be compatible across the entire family. It is not necessary to store machine instructions sets in silicon—they can be in software, for instance—but with the great success of the 360, the concept of committing instruction sets to microcode almost immediately became standard practice for most computer manufacturers.

The development of useful instruction sets, particularly microcoded instruction sets, was an important advance in improving the capabilities of computers and the ease of programming them. But good ideas are usually carried to excess, and in the late 1960s, when Cocke began to focus on the problem of building faster processors, he found that the growing complexity of instruction sets was hogging a major share of processor time and acting as a serious drag on computer performance. Cocke had always been interested in optimizing the interaction between hardware and software, and he focused on the instruction set problem with a jeweler's eye. He found that if he greatly simplified the instruction set and tuned it so each instruction was completed in one processor clock cycle, computers could run much faster. (Instead of a complex instruction like "Drive to the corner, pause for the stop sign and turn," a RISC processor will use a sequence of simple, one-clock-cycle instructions: "drive-drive-stop-turn-drive.")

Cocke's work at IBM was kept secret for more than a decade, but by the end of the 1970s, similar ideas were bubbling up in the academic computer science community, particularly at Berkeley, through the work of David Patterson, and at Stanford under John Hennessy. (Both had students who had worked at IBM Yorktown as summer interns.) Patterson spent a sabbatical at DEC in 1979 and was impressed with the great complexity of the VAX microcoded instruction set; he was probably the first to realize that reducing microcode was especially important for microprocessor design, since it regularized circuit layout and conserved scarce silicon real estate. In 1980, with the help of a Defense Department grant, he and a graduate student designed a new microprocessor called RISC I—the first use of the name RISC. IBM disclosed its own work on RISC only in 1982, and then very guardedly, at a conference at which all the main academic players were present. Patterson's work led directly to Sun Microsystems' highly successful SPARC RISC microprocessor, while Hennessy left academia to cofound MIPS. MIPS and Sun processors dominated the RISC market during the last half of the 1980s.

Cocke, on the other hand, worked on RISC for almost fifteen years before IBM introduced a product—the 1986 RT PC workstation, an abject failure. The story of how IBM squandered a decade's head start in RISC holds important clues about what was going wrong at the company.

Burying RISC

Cocke first developed his RISC ideas as part of a research effort in California under "Black Jack" Bertram, one of IBM's most respected, and feared, development managers. The team was charged with developing a fast scientific computer. (Computers use floating point arithmetic, basically scientific notation, to handle the large numbers characteristic of scientific calculations; for various reasons, accelerated floating point is often not appropriate for commercial machines, so until very recently, scientific and commercial machines usually had different processor designs.) By 1968, Cocke's team had built a prototype computer called the ACS that incorporated early versions of the key RISC concepts. The ACS computer was quite fast, although it was expensive. Much more important, Cocke had designed an ACS instruction set that was not compatible with the 360's. Incompatibility with the 360 was a fatal defect at IBM, so the project was canceled.

Cocke returned to the East Coast, still under Bertram, and took on a new assignment to design a high-reliability, low-maintenance computer. He had a new machine running in 1974 or 1975, called the ServiceFree. RISC was ideal for a low-maintenance product, since it minimized the number and complexity of circuit boards and simplified the entire design.

The ServiceFree was a small computer, potentially quite inexpensive, and screamingly fast. Cocke, who is cautious in the extreme about making claims, has reported that the Service-Free ran at 80 mips—that's about fifty times faster than IBM's fastest mainframes at the time. Supercomputers did not reach speeds of 80 mips until the early 1980s, almost ten years later. RISC workstations first hit 80 mips about 1990.

This time, Cocke understood that management would accept no computer that was not 360/370 compatible. So his team devoted considerable effort to emulating 370 instructions, even though that effectively meant putting back much of the software overhead that had been stripped out to make the ServiceFree run so fast in the first place. They succeeded in getting the ServiceFree to run 370 code very fast, if not nearly as fast as the 80 mips it could hit in its native mode. They also began work on a library of routines that would allow the machine to switch gracefully back and forth between 370 and native code. When speed was of the essence, customers could run programs optimized for the ServiceFree's architecture, but they could still run 370 programs if they wanted to.

IBM, however, had no interest in the ServiceFree. F/S was in full swing, consuming an enormous share of resources and scientific attention. At the same time, the mainframe division, alarmed at the slippage in 370 development caused by F/S, was squeezing resources to enhance the 370. The Service-Free, like the ACS, was killed.

After the death of the ServiceFree, Cocke developed statistical analyses of IBM program runs, and showed that the vast majority of the standard microcoded instruction sets were almost never used. The analysis allowed Cocke to demonstrate theoretically that his new architecture, assuming equal hardware technology, would run standard programs at least two to four times faster than the best conventional computers, and six to eight times faster than a 370, which was already an old processor design. Joel Birnbaum, Cocke's supervisor at Yorktown, authorized yet another project in 1976, originally aimed at building a fast telecommunications switch, that by 1978 produced a computer prototype called the 801, named after the number of the laboratory building where Cocke worked. That is the event that is usually designated as the invention of RISC. The 801 was a minicomputer that Cocke and his team assembled from standard components to shorten the design period. Its microcode and compilers (software that helps translate higher level code down to machine language) were considered very primitive, but it was still a very fast machine.

The technical side of IBM—Lewis Branscomb, the chief scientist; Ralph Gomory, the chief of research; Birnbaum; and a small number of others—had by this point been selling RISC indefatigably for more than five years. At first they were drowned out by the Sturm und Drang surrounding F/S. Then, when F/S was finally killed, they ran into a solid wall of resistance from the mainframe division, who were fuming at the loss of a product generation because of F/S and resolved never to let anyone meddle with their beloved 370 architecture again. But RISC was by now slowly gaining a following within IBM, and the 801 was clearly too important a development to be ignored or canceled like the ACS and ServiceFree. But it was still ten more years before a marketable 801-based product would emerge from the ever-murkier gloom of IBM's evolving interdivisional politics.

The 801 design finally found a constituency in IBM's Austin Laboratory, the development arm for IBM's office products division, the unit that included typewriters, copiers, and the Displaywriter word processor, oddly remote from the mainstream of IBM's computer technology. The Austin group executed part of the 801 design on a microprocessor, called the ROMP (Research/Office Products MicroProcessor). It was fabricated at the Burlington, Vermont, semiconductor plant about 1980, making it the first RISC microprocessor, completed at least a year before Patterson's RISC I was designed at Berkeley. Burlington's execution of the ROMP was flawed, but the chip was still the fastest microprocessor in the world by a wide margin, probably five or ten times faster than any other chip on the market.

RISC also gained a powerful, if tainted, ally in top management about 1980 in the person of Bob Evans, a harder man than Cocke to ignore. Evans no longer had his old direct authority over the technology of IBM's divisions, but he had been assigned a critical coordinating role, charged especially with flagging technical issues of corporatewide significance. Although he had not been an early RISC advocate, Evans seized on RISC as a potential solution to the growing problem of incompatible systems and architectures proliferating throughout the divisions. Besides the 360/370 architecture, there were more than a half-dozen lines of minicomputers and, of course, the new PC. All of them used their own mutually incomprehensible software and operating systems, so the forces of Babel reigned. Without greater architectural coherence, Evans feared, the company faced an explosion in development costs—good software could not be transferred from one system to another—the very same problem that had prompted the development of the 360 in the first place. Other companies like DEC and Hewlett-Packard were emphasizing the compatibility of all their machines in the mid-range market and rapidly gaining market share from IBM.

In a series of presentations to senior management committees between 1980 and 1983, Evans proposed a new IBM architecture centered around RISC processing. The architecture—that is, the instruction set, the hooks and handles for software writers, and the design of the operating system and other fundamental rules of the system—would be controlled centrally to ensure compatibility, but specific implementations would be left to the product divisions. Evans also proposed aggressive development of a line of IBM RISC microprocessors, including sales of microprocessors on the open market to create a new IBM standard. Although these were still the early, giddily successful, days of the PC, Evans and a number of other executives in the company were already worried about the potential danger from clones if Microsoft and Intel controlled the PC architecture.

RISC's technical advocates were happy to get Evans's support but worried about his proposals; they wanted a simple commitment to a clean RISC design to show what the technology could do. Evans was freighting RISC with the politics of centralized versus division-level architectural development,

which had been fought out bitterly during the decentralization move in the mid-1970s. And although Evans's technical
and marketing arguments were powerful ones, the thudding
failure of F/S still hung heavily over the corporation, and
Evans's complex development plan would have delayed the
commercialization of RISC. For its part, the mainframe division was unmoved: it would have nothing to do with big central projects, with Evans, with RISC, or with microprocessors.
At the other extreme, PC executives were fiercely jealous of
their hard-won independence from central directives; despite
repeated presentations in Boca Raton, Estridge had no interest in RISC microprocessors, no matter how fast they were.

Cocke kept making his technology harder to ignore. The
Aspen conference in 1982 confirmed his argument that RISC
conferred a two to four times speed advantage over conventional processors (now dubbed CISC, for "Complex Instruction Set Computing"). More important, a Yorktown team
quietly joined with Austin's ROMP developers to quell any
remaining doubts about RISC's usefulness for real-world
computing problems. By eliminating most of conventional
processors' microcode, RISC placed a much greater burden
on the compiler software, the software that helps convert high-
level languages into machine instructions. The compilers for
the ACS, ServiceFree, and 801 were only prototypes. About
1982, however, the Yorktown/Austin group produced the
"Austin Compiler System," software that would compile instructions from four major languages in wide use at IBM—
PL.8, PL/1, FORTRAN, and C—to run efficiently on the 801,
or for good measure, on the 370 and the 68000 microprocessor from Motorola as well. It was an elegant and impressive
achievement; not only did it make RISC a realistic computing
solution, it would allow IBM software to run on either 370 or
RISC systems.

There was a problem with the Austin Compiler System,
however, which spoke volumes, not only of the limitations of
the 370, but also of the status quo mind-set that had begun to
permeate IBM. The 370, for all the mainframe division's fall-
on-the-sword insistence that it was and would always be the
quintessential IBM product, was getting long in the tooth.
Because of its original internal processing design, its main

memory, or RAM, was limited to 16 megabytes (the problem was only solved with improved hardware and software a few years later). This was very small for a big workhorse mainframe; by comparison, a standard PC that runs Windows/DOS needs almost five megabytes of RAM to operate efficiently. The Austin Compiler System, which was much more complicated than Windows, needed 10 megabytes, which was too much for the memory-starved 370. In a former IBM, if an obsolescing technology stood in the way of adopting something newer and faster, there would have been little doubt of the outcome. But now, although RISC's potential was beyond dispute, no one was prepared to tell the mainframe division to fix the 370's memory or move on to a better architecture. RISC and the Austin Compiler System were disruptive technologies. Sales of the 370 were holding up fine; the mainframe executives, mostly salesmen, had no interest in rocking the boat. The Austin Compiler System was shelved.

A shaky RISC compromise finally emerged from the continued rounds of senior management discussions in 1982 and 1983. The mainframe and PC divisions opted out of RISC, but two divisions were prepared to go forward—the Austin office products division, which had designed the ROMP, and the minicomputer division, which housed the largest number of incompatible architectures. Two projects were approved. The first was called Olympiad; it was housed in Austin and assigned to develop a workstation based on the ROMP microprocessor. The second, called Fort Knox, was to develop a RISC minicomputer family. Evans viewed the compromise as a major mistake, since it did little to solve the cross-divisional compatibility problem. He continued to press the issue until he was harshly dressed down by Opel at a senior staff meeting in 1984; shortly thereafter, he resigned in disgust.

OLYMPIAD AND FORT KNOX

The Olympiad project was star-crossed from the outset, an example of how a promising development program could get ground up in the process machinery that was increasingly substituting for management at IBM. The original mission was straightforward: design a ROMP-based, high-speed workstation for power users in the scientific and academic communities. It was taken for granted that it would run on a UNIX operating system. UNIX had been designed at AT&T and was widely licensed throughout the university community. The senior managers who were well disposed toward RISC placed great hopes in Olympiad. It offered a chance for a clean demonstration of RISC's power free of the entanglements of divisional politics. Or at least, so it seemed.

There were, to begin with, design and process problems with the ROMP. The chip was fabricated at the Burlington semiconductor plant and may have been Burlington's first microprocessor. Burlington had an outstanding record in memory chips, where IBM technology led the world, but the requirements for microprocessors were different; they ran better on CMOS chips, for example—which Burlington still didn't make—and used different gate, or logic circuit, technology. Although Austin's high-level ROMP design generally gets good marks, Burlington insisted on building it with a poor layout and with memory-oriented processes, which significantly degraded its performance. Both Austin and Burlington were fully aware of the implementation's deficiencies, but, as far as we can discover, neither ever considered contracting the chip to an outside microprocessor specialist like Intel or Motorola. Still, the early ROMP chips were certainly good enough. They were running at about 2.5 mips in 1982, faster than a big DEC VAX computer, and about as fast as the Intel 386 chip that was introduced only in 1986.

The planned use of UNIX quickly became another major problem. It was clearly the right choice for a scientific workstation, but since UNIX was owned by AT&T, management began to worry about creating future AT&T dependencies. The Justice Department and AT&T had reached a settlement of their prolonged antitrust action in 1982, just about the time Olympiad was getting under way. AT&T had made no secret of its intent to enter the computer business once the antitrust case ended, and IBM expected it to be a formidable rival. It was decreed therefore that the ROMP workstation would have a custom IBM software layer, called the Virtual Resource Manager (VRM), standing between the ROMP and UNIX, so third-party software developers could choose to write to one or the other. The logic was apparently that if AT&T ever began to assert control over UNIX, the VRM layer could be expanded upward into a proprietary IBM operating system. While technically feasible, that would have required a major effort on IBM's part. In any case, the first version of VRM was a performance hog and slowed the ROMP badly; worse, writing it delayed the project for at least a full year, effectively eliminating its first-to-the-market advantage.

It got worse. IBM had a corporatewide graphics program oriented around mainframe users. Somehow, the internal sponsors of the graphics architecture, in North Carolina, managed to have their software mandated for Olympiad. (The Olympiad managers we interviewed have no idea of the source of such edicts, only that they came down "from on high." The most senior manager on the project, Frank King, has refused comment.) There was nothing technically wrong with the IBM graphics standard but it imposed a complex coordination process that added further substantial delays. The ROMP workstation was turning into a toad. The graphics decision was characteristic of IBM's new management. No one would press a course on a reluctant division executive; if mainframe and PC executives chose to ignore RISC, they could. But if a decentralized division actually initiated a new project, coordinative salvos came from every side. A kind of reverse Darwinism was stunting development. Any new idea could be vetoed by the divisions; but if a project actually got under way, it had to run a gauntlet of corporate mandates, which, often as not, crippled the original idea.

Then the ROMP workstation's mission began to shift. Austin, after all, was the development site for office products, such as typewriters and copiers, and their original interest in the ROMP had been for a networked office workstation to replace the Displaywriter, its stand-alone word processor. Olympiad, however, was targeted for the scientific world, not Austin's natural market. But parallel to Olympiad, the division was still working on a Displaywriter successor. Inevitably, about a year into Olympiad, a decision was made to revert back to the old plan. Shifting the design back to an office product had radical design implications. The advanced mathematical capabilities that were being built into the machine were no longer needed, and the graphics requirement would be much reduced; on the other hand, a network architecture became much more important, as did inquiry capabilities into mainframe storage files. So Olympiad changed direction and started building an office workstation. Then about 1984, it was decided that the office workstation was a bad idea after all, and the design team dutifully switched back to the original scientific concept. But by now it was too late to add back mathematical and graphics capabilities that had been scuttled for the office project.

There were still other problems. Almost no one in the top management layers of Olympiad had managed systems development projects before. Key members of the design team had experience only with the electromechanical products from Austin's more standard portfolio. The project was plagued by a blizzard of adversarial audits and information requests from the corporate level—the hostility that RISC generated in so many quarters of IBM is astonishing and, in its intensity, finally inexplicable. It is remarkable, perhaps, and a tribute to the tenacity of the working-level design team, that Olympiad produced a working computer at all. But the RT PC was an embarrassment—years late, with capabilities weirdly mismatched to its proclaimed market, very expensive, and most damningly, slow. Top IBM managers were shocked when the Sun Microsystems SPARCstation, released just six months later, decisively outperformed the RT PC, often by several factors, on every count.

Sadly, if anyone was at all vindicated by the RT PC fiasco, it was the managers of the PC division. They have been much criticized, and deservedly so, for repeatedly insisting on inferior non-IBM technologies for the PC, ultimately at the great cost of handing over the PC architectural franchise to Microsoft and Intel. But the history of the RT PC was a stark object lesson on the perils of letting a product become hostage to the Grendel-like beast that the IBM management system was turning into.

• • •

The Fort Knox project was a less traumatic failure than Olympiad only because it was less public. The project was of only two or three years' duration. The most modest estimate of its cost we have heard is $100 million, but it may have been several times that. Once again, RISC's advocates hoped to build an elegant, very fast minicomputer that would be an IBM breakthrough. Instead, the 801-based minicomputer was required to tie together the different software environments in the minicomputer division as well as the low end of the 370 architectures. Instead of producing a clean, fast 801 that would run in its native mode, the first machine was required to run in at least three other modes, to ensure that no existing installation would be disrupted by the new machine. But the division's various minicomputers and the 370 were all very different computers, with drastically different approaches to operating systems, processor design, instruction sets, and even manufacturing technology. Piling it on, the project plan called for accomplishing all the emulations at once. Slick as the 801 was, that was too much of an overhead burden to carry. In the end, the project became too big, too unwieldy, too freighted with multiple conflicting agendas ever to succeed, kind of a mini-F/S, if not nearly as expensive. Killing it was an act of mercy.

As Olympiad and Fort Knox lurched toward their inevitable demise, there was an exodus of IBM's key RISC designers. Joel Birnbaum, who was in charge of Cocke's 801 effort in the late 1970s, took a design team to Hewlett-Packard, where he is now head of development. HP's RISC-based workstations and minicomputers are arguably the most advanced in the industry, and the company has used RISC to assert itself as a force in computers after a long period of decline. John Moussouris took a leave to work with John Hennessy at Stanford and, along with Hennessy, eventually became a cofounder of MIPS. Sun and MIPS set the RISC microprocessor standard during the last half of the 1980s.

Ralph Gomory, who had become IBM's chief scientist, mounted a last-ditch effort to save RISC after the failure of the RT PC. After fierce lobbying, a new project was funded, headed by Andy Heller. Gomory made an impassioned speech in the auditorium at Yorktown: if the people who had devoted their professional lives to RISC would join Heller's team, Gomory promised, they would get one clean shot at showing what they could do. Many took the chance and the result, in just about three years, was the RS6000 line of workstations, among the best in the industry.

Twenty years after ACS, fifteen years after the Service-Free, and ten years after the 801, IBM finally produced a competitive RISC product. The RS6000 was everything the RT PC was originally supposed to be. It ran on a very fast, internally supplied, 801-derived processor. It had a clean UNIX-derived operating system, IBM's AIX. It was competitively priced. From an initial product base in the scientific and engineering communities, it steadily expanded into the office network market and is an important component of IBM's strategy in the 1990s.

By common consent, Heller gets the major share of the credit for the RS6000; instructively, he is no longer with IBM. Heller is a superb technologist who did not fit well with the IBM culture. (He once rode his motorcycle through a division headquarters hallways on a Saturday—"There was a sales meeting, and the salesmen were all wearing their suits on a Saturday!" he told us. "It was absurd. What would you have done?") Heller's general outrageousness and single-minded insistence on keeping the RS6000 on track, say insiders, offended too many executives for him to remain at the company. He is now the president of HAL, a promising Japanese-financed start-up in California developing high-speed parallel machines using SPARC RISC microprocessors.

The ultimate cost of fumbling RISC, ironically, may be heaviest not in PCs or workstations, but in mainframes, long IBM's flower and glory. As of 1992, high-speed computer designs are moving decisively to arrays of RISC and microprocessor-based architectures. IBM, however, has remained stubbornly committed to a by now very creaky 370 architecture and is facing a major migration problem. The mainframe and PC divisions' monolithic refusal to develop RISC will weigh on IBM for the rest of the decade.

4

THE RISE OF THE CLONES

The best ideas are the obvious ones; the trick always is to get there first. When sales of the IBM PC took off like a rocket, cloning was inevitable. Three Texas Instruments engineers with dreams of starting their own business, Rod Canion, Jim Murto, and Bill Harris, saw the opportunity first, moved fast, and executed it brilliantly. They called their company Gateway Technologies; later, when they could afford an advertising agency, the name was changed to Compaq.

There were lots of manufacturers of non-IBM personal computers before Compaq, but they all sought brand definition by making their machines run differently from everyone else's. Compaq imitated IBM *exactly*; the key insight was that once IBM had the lead position, it was more important to reassure buyers that a non-IBM machine would run all the important PC programs. Canion, Murto, and Harris didn't start out with the intention of taking on IBM directly—nobody would have funded them—but thought there was an opportunity for an IBM-compatible portable. They inspected an

IBM PC at a Houston trade show, then, in one of the industry's favorite legends, sketched out the first portable on the place mat of a nearby restaurant. (Compaq later used that sketch in an ad campaign.) Venture capital flowed easily in these early heady days of the PC industry: within a few months, the trio had cobbled together $1.5 million in start-up financing and plunged headlong into getting a product out the door. The legendary venture capitalist Ben Rosen, who also financed Lotus and Borland, was one of the first investors.

IBM executives, both at Boca Raton and headquarters, had always worried about cloning—mainframe clones had been a sizable industry for years. Since the PC was such an open architecture, with so many third-party components, it was obviously much more vulnerable to clones than mainframes could ever be. But they thought they had two major defenses. The first, which much impressed Opel, was that IBM would always be the low-cost producer. The theory was that as the largest-volume purchaser IBM could always exact the lowest prices. That turned out to be precisely wrong. What happened instead was that IBM put its suppliers into the high-volume business and so bore their start-up and learning curve costs. The clone-makers then rolled in behind IBM and bought suppliers' excess capacity, so their costs were usually *lower*. (Clones got no free rides from Microsoft, who charged whatever the traffic would bear, and always more than IBM's contractual price.) In addition to their lower costs, cloners such as Compaq, Dell, AST, and Leading Edge ran very lean operations, with none of the expensive planning, human resources, and other corporate functions that IBM was so proud of. Finally, slow design cycles can raise costs sharply in the computer business, because older technology is always more expensive. Even in 1992, after years of aggressive cost-cutting, the IBM cost disadvantage is still about $200 to $1,000 per PC.

IBM's second layer of protection was its BIOS software (basic input/output system) that sat in a microchip on the PC's motherboard (the main circuit board). The BIOS translated signals from the operating system and other software for the PC's keyboard, display, and printer connections. It was copyrighted and not for sale; without it, no one could make a completely IBM-compatible PC, or so IBM thought. But Compaq spent most of its first round of financing reverse-engineering the IBM BIOS. A team of programmers who had never seen IBM BIOS specs took the thirty leading software applications, such as Wordstar and Visicalc, and analyzed the signals each program sent to the PC hardware and the responses it needed to get back. Then they wrote software that supplied all the right responses; it performed exactly like the IBM BIOS, but with completely different code, skirting any copyright issues.

Armed with its own BIOS, Compaq needed only to buy 8088 microprocessors from Intel, who was eager to sell them, and IBM DOS from Microsoft. Surprisingly, Gates resisted at first; he was used to customizing his software for each buyer. But he quickly caught on that the more clone-makers used identical Microsoft software, the greater Microsoft's leverage on the industry. As soon as he made his deal with Compaq, Gates stopped a long string of customizing projects and insisted from then on that every clone-maker buy the identical DOS. From that point, the IBM PC stood naked before the world.

Compaq hired Sparky Sparks from Boca Raton, who had built the PC's distribution network, to repeat the performance. Since IBM's factories still had not caught up to the flood of PC orders, dealers snapped up the new compatibles—Compaqs were cheaper than IBM PCs and dealer margins were higher. In 1983, its first full year, Compaq racked up $111 million in sales, the most first-year sales of any company in history, and started expanding its product line beyond portables. Canion emerged as a management star, and Compaq quickly gained a reputation for the highest-quality, best-designed machines in the industry. In just its third full year, Compaq burst into the Fortune 500 rankings—sooner than any other company; its peak sales year came in 1990, at $3.6 billion. In 1992 the savage PC price wars engulfed Compaq, Canion was fired, and the company is struggling to redefine itself. It was a short and giddy, but most impressive, run.

IBM had never expected to be vulnerable on quality. But the early successes of the PC and the PC-XT were followed by a long series of embarrassing snafus. The PC team badly misjudged the market for the PCjr., an attempt to produce a low-end home computer less capable than the current PC and XT standard. Estridge insisted on reducing its capabilities before it was shipped, stubbornly conforming with mainframe-derived IBM "rational pricing" rules—cheaper machines were supposed to do less, or else they might cannibalize higher-margin products. A PC reviewer said the keyboard looked like chewing gum Chiclets, and the name stuck; on top of some serious quality problems, it made the machine a laughingstock. A massive Christmas advertising campaign didn't help and cost a fortune. The next year, an IBM PC portable proved expensive and slow, and had to be withdrawn.

Boca Raton seemed to recover its touch with the PC-AT. Introduced in mid-1984, it featured the very fast Intel 80286 processor and a number of other advanced features, including a Selectric-style keyboard (at last) and a built-in 20-megabyte hard disk. But an enthusiastic initial reception was dampened by inexplicable disk crashes. It took nine months to track down and fix the problem, a faulty chip from a small supplier. IBM's reputation was badly tarnished, while Compaq moved in with a full line of high-quality, 286-based machines and snatched away a healthy piece of the business market. By now, the clone industry was developing its own infrastructure. Gordon Campbell, an Intel alumnus, hit pay dirt with his second consecutive start-up, Chips & Technologies. He reduced the sixty-three chips on an IBM PC-AT motherboard to five. At just $72 a set, clone-makers could buy motherboards that were faster and more reliable than IBM's, and much cheaper than the ungainly Boca Raton design.

Boca Raton's proudest boast was that it had met an almost impossible PC rollout schedule by completely shedding the bureaucratic IBM management style. The story of the "wild ducks," the impatient mavericks whom Don Estridge had culled from throughout IBM, and Estridge's project-team style of organization were already business school legend. But Estridge seems to have been overwhelmed when PCs ballooned into a $4 billion business. Promoting Estridge to head a new division combining the PC with office products didn't help. In the early days, Estridge's direct involvement with the project teams and flair for pep rallies was a major morale factor. After the promotion he began to slip back into a more traditionally remote IBM managerial style. PC employees were also looking green-eyed at the money being paid in start-up companies, and defections were rising. Estridge had made promises about a high-powered bonus program just for PC staff, but was never able to deliver.

The Boca Raton solution to any problem was to add a project team. Bill Lowe came back as the PC division head in 1985, when Estridge was finally moved out to a corporate staff assignment. (Shortly thereafter Estridge was killed in a plane crash, along with several other IBM executives.) Lowe says that he found twenty-seven major development teams all working separately on various PC-related products. Out of ten thousand employees, there were only two officially designated to coordinate the PC's overall systems architecture. But Lowe did little to fix the problem. In his own major development program, the PS/2, each of the four different models had its own team negotiating with its own component suppliers. Components bought for one machine wouldn't always work in another. The buying clout that IBM expected from its leading market position was frittered away by sheer disorganization.

The psychological watershed came in 1986, when IBM passed up Intel's very fast 386 processor in favor of sticking with the 286. This time, instead of waiting for IBM to lead the way, Compaq charged ahead with a 386 offering of its own that ran much faster than anything IBM had. In the PC magazines, machines now became designated by their processor type more than their brand name; IBM began to be lumped with the clones as just another IBM-compatible player; and its share of the personal computer market began a steady slide from about 50 percent in 1984 to about 15 percent eight years later.

TAKING ON THE CLONES

Management by intimidation has a long tradition at IBM. It is a Darwinian process that produces combative, hard-driving executives. In Watson's day, the spirit of contentiousness assured that all ideas, no matter whose, were constantly under challenge and had to prevail on their merits. Later, when dissent was less tolerated, managers trained in the Watson tradition could become merely overbearing. Tough managers forcing through critical technical decisions they do not understand can be very destructive. Bill Lowe was a forceful manager who, by common consensus, had little understanding of technical issues. During the three years he headed the PC division, he was responsible for a series of critical decisions that effectively sank any last hopes IBM had to succeed in the personal computer business. He didn't work in a vacuum, of course; all key decisions were hashed out by a small group of senior executives that included Lowe's immediate boss, Mike Armstrong, another former marketer, and Jack Kuehler, IBM's president. Significantly, Kuehler is the only executive in IBM's operational management chain who came out of the technical side of the company.

By the mid-1980s it was clear that the personal computer market was following a power trajectory all its own. Mainframes, and even minicomputers, were purchased by a small closed elite of computer professionals; technical progress was very fast compared to most industries, but high price tags and an ingrown user community moderated the pace of change. Personal systems, by contrast, were cheap, open, and democratic. Thousands of software programs followed the PC onto the nation's desktops, wresting the technology away from the professionals. The PC-AT, which had appeared so astonishingly fast at first, looked fairly poky when financial analysts started toying with multidimensional spreadsheets; a secretary with a long mailing list could make an AT hit a wall. Novices liked graphic user interfaces, but they are performance hogs. No matter how much power was built into personal computers, in short, it was quickly exploited by legions of software writers, leaving the machines gasping for more speed.

The AT, IBM's top-of-the-line PC, was a 16-bit machine, and the 286 chip was a 16-bit microprocessor; in addition, the "bus," or the data highway between the 286 and the rest of the machine, could handle only 16 bits at a time. Shortly before Lowe took over, the PC division conceived of a new family of IBM PCs, to be called the PS/2 (for the second generation of personal systems), to create a new standard for the industry and put the clones in their place. The top machine, which would set the architectural standard for the new family, was to be a spectacularly fast 32-bit design, with a 32-bit microprocessor and a new 32-bit bus. For good measure, it would have a much sharper display, a new 3.5 inch diskette standard, and a number of other features. It all seemed to make good sense. What actually ensued was nothing less than a horror story. Top management meddling was always a problem, but hardly the root cause. Boca Raton's execution, initially under Estridge and then under Lowe, was utterly confused.

The first blunder was to pass on the 386, Intel's new 32-bit microprocessor. This was the opening for Compaq to seize the banner of PC standard-setter. That was not necessarily a disaster. As one top executive put it, "We didn't think it mattered much if we weren't first, as long as we were there relatively soon and we were clearly the best." Widely accepted as the 286 was, however, there were powerful technical arguments against making it a core IBM platform. Although it was much faster than Intel's previous chips, it was universally regarded as a poor design. It was originally intended for a UNIX machine, and incorporated awkward and complicated compromises that severely limited its performance and made it very hard to program. But one technical manager who was at Lowe's meetings at Boca Raton said, "They had these market projections showing all the world running on 286s for years. They didn't care if we thought it was a bad chip." Lowe decided to plant a flag on the 286, and that was that. (The great success of Compaq's 386 machine, however, eventually forced IBM to include a 386-based PS/2 in its initial release.)

IBM's top managers did not realize what a technical dead end the 286 was. Nor did they understand the market's insatiable demand for more desktop power. The fact that concentrating development on the 286 might hinder a graceful migration to new generations of platforms just didn't seem important. The 286 was considered very fast for a PC; IBM was planning to make 286s itself and expected them to be even faster. (In fact, they failed.) There was some fear that a 386 would encroach on IBM's minicomputer sales. More important, most IBM executives had spent their working lives selling mainframes; very few of them had PCs on their desks, and few of them, apparently, knew how to use them. That this innocuous little box that Boca Raton had cobbled together in a crash project barely five years before was gnawing voraciously away at the whole substructure of the computer industry was simply incomprehensible—the 370 mainframe was not even entirely a 32-bit machine.

The 286 decision had a host of unhappy consequences. The first was that a new operating system, OS/2, which IBM hoped would replace DOS, had to be written around a poor chip. But OS/2 was a complicated catastrophe in its own right, one we will cover in the next chapter.

Secondly, the 286 decision made nonsense of the new 32-bit bus IBM was developing for the PS/2, called Micro-Channel. A 32-bit processor like the 386 ran much faster than its 16-bit cousins, but would go faster with a 32-bit bus. (The gain in the early years, however, was quite minimal; a 32-bit bus didn't help much if all the peripheral device chips were 16-bit. It was some years before PCs were optimized for 32-bit performance throughout.) There is no real advantage, however, to a 32-bit bus without a 32-bit processor; that is like building a superhighway for a go-cart. IBM designed its new bus when the PS/2 was still conceived as a 32-bit architecture, but after the decision was made to focus development around the 16-bit 286, IBM went ahead with the new bus anyway.

There was a problem. MicroChannel was an excellent bus, but it was not compatible with most expansion and interface cards supplied by third-party vendors for IBM PCs. The cards added functions to the PC, such as connections to mainframes or networks, or special graphics for professional designers. In big companies, the investment in cards could easily represent $1,000 per PC. IBM's designers knew this, so they prototyped the first PS/2s with both the PC-AT 16-bit bus and Micro-Channel. After the 286 decision was made, they did even better than that, and redesigned MicroChannel so it would be compatible with the old cards. But Kuehler, with Lowe and Armstrong concurring, axed the new compatible design. "Jack decided it was time to take on the clones directly," said an executive who was at the critical meeting. The market, that is, would be forced to accept MicroChannel, even though it cost more, provided no advantage for a 286 machine, and required customers to scrap their expansion cards. (To make matters worse, IBM's expansion cards for MicroChannel weren't ready for months.) It was the old IBM arrogance: "They still didn't realize they were in a competitive world. They thought we could ram anything down customers' throats," one former executive said. Adding insult to injury, IBM peremptorily discontinued the popular PC-AT so customers would be forced to buy the PS/2.

Not surprisingly, customers were less than delighted with MicroChannel. The only one of the initial PS/2 offerings that sold at all well was a low-end model with an 8086 chip and the old bus. About a year after the MicroChannel release, a consortium of clone-makers, led by Compaq, financed the development of a new 32-bit bus that was compatible with customers' installed base of equipment. The EISA standard, as it came to be called, quickly became the industry norm.

It got worse. A top-of-the-line, extra-sharp display system was made available only through a special expansion card costing about $2,000. There were almost no takers. Emboldened by the success of EISA, another consortium developed a new, open video standard similar to, but much cheaper than IBM's, which again quickly became the IBM-compatible norm. Still worse, the OS/2 software that was supposed to be ready for PS/2 was months late, and an expensive failure when it was finally released. The much-advertised mouse came without any base of third-party software that used it.

When the smoke cleared from the PS/2 debacle in 1988, IBM had lost on all fronts. It had spent three years developing an entirely new standard for PCs. That was at least twice as long as the PC market was coming to expect from the best clone-makers like Compaq. The result of all the effort was that IBM had lost control of all four of the important personal computer standards—the microprocessor, the operating system, the bus, and the graphics system. IBM was just another clone-maker, but the one with the most pretensions, the biggest overhead, the highest prices, and a rapidly falling market share.

GAVOTTE WITH INTEL

Kuehler commented in mid-1992: "When you sell a personal computer today, the people who make the money are the microprocessor maker and the operating system supplier." IBM's PC business probably loses money, or at best breaks even, while the rest of the PC clone-makers wage savage price wars for razor-thin margins. Microsoft's 1992 after-tax profit rate, in the meantime, is closing in on $750 million on almost $3 billion in sales, while in 1991, Intel, with sales of $5 billion, made $1 billion in profit and spent $1 billion on R&D. Those are very fancy numbers indeed; at the time of Kuehler's comment, the two companies together had $5 billion in cash on their balance sheets, more than IBM. Kuehler was speaking, in fact, in the context of an announcement that Intel and IBM would finally begin to go their separate ways. IBM would thenceforth diversify its base of microprocessor vendors and supply more of its needs internally. Intel has always sold its chips to all comers. To both companies' credit, the divorce—if that is the right word—was a friendly one, with none of the imputations of bad faith that soured the last years of IBM's alliance with Microsoft.

IBM's consistent support of Intel throughout the 1980s was motivated partly by public-spirited national policy concerns and partly by its own long-term interests. Intel had pioneered not only the microprocessor but also the first mass-produced DRAM, the SRAM (a memory device), and the EPROM (a device for permanent storage of software in silicon)—the three key inventions that made microcomputing possible. Its top executives, Robert Noyce—co-inventor of the integrated circuit—Gordon Moore, and Andrew Grove, were greatly admired by IBM's managers. In 1982, IBM paid $250 million for a 15 percent equity stake in Intel (which it later sold). Intel's primary business in the early 1980s, however, was memory chips, which were becoming low-margin commodity products. When the Japanese attacked the American memory chip market during an industry recession in the mid-

1980s, Intel was pushed to the brink of insolvency. IBM was alarmed at the potential loss of the nation's semiconductor manufacturing base. In its own self-interest, it needed healthy American semiconductor makers to support domestic chip manufacturing *equipment* makers, because it feared becoming dependent on Japanese equipment makers. Intel and IBM played a leadership role in organizing Sematech, a government/industry chip manufacturing technology consortium. Noyce served as its first director. IBM was the only computer-maker that could afford to take such a long-term view; since it is the only company that makes most of its own chips, it stood to make substantial short-term profits if its competitors had trouble finding supplies.

Regardless of IBM's motivations, it still became needlessly reliant on Intel, at the time a technically inferior outside supplier, for one of the keystones of the PC architecture. In the course of its relation with Intel, IBM transferred substantial technology and received little for it; and when the microprocessor business became hugely profitable, IBM got almost no benefit from it. This was quite out of character for the old IBM, which was famous for its skill in disciplining suppliers, even without all the leverage it enjoyed over Intel. By the 1990s, when IBM first began seriously trying to establish itself in the microprocessor business, Intel had become a far more formidable and resourceful competitor.

The original choice of Intel to supply the PC microprocessor was almost casual. As soon as PCs bloomed into a multibillion-dollar industry, however, with most software designed for the Intel chip, Intel's strong position was obvious. Therefore, very early in the PC game, top management began debating what to do about Intel.

Three partisan camps emerged in the constant meetings on microprocessor policy throughout the 1980s. The first were the "RISC bigots," as one designer called them, the flag bearers for the ROMP. They never pressed the case for a PC ROMP as vigorously as many observers hoped—RISC advocates "were so convinced that good architectures always win out over bad that they were willing to wait. They didn't see how they could lose." In the event, the energies of the Austin

ROMP group were dissipated in the ill-fated Olympiad/RT PC project.

The second natural interest group was the semiconductor division. The ROMP came from the Burlington foundry, and the division's executives had a continued interest in capturing more of the PC business. But, like the ROMP partisans, they were at best halfhearted advocates. As a senior semiconductor executive told us, "We thought like an in-house foundry. We tended to wait for people to bring business to us. We weren't used to going out and fighting for it." Just as important, although IBM had probably the best semiconductor process and packaging technologies in the world, it was still weak in microprocessor design, and its chip manufacturing technologies were heavily oriented toward memory chips. Aware of their problems, Burlington put together two talented microprocessor teams in the early 1980s, and by about 1982 designed an improved ROMP to run at 9 mips, startling for the day. But Opel was looking to reduce expenses in 1982 and ordered the project killed and the teams disbanded. The lack of the highest-quality microprocessor design skills within IBM still handicaps the RS6000 RISC chip set, good as it is. IBM finally joined with Motorola in 1991 to design its advanced RISC chips.

The old IBM arrogance didn't help. Intel and IBM entered into a major technology agreement in 1986. Intel got a number of IBM's technologies, such as chip packaging, where IBM was the best in the world. IBM got the 386 designs and the right to make up to half of its own 386 requirements. In addition, IBM got the right to make enhanced 386 designs, not only for internal consumption but for outside sales as well. IBM could not sell single chips, but could sell the enhanced designs as part of integrated modules, like motherboards—in short, it could have gone into competition with Intel in a serious way. But as an Intel executive put it, "We really never worried much about IBM selling our designs. The NIH [not-invented-here] mentality in Burlington was so strong, we could trade them anything and be pretty sure they'd never use it."

While Burlington and Austin pressed the case for recapturing the microprocessor standard without much fervor, the PC division stood consistently, unalterably, opposed to any change in the relationship with Intel. At one point, after Austin was folded into the PC division, Estridge forbade them to work with Burlington on technologies aimed at replacing Intel. Even after Burlington got the right to make 386s, the PC division refused to buy them, arguing, apparently with a straight face, that they feared becoming dependent on a possibly unreliable sole-source internal supplier. (In their defense, it is not clear that Burlington could yet beat Intel on price.)

Between 1986 and 1989, there were at least three, and probably more, attempts to reduce dependence on Intel, apparently all of them debated at the Kuehler level. The first was simply a proposal from Burlington to make unenhanced 386 chips, as its agreement with Intel permitted. The PC division fought it all the way to Kuehler before grudgingly assenting to buy about 20 percent of its requirements internally. (IBM is apparently fully exploiting the agreement's 50 percent limit in 1992.) But internal politics and the PC division's lack of interest shot down the second Burlington proposal to make multichip modules with enhanced 386s. IBM's process technologies were sufficiently superior to Intel's at this point that, armed with Intel designs, they could have made more highly integrated, faster components than Intel, and either captured a profitable share of the clone market or at least distanced themselves from their PC competitors. Our Burlington sources concede that they stopped pushing the proposal when the PC executives objected adamantly.

The third and most ambitious proposal, informally dubbed L86 for "last x86," was actually approved and funded by Kuehler over the PC division's objections. It originated with Glenn Henry, a creative software and logic designer and a prestigious IBM Fellow. In 1987, Henry demonstrated a chip architecture that could use a RISC core to run in either a RISC or x86 mode. In the x86 mode, it would be twice as fast as Intel's best chips at the time. Two separate corporate audits pronounced the project technically sound. Since it promised independence from *both* Intel and Microsoft (in its non-x86

mode, it would be liberated from DOS), it provoked a continuing controversy at the highest levels, not only on advis-
ability and feasibility but also on the details of the approach.
Despite the project's importance, when Henry gave up in frus-
tration and accepted an offer from Dell, no one picked up his
cudgels, and the project was simply dropped—a depressingly
familiar story.

The PC division's steadfast opposition to internal microprocessor solutions was an unattractive combination of cynical realpolitik and narrow self-interest. By the mid-1980s,
based on fiascos like the RT PC, they certainly had reason to
fear asphyxiation within the constrictor coils of centrally mandated IBM projects. But that can be no excuse for their failure
to exercise a leadership role in developing competitive internal sourcing—the PC division was big enough to justify its
own foundry—either in partnership with or in opposition to
Intel. The real reason for their obstructiveness, it appears, is
simply that they preferred their independence. Swinging with
the stars in Silicon Valley was a lot more fun than blue-suited
planning marathons in Armonk.

Don Estridge and the other members of the original Boca
Raton team deserve full credit for the initial IBM PC, an
achievement of historic significance. But after 1983, the PC
division did almost everything wrong. Product development
was chaotic and slow. Quality was only average. Relations
with critical suppliers were mismanaged, much to IBM's detriment. Fundamental strategic decisions were almost all
wrong, much to the benefit of Microsoft and Intel. They took
no interest in developing the internal supply regime necessary
to discipline third parties. PCs were a tough business, and
these were all hard issues. But the PC division got almost
none of them right.

It was not until 1991 that IBM finally introduced an enhanced 386 design, the 386SLC, as permitted by the 1986
agreement with Intel (the 486SLC followed in 1992). In what
may have actually been a countermove, the PC division
opened a joint IBM-Intel design center, called the Noyce Center, in Boca Raton, pointedly without the participation of the
semiconductor division. IBM will have only four-month ex-

clusivity on new designs coming out of the center. It is too soon to speculate on the future relation between IBM and Intel, but the fact that IBM, the world's biggest semiconductor maker, has no substantial position in microprocessors more than ten years after it virtually created the PC industry is nothing less than a scandal.

Stormy as the relations between IBM and Intel sometimes were, the executives of the two companies fundamentally liked and respected each other. By the mid-1980s, however, relations between IBM and Microsoft, the other important PC supplier, had become toxic.

5

REVENGE OF THE NERDS

When the IBM PC team first visited Bill Gates in Redmond, Washington, in 1981, they thought the skinny twenty-six-year-old and his little stable of hackers were very bright and competent, but hardly an industrial-strength software shop. "They were just a bunch of nerds, just kids," said one IBM manager. "They didn't know how to write code. They had no test suites [automated debugging routines], nothing." But the minnow that IBM pulled aboard its PC ship turned into a whale shark that is eating the crew, the other passengers, the boat, everything.

Gates is the most respected and feared man in the computer industry—and the most hated. He has been accused for years of using his control over the DOS operating system to ambush his software competitors—"DOS ain't done till Lotus don't run" was the reported slogan for the young programmers working on DOS 2.0. Microsoft doesn't invent software, it commercializes it; Gates has built an empire on his competitors' best ideas. DOS came from Seattle Computing; the ideas for Windows from Apple and Xerox, for TrueType from Adobe, for Word from Xerox, for PenWindows from Go/Penpoint. The list goes on and on; as one erstwhile partner put it, "A partnership with Microsoft is like a Nazi non-aggression pact. It just means you're next." No one has ever accused Gates of losing gracefully. His colleagues and partners speak with awe of the uncontrolled, scarlet-faced, screaming fits. One of IBM's top technologists argued with Gates one night in California and refused to give in. "The next morning," he said, "Gates stormed into Akers's office in Armonk—he must have caught a plane and flown all night—and demanded that I be fired."

But Gates is a visionary. Very early in the history of the PC, he evolved a strikingly clear concept of where the industry was headed, and he has pursued that vision—despite many tactical setbacks—unwaveringly, relentlessly, and ruthlessly. To Gates, the only limit on the growth of personal computers is that they are still hard to use. Like everything at Microsoft, it is not an original idea; Steve Jobs and the researchers at Xerox PARC had it first. But Gates has pursued it the furthest. With cheap microprocessor power growing limitlessly, all but the most rarefied computer applications will move to the desktop as soon as ordinary users, people who are not computer science professionals, learn how to run them. Software is the democratizing trumpet that is blowing down the walls of mainframe computer centers. It is the nexus between people and machines; humanize the software, Gates argues to anyone who will listen, and the industry's potential is limitless— and who controls the software controls the industry.

IBM and Microsoft have been inextricably linked through the PC's history, first as partners, then as bitter rivals. But the process mire that IBM had created by the mid-1980s had no room for a vision to compete with Gates's own. With thousands of remarkably talented people, bright ideas would bob hopefully around the company, then slide under the viscid bureaucratic layers. No one at the top had the technical confidence and personal authority to impose coherence and focus on the contentious product baronies. No one at the bottom had the freedom or the resources to cleave a new course through the administrative muck. The computer industry was evolving rapidly in the 1980s, and IBM evolved along with it, but in a kind of Brownian motion, an ungainly flopping from one product generation to another—spastic, late, confused. Gates's early deference toward IBM slowly shifted to derision. As a former Microsoft executive put it, "Bill always thought he needed IBM, because IBM was the standard-setter. Then about 1987 or so, he realized he could set the standard all by himself."

THE DEAD WEIGHT OF DOS

Microsoft's strategic position in the computer industry re-volves around its control of the most popular operating sys-tem, MS-DOS, with more than 80 percent of the market. Nobody has ever pretended MS-DOS is good software. As one leading text puts it, MS-DOS is "obsolete, primitive . . . a bad dream . . . dragged to a fame it never deserved."

An operating system is the traffic cop that directs all the events going on inside a computer—the flow of signals from the keyboard to the processor to the display, moving files back and forth between RAM and the hard disk, allocating mem-ory space, and so forth. A good operating system will make hardware run even better than its design; a bad one not only accentuates the hardware's weaknesses, but can cripple its best features.

The attributes of a good operating system are well estab-lished. For example, it should have virtual memory. A PC motherboard comes with silicon memory called RAM; avail-able RAM limits the amount of data a program can work with at any one time. Virtual memory is a software trick that con-stantly trades data between RAM and the hard disk, so the user never notices a memory shortfall. An operating system should also have multitasking, so a user can work with two or more programs at a time, switching data from one to the other. It should protect the internals of the circuitry so data from one program can't damage another. The list goes on. But if one wrote down attributes of a good operating system, DOS would have none of them. The Intel 386 microprocessor, for example, probably DOS's most important platform, was specifically designed for virtual memory, but when it runs under DOS, the capability is wasted. The latest versions of Microsoft's Windows repair some of DOS's deficiencies, but only in a limited and tentative way.

The first DOS, MS-DOS 1.0, was a signal achievement, not because Gates and his little stable of hackers did it well but, like the dog walking on its hind legs, because they did it at all. It was written in a state of emergency; IBM didn't ask Microsoft for an operating system until very late, after IBM's original plans had fallen through. There were actually three operating systems available, however, when the PC was launched. MS-DOS won out partly because it was cheapest, partly because IBM began bundling it with the PCs, and partly because Lotus, the PC's first true blowout software product, was written specifically for it. By 1983, after almost all software for the IBM PC had come to be standardized on MS-DOS, it was effectively the only game in town.

Writing a good operating system is very hard. The great success of some of the software packages turned out by youthful virtuoso hackers gives a misleading impression of how complex and capital-intensive software production really is. Early personal computers had very limited capabilities and could make do with very limited software. It took only eight weeks for Gates and Paul Allen to write the version of BASIC that launched them in the personal computer business. Their work on DOS 1.0, starting with a hacker friend's program, took a small team about six months. But the creation of NT, Microsoft's replacement for DOS scheduled for release in 1993, has taken at least five years and has involved hundreds of programmers at a cost in the hundreds of millions of dollars. IBM's OS/2 2.0 took at least that long, consumed four hundred programmers, and may have cost $1 billion. The entire DOS 1.0 was only about 30,000 bytes long; modern fully functional operating systems require millions of bytes, and complexity rises exponentially as the code gets longer.

Very early on, DOS 1.0 became a serious constraint on the PC's usefulness. IBM, with Microsoft's full concurrence, decided that a follow-on was an urgent necessity. But the software experts at IBM were sure—with good reason—that

Microsoft did not have the industrial programming skills for the challenge. Boca Raton, however, wanted to continue working with Microsoft. With almost an audible sigh, IBM mounted a major effort to transfer programming technology and skills, like automated debugging and testing, to Gates's little company. Gates also supplied the DOS source code to Boca Raton, and a substantial amount of the actual coding of DOS 2.0 was done by IBM employees. The final version was still far from a modern standard, but at least the most egregious shortcomings of DOS 1.0 had been patched over.

Gates and his team proved quick and astute learners. One former Microsoft programmer remarked on their amazement at the stringency of IBM's testing procedures. IBM deployed one tester for every programmer; at Microsoft the ratio was one to twenty. But within a year or so, Microsoft's ratio was close to one-to-one as well. Although Microsoft remained dependent on IBM's help for DOS enhancements until the mid-1980s, Gates spent whatever was necessary to turn Microsoft into a world-class software factory, and was reaching out for top talent, such as Charles Simonyi and Scott MacGregor, both from Xerox's PARC. Simonyi, widely regarded as one of the industry's true geniuses, is still Microsoft's top designer.

By the time DOS 2.0 came out in 1983, a number of senior IBM managers were having second thoughts about Gates. People like Bob Evans had long been warning about excessive dependence on outsiders. Microsoft was not yet a public company, but everyone knew that Gates and his young acolytes were getting very rich, which engendered much resentment. In business negotiations, Gates often seemed too grasping, too shrewd, too ruthless to be entirely trusted. Still, during 1983, at the same time that it was helping Microsoft with DOS 2.0, IBM initiated far-reaching discussions aimed at merging DOS with Xenix, Microsoft's version of UNIX, which would have given Gates a potentially massive new franchise.

The surface cooperative relationship concealed a festering tension between the two companies. Astonishingly, for all its dependence on Microsoft and DOS, IBM had never secured the rights to the DOS source code; that is, as far as IBM was officially concerned, DOS was effectively a black box. Without the source code, IBM would be unable to modify DOS on its own and would always have to purchase enhancements from Microsoft. (Senior executives were unaware of the source code in Boca Raton during the DOS 2.0 push, which might have compromised Gates's rights.) It was a fundamental error, and not at all standard practice in software licensing. The only plausible explanation we have received is that Estridge and his key executives were determined to keep IBM out of software. That was arguably a sensible decision as far as *applications* software was concerned, since IBM wanted to encourage third-party developers. But it made no sense for the operating system. The PC division had the initial insight that the PC should be an open architecture, but were usually muddled about *what* parts needed to be open and which were important for retaining architectural control.

Failure to secure the rights to the DOS source code was clearly an error, but it was certainly an understandable one. It was made during the extraordinary rush to get the first PC out of the door, before the Justice Department's antitrust suit had been settled, at a time when IBM was extremely sensitive to even the appearance of having an unfair advantage over a small supplier—the kind of mistake, perhaps, that anyone could make. And normally, given the relative power of the two companies, it would have been easy to repair—simply negotiate a fair price for the source code. But the partnership with Gates was not so simple, and the failure to secure the source code at the outset, seemingly such a minor error, turned into one of the more portentous of IBM's many missteps in the 1980s. The growing acrimony between IBM and Gates was well known, and it is usually assumed that IBM stuck with Gates and DOS, despite their growing unhappiness with both, because there was no other choice. That is emphatically not the case. IBM, in fact, was on the verge of creating its own operating system standard in the mid-1980s, but Gates played hardball with the source code and faced down the assembled brass at Armonk with a degree of brazen cheek that no thirty-year-old captain of a small software company should have been able to muster.

MERMAID ON THE ROCKS

A small group of software researchers at IBM's Yorktown Heights, the same laboratory where John Cocke worked, were presented with an interesting challenge sometime in 1982. IBM had built a PC called the 3270-PC that could connect with its mainframes, so a worker could reach into the mainframe for data that she could then manipulate on the PC, with Lotus, say. Before the 3270-PC, IBM's mainframes and PCs could not talk to each other, because mainframes used an unusual convention for converting digital signals into information. The 3270-PC bridged the language gap with some special software and hardware. But that meant it could not run under DOS alone. The Yorktown group were asked to solve this problem, which they proceeded to do.

The Yorktown group wrote an elegant little operating system for the 3270-PC that they called CP/88. To the user, it looked just like DOS, but it allowed the 3270-PC to run as either a mainframe terminal, a PC, or better yet, both simultaneously. The display screen had a windowing capability—a user could work in a PC mode but keep a window open to the mainframe so he could easily switch back and forth between the two. When the PC-AT was introduced, the Yorktown group completely rewrote CP/88 and changed its name to CP/286, which they later upgraded to CP/386 (or more generally, CP/X86).

The Yorktown group then folded in a second project, originated in Boca Raton, called Mermaid. Mermaid was a GUI (a "gooey," or Graphical User Interface), a pictorial program that sat on top of DOS or CP/X86; it let the user call up files or functions by pointing to pictures rather than typing out their names. "Basically, in 1984 or so," one designer told us, "we had Windows 3.0." (Windows 3.0, introduced by Microsoft in 1990, was a blowout success.)

Taken together, CP/X86 plus Mermaid had all the features power users would insist on. It was compact code that ran efficiently on the PC. It had virtual memory, as DOS still does not. It had multitasking, so the user could run multiple PC applications simultaneously, each in its own window. Windows 3.0 can support multitasking in a limited way. Even better, CP/X86 had "virtual machine" capabilities. Put simply, it could pretend to be almost any machine the user pleased. If the user liked DOS, for instance, or needed DOS to run some application software, CP/X86 could call up DOS and run it as a subset of itself. CP/X86 also had a "bit-mapped" display processor. Before Windows, a DOS-controlled screen could show only a limited array of predetermined characters. Under CP/X86, the display would work like an Apple Macintosh, and be able to show any picture or character shape at all, even ones that users invent themselves.

Finally, and perhaps most important, CP/X86 was portable, as DOS/Windows still is not. When Microsoft wrote the first DOS, they knew IBM was going to use the Intel 8088 processor, so DOS was written in Intel assembler. Assembler languages are close to the machine level and designed only for a specific processor's circuitry. Assembler is very hard to work with, and instructions are much longer and more intricate than in high-level languages, but it can often be made to run faster than code that has been compiled from a high-level language. But the consequence of writing in assembler was that DOS could run only on processors of Intel's design—it was not a portable operating system. CP/X86, however, was written in PLAS, an IBM high-level language. By using compilers for different processors, it could run on any machine, including a RISC workstation.

CP/X86 and Mermaid began to develop a following within IBM; CP/X86 itself was eventually used on more than twenty IBM products, mostly peripheral devices. There is no question that it worked; everyone agrees, in fact, that it worked very well. The advantages to IBM of adopting an excellent, portable, IBM-controlled operating system would appear overwhelming. The IBM standard would no longer be tied to any particular processor. The company could continue to work with outside vendors, but would no longer be in danger of losing control to any one of them. Most important, the quality of the computing power available to users would have been sharply improved. CP/X86 was not the only choice for an internal operating system—there were a number of competing UNIX programs as well—but it was clearly the front runner. In 1984 a three-day CP/X86/Mermaid strategy conference was held in Boca Raton, attended by more than fifty technologists and managers. CP/X86 was also much discussed at the very top of the company in the shorthand "VM for the PC." VM was the name of a mainframe operating system that IBM was very proud of. Technically, the parallel was nearly exact. There is no doubt that IBM knew it had a high-quality internal operating system with advanced features that could be a major competitive advantage.

When IBM decided anyway to partner with Gates to develop a new follow-on to DOS, to be called OS/2, there was a near-revolt among the technologists. "The bitterness was unbelievable," one former designer told us. "People were really upset. Gates was raping IBM. It's incomprehensible."

The decision was made by a small group of top managers, including Kuehler, Armstrong, Lowe, and several others, who debated the operating system issue through most of 1984. (Our information comes from two executives who attended most of the meetings.) There were four alternatives on the table. Do the new OS/2 with Microsoft. Adopt CP/X86 as the IBM standard. License, or give, CP/X86 to Microsoft. Do one of the UNIX alternatives. Of the possible system choices, of course, OS/2 was the only one that did not even exist; it was just a plan. In the final analysis, the choices came down to two. Do OS/2 with Microsoft, or go it alone with CP/X86, since Microsoft insisted on its own code in any system it sold. OS/2 was chosen for one simple reason: Bill Gates had made it plain that if IBM introduced a successor to DOS that was not codeveloped with Microsoft, he would never release the DOS source code.

That Gates could so brazenly face down IBM's top executive firepower is astounding. What would have happened if he had actually carried out his threat? It could have meant a war between DOS and CP/X86 for control of the operating system standard. DOS's initial large installed base would obviously have been an advantage; but CP/X86 was so superior that it would almost certainly have become the primary design target—at this time IBM was still the unquestioned market leader. CP/X86, anyway, could run in a DOS mode, and IBM had already emulated the DOS commands. (A Yorktown summer intern did it in a couple of months.) To win in the long term, Gates would have had to produce DOS enhancements that outperformed CP/X86, which was extremely unlikely— IBM certainly knew firsthand how limited Microsoft's capabilities still were. There were no outstanding antitrust concerns; the Justice Department's suit had been settled for two years. In a showdown, Gates could have expected little sympathy from the rest of the software community. A long list of software vendors, such as Lotus or Borland, would have been delighted to ally with IBM to market CP/X86 and assist in its continued development.

That IBM backed away from CP/X86 in the face of Gates's threats speaks volumes of the confidence, guts, and determination of both of the parties. To make matters much worse, OS/2 proved to be an almost unmitigated catastrophe.

DIVORCE IS UGLY

OS/2 was the precipitating event in the long and painful breakup between IBM and Microsoft. But as Andy Heller points out, the relationship was "inherently unstable from the start." Microsoft's ambition was to become the software standard setter; to do so, it needed to treat all hardware platforms equally. But IBM was aiming at hardware supremacy and needed a software standard that served its own ambitions, not Microsoft's. The frictions had been building for years. IBM executives greatly resented Gates's enthusiastic courting of the clones, his great success with software that IBM had helped develop, and his then close relationship with Apple. (Opel was outraged when he saw a trade press photo of Jobs and Gates wearing Macintosh sweatshirts.) Some of Microsoft's best software, such as Microsoft Word, the Excel spreadsheet, and the TrueType printer and display fonts, were originally developed for the Macintosh. For his part, Gates "went ballistic" when IBM bought NeXtStep, a Windows-like graphical user interface from Steve Jobs; bought type font software from Adobe instead of using his TrueType; and sponsored an industry UNIX consortium in 1987. The negotiations over the DOS source code were "very acrimonious"; as relations continued to deteriorate during the OS/2 development process, IBM flirted with Metaphor, a small software house with a Windows-like GUI for the PC.

The new OS/2 program was to be rolled out with the ill-fated PS/2 computers. Right from the start, therefore, OS/2 was compromised by the decision to focus PS/2 development on the 286 processor. Gates was horrified. He regarded the 286 as a "brain dead" chip; the decision undercut the whole idea of moving to an advanced architecture. Gates appealed the decision aggressively until he was faced down directly by Lowe: management had placed a flag in the ground on the 286, and that was that. The unwonted meekness of Gates's final acquiescence is surprising. A former Microsoft executive suggests, however, that "Bill was convinced that IBM would set the standard, and he was determined to stick with them so he would have his share of it." In that light, Gates's behavior is perfectly consistent: he had gone to the wall to ensure that Microsoft would always be co-owner of the software standard; but with that argument settled, he could play along, at least temporarily, if the standard-setter insisted that the standard be brain dead.

Developing OS/2 for the 286 was a retrograde step, but barely defensible because of the chip's wide market acceptance. The real crippler, however, was the decision to write OS/2 in 286 assembler. Because of the odd layout of the 286, a 286 assembler program would be gnarly, complicated code—hard to write, hard to test, forever limited to Intel chips, and because of its deep-level ties to the 286, forever a drag on the performance of the 286's much superior successors. "Pretty crazy, isn't it?" said a top IBM executive.

But *that* decision—to develop in 286 assembler—was made by Microsoft. The IBM technologists unanimously railed against it. Lowe and the higher-ups seem to have missed its significance. Lowe told us it was made at the "techie" level, and he assumes "there was some good reason." Microsoft does not return phone calls or letters on the question.

Choosing to write OS/2 in 286 assembler is a most peculiar decision and, superficially, appears very much against Microsoft's own interests. Gates had every reason not to tie OS/2 so tightly to the 286, especially since he was so scornful of the chip. By this time he was standardizing all of Microsoft's new software on the computer language C because of its portability, and he was very proud of his new C compiler especially for Intel chips. He had also created new C development tools that allowed a programmer to work at an even higher level than C and write code very quickly that was then compiled down to C and from there to assembler. C also makes it easy to incorporate small sequences of assembler when absolutely necessary. OS/2, purportedly, was going to be Microsoft's new flagship; if it was written in C, Microsoft could eventually attack a much larger market just by adding compilers, even for Apple and RISC machines. CP/286 had already proved that a high-level language could be efficiently compiled for the 286; Microsoft itself had released a version of UNIX, in C, that compiled for the 286.

Furthermore, there is no question that Gates knew what an important chip the 386 was going to be. He had fought for the PS/2 being standardized on the 386 in the first place. Intel began circulating prototype chip sets of the 386 in the summer of 1985. Both IBM and Microsoft had them, and Microsoft immediately began working with Compaq and other clone-makers on a DOS version for their 386 machines—DOS 3.0, released in 1986, with specific features for the 386. IBM also knew about the Compaq effort and, as Gates knew, was wavering on its own 286 decision; the eventual first release of the PS/2, as we have seen, did include a 386 machine. Finally, about 1985, Gates started developing a new program, called Visual BASIC, first released in 1991, that greatly increased the power of Windows, partly by making use of the most advanced features of the 386. If anyone in the world could be expected to know that tying OS/2 tightly to 286 assembler was a killer decision, it was Bill Gates.

Language decisions in complex software development

evolve; they are not made in a single sitting at the outset of a development program. When OS/2 got under way, Microsoft was still in the process of converting from assembler languages to C. The OS/2 core was assigned to the DOS team—"macho assembler" types—as opposed to the Windows team, who were working in C. Programmers are notorious for solving problems as specifically as possible. If programmers as wedded to assembler as the DOS group are handed OS/2 specs and told only to put them on a 286, they will inevitably home in on the tightest processor-bound design possible. If graceful migration to the 386 and other architectures is an explicit project objective, they will behave much differently: they might still use some 286 assembler, but would keep it—or be forced by their managers to keep it—to the minimum necessary. In a major project like OS/2, there were many checkpoints where the programming strategy would have been specifically reviewed by Gates. Indeed, Gates is famous for reviewing, sometimes even editing, almost every line of code that goes out of Microsoft. This was supposedly Microsoft's single biggest development effort; there is no question that Gates watched the OS/2 code get more and more tightly tied to the 286, and did nothing about it.

Why would he let that happen? There is no way to know for certain what was in Gates's mind, but the circumstantial evidence points in only one direction. To begin with, there is a pattern of software development at Microsoft, which Bob Cringely, the influential columnist of *Infoworld*, has pointed out. The first version of a new product is just "market research." It works badly, if at all, but lets Microsoft find out what customers really want. The second is a more serious attempt, but still a learning exercise. The third time is when Gates finally gets it right. Windows has followed this pattern, and so did Microsoft's word processor and spreadsheet. In this paradigm, DOS would have been market research for operating systems. OS/2 would have been the serious learning exercise. And true to form there is, indeed, a third version—Microsoft's NT, a brand-new, portable, apparently highly functional operating system that is Microsoft's very own, due to be released in 1993.

Add to this pattern the state of relations between IBM and Microsoft. Bill Gates is the most visionary man in the industry. The divergence of interests between IBM and Microsoft was obvious; a breakup must have seemed inevitable. Gates had needed to bully IBM into the OS/2 partnership in the first place; the acrimony over the DOS source code made the atmosphere only tenser. Gates's intelligence network is legendary: he knew all about CP/X86, Mermaid, the various UNIX endeavors, the courting of Metaphor. Nor has Microsoft ever shrunk from putting its own interests over those of its partners; according to a famous internal memo at Lotus, Gates "admitted that Microsoft is dragging its feet" on a later OS/2 release to get a new version of Windows to market first. (Gates later denied it.)

Bluntly, if Gates expected ultimately to break with IBM, he had every interest in ensuring OS/2's failure. In that light, tying the project tightly to 286 assembler was a masterstroke. Microsoft would have acquired three years' experience writing an advanced, very sophisticated operating system at IBM's elbow, applying all the latest development tools. After the divorce, IBM would still own OS/2. But since it was written in 286 assembler, it would be almost utterly useless.

For its part, the by-now finely honed IBM bureaucratic machine did everything in its power to infuriate Gates and help OS/2 fail. In order to parcel out the action among all the potential political interests at IBM, there were at least four different IBM teams working on pieces of OS/2, one of them in England. For all practical purposes, the only code that got into the final version was Microsoft's, but the dispersed responsibilities allowed Gates to play one IBM team off against the other; from a development standpoint, the coordinating process was maddening and added at least a full year to the development cycle.

Then OS/2 got entangled with an IBM software monster called SAA, or Systems Applications Architecture. SAA was an unwieldy congeries of software projects aimed at linking together all of IBM's computers, from mainframes to PCs. SAA is typical of the projects emanating from Armonk in the last half of the 1980s. After the failure of Fort Knox, IBM never again asked a division to change its basic architectures; instead, Armonk satisfied its coordinative impulses by having divisions *add* IBM-standard embellishments and ornamentation, which almost always interfered with the basic architecture's performance. When the PC was dubbed "an SAA platform," OS/2 was burdened with a long list of mainframe-oriented development rules (designed, for example, to improve security), with little or no relevance to PCs.

The rules of SAA also decreed that the user interface for OS/2 would not be Gates's beloved Windows, but a mainframe-derived program called Presentation Manager. It descended from software written for computer professionals working at remote mainframe graphics terminals and lacked the intuitive, user-friendly feel Gates was striving for in Windows. The hooks and handles it offered to outside software developers were not at all like the ones PC software vendors were used to working with. Gates did succeed in adding his own PC-oriented graphics to Presentation Manager, but only at the cost of slowing down OS/2 considerably. Having first placed itself at Gates's mercy, IBM was doing everything in its power to turn his initial irritation into cold, derisive anger.

Perhaps even more fatefully, apparently as a consequence of IBM's interest in SAA, in about 1986 management of the relation with Microsoft was shifted away from Boca Raton to Armonk, in the first instance to an executive named Dick Hanrahan, the SAA project leader, and then increasingly to Kuehler himself. Both men, of course, are intelligent and able executives, but they had a lot on their plates, and they went home at nights. In Gates, they faced a partner—and now more often an opponent—whose knowledge of his field was matchless and whose commitment was extreme. It was about this time, many senior IBM executives feel, that Gates's relation with IBM shifted from guarded co-operation to cynical exploitation.

The first release of OS/2 in late 1987 was not auspicious. It was announced at the same time as the star-crossed PS/2, although it was not actually ready until months afterward. When it was finally delivered, it ran very slowly on both 286 and 386 machines, and slowed down even standard DOS applications. The cost of additional hardware to speed up OS/2 could run as high as $2,000. The third-party software community, after an initial burst of interest, reacted coldly. The first major software package written for OS/2, Lotus 1-2-3/G, was a bomb. Much to IBM's irritation, although Gates continued to speak enthusiastically about OS/2 in public, Microsoft was conspicuously absent from the ranks of OS/2's third-party software developers. By 1990, OS/2 accounted for only about 1 percent of the installed base of operating systems. In 1992, after living apart for some years, IBM and Microsoft agreed on a final divorce. IBM would continue to sell OS/2 by itself. Gates got the rights to any code he could use from the project.

It took IBM five years, the efforts of some four hundred programmers, and the expenditure of perhaps $1 billion to extricate the OS/2 that Gates had bequeathed them from the Laocoön coils of 286 assembler. IBM finally released a new version, OS/2 2.0, in early 1992. It is now written in C, and has enjoyed a favorable critical reception and some modest commercial success, with a million copies sold by mid-year. Windows 3.1, in the meantime, was selling a million copies every two weeks.

A handy fever chart of Gates's devotion to OS/2 is the resources he allocated to Windows. Gates never stopped Windows development, even in the first flush of the agreement on OS/2, although he cut the programming staff to skeletal levels to free resources for OS/2. Gates's first Windows release had been a failure. Windows 2.0, however, released in 1986, began to draw some respectful interest from third-party software vendors and sold a million copies its first year. By 1988, shortly after the first OS/2 release, it is clear that Microsoft was working full bore on Windows 3.0, destined to be the most successful software product in history. It was released in May 1990 with a vast array of supporting third-party software, including a long list of excellent applications from Microsoft that had somehow never gotten developed for OS/2. Within a few months, sales exceeded a million copies a month.

Windows 3.0's successor, 3.1, is now bundled as standard software by every leading IBM-compatible PC-maker except

IBM itself; and Bill Gates is well on course to become the richest man in the planet's history. IBM futilely points out that Windows is still linked to the deficiencies of DOS, but to little effect. In any PC software catalog, Windows applications outnumber those for OS/2 by ten to one. Somewhat forlornly, OS/2 2.0 ads boast of how well it runs Windows.

More ominously for IBM, by 1988 Microsoft had also begun an intensive development effort on its new operating system, NT, for "New Technology," scheduled for release in early 1993. It was developed under the direction of Dave Cutler, the creator of DEC's VMS operating system and perhaps the country's top operating system developer. Prototypes have been circulating in the third-party software community for some time; an NT software convention in mid-1992 drew more than four thousand developers. Early reports are that this time—consistent with the third-pass development pattern—Gates has done it right. Interestingly, Gates seems to be betting that Windows/DOS will continue to control the single-user desktop, even after NT. NT appears aimed at network and minicomputer users, particularly systems with multiple processors. Prototypes have already been demonstrated running on the 16-processor Sequent superminicomputer. DEC has announced that it will use NT in addition to its own operating systems on its new superfast Alpha RISC machines. If NT becomes the preferred RISC and/or multiprocessor operating system, Gates has a real shot at controlling the software environment from PCs all the way up to mainframes. Pointedly, while NT is Windows-compatible, it will not run OS/2 Presentation Manager graphics. The extent of the damage that IBM allowed to be inflicted—indeed, helped to inflict—on itself is only now becoming clear.

For IBM, the OS/2 story is a Greek tragedy. The original error, seemingly a small one, was the failure to secure DOS source code rights in 1981. When Gates used the source code as leverage in 1984, a collective failure of nerve in Armonk handed over control of the most critical PC architectural standard to Microsoft. Then Gates, with malice aforethought or not, used that development program to sink

IBM's last hopes of controlling the PC industry. Long ago, in 1976, an IBM senior staff planning exercise forecast that personal systems would be a $100 billion market in the 1990s, which is close to being right; and they concluded that if IBM could control half of that market, it would be a $100 billion company now. The market evolved almost exactly as forecast—in fact, IBM made it happen—but instead of owning half of it, IBM's share is only about 15 percent of hardware sales and much less than 10 percent of the total. Its grip even on that is tenuous. That the industry which it created and failed to control, the IBM-compatible PC, still bears IBM's name is a constant mockery.

6

Picking Through the Shards

If a modern-day Dante were taken on a tour of Businessmen's Hell, he would doubtless encounter, deep in the gloom, writhing executives from American basic industries, the Lee Iacoccas of the world, who let both their technologies and their businesses slip into second-rate status. But in an even deeper ring he would find a separate group of blue-suited men whose crime was far worse: they had had the finest technologies in the world, but let their company founder anyway.

The fall of IBM is not the conventional American story of underinvestment, slipshod standards, and lagging technology. Even with all the recent defections, it still has outstandingly talented employees. Its rate of investment through the 1970s and 1980s was massive; R&D spending in the last half of the 1980s averaged almost $6 billion a year. No other company in the history of the world has spent that much. But still the loss of market share has been precipitate in every major product category. The charts on the next page show how serious the erosion has been.

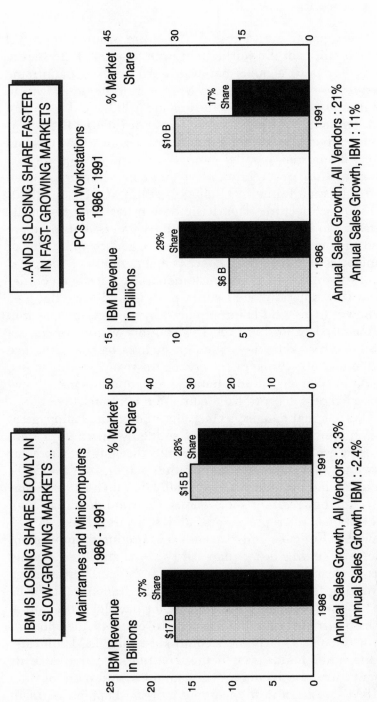

IBM IS LOSING SHARE SLOWLY IN
SLOW-GROWING MARKETS ...

Mainframes and Minicomputers
1986 - 1991

% Market
Share

IBM Revenue
in Billions

28%
Share
$15 B

1991

37%
Share
$17 B

1986

Annual Sales Growth, All Vendors : 3.3%
Annual Sales Growth, IBM : -2.4%

...AND IS LOSING SHARE FASTER
IN FAST- GROWING MARKETS

PCs and Workstations
1986 - 1991

% Market
Share

IBM Revenue
in Billions

17%
Share
$10 B

1991

29%
Share
$6 B

1986

Annual Sales Growth, All Vendors : 21%
Annual Sales Growth, IBM : 11%

Source: McKinsey Database

The slippage cuts across IBM's entire product line. IBM held two thirds of the world mainframe market at the start of the 1980s; now it holds barely a third, and its mainframe revenues are dropping. There will be little or no growth in mainframe computer sales during the 1990s, and a host of new competitors, using parallel arrays of Intel or RISC processors, are challenging the traditional designs. IBM has had powerful internal parallel processing technologies for ten years, but has never introduced them in a major product. Worse, its mainframe technology is still based on the 1960s 360/370 architecture. That basic design has been heroically stretched and extended for almost thirty years, but there are limits to how far the old mule can be flogged up a hill. One of its major competitive advantages is a generation of computer center executives, its prime customers, who have been bottle-fed on IBM solutions their entire professional lives. But they are now retiring and being replaced by younger people who are not used to pushing the IBM button when they have a problem. Once-reliable customers such as banks, insurance companies, and brokerages are aggressively cutting costs, reining in their mainframe data centers, and looking at new, much cheaper, decentralized computer solutions.

There is real danger, in fact, that the gradual slippage of IBM's mainframe position could suddenly turn into a rout. The slow evolution of the 370's architecture has been a major opportunity for Japanese mainframes selling into the 370's market. Asian manufacturers typically do much better in stable technology regimes—televisions, for example, rather than workstations, microprocessors, and software. There is evidence that Fujitsu's and Hitachi's 370 product improvement cycles are getting faster than IBM's own, and their market share is steadily rising. Thus the 370 is trapped between two converging forces. On the one hand, its franchise could be taken over by fast, inexpensive RISC or parallel processors—processors more than fast enough to emulate the old 370 instruction set, so customers could keep their IBM software. On the other hand, even if the 370 market survives in its present form, the Japanese will take more and more of it.

IBM's position in minicomputers is no happier. Its main

offering, the AS400, is an excellent machine, easy to install, easy to use, with a good software base; it won't disappear overnight. But a top-of-the-line AS400 costs almost $1 million; and customers are beginning to catch on that RS6000 workstation-based networks can do the same job for a fraction of the cost. They get irritated when they ask about workstations and the IBM salesman starts pushing the AS400; so they call Sun or Hewlett-Packard instead. At least a dozen competitors, including small companies such as Dell and AST, have already announced multiprocessor Intel 486-based machines that migrate easily from a PC environment into minicomputer processing territory; IBM is working on commercial multiprocessor products, but they are stubbornly 370-compatible, which will almost certainly limit their performance and their market impact. If Microsoft's NT establishes itself as a multiprocessor standard operating system—as Gates seems to intend—and PC software vendors like Borland succeed in bringing minicomputer-sized data bases within the reach of dBase and Paradox—as they are trying to do—IBM's position will be very vulnerable.

The future of IBM's workstations looks only a little brighter. Squandering its ten-year head start in RISC computing is among IBM's more breathtaking failures. The RS6000 is a good product selling into an intensely competitive market, against outstanding products from Sun, DEC, and Hewlett-Packard. For the most part, IBM still stubbornly refuses to allow its workstations to cannibalize its mature product lines. For example, the workstation division has developed software to allow the RS6000 to run all the AS400's minicomputer applications, conferring a major competitive advantage in a hotly contested market. But the software is still locked up in an IBM safe. A positive sign is that in mid-1992 IBM permitted its excellent mainframe transaction processing software, CICS, to be ported to the RS6000. But it must be much more aggressive if the RS6000 is to succeed.

Finally, of course, IBM's position in PCs and PC operating systems and microprocessors is lamentable. The only vestige of its brief former glory is the "IBM-compatible" name that the PC industry still wears.

IBM's unhappy position sums up like this: Sales of mainframe and minicomputer hardware and related software, maintenance, and services constitute about 65 percent of IBM's revenues. But the 370's hold on the high-performance computer market is slipping; a complete rout over the rest of the decade is not implausible. IBM's minicomputer position is fragile. In workstations, it is in the middle of a very fast pack. The PC battle has been lost. We are not making forecasts. But there is a reasonable question whether IBM is on the brink of a colossal Wang-like implosion. The possibility is all too real.

EXTENUATIONS

There is no exonerating IBM executives for their company's sudden decline; but it is only fair to point out that for some thirty years IBM's business was carried on in the face of official hostility on the part of the governments of almost all industrial countries, most particularly those of Japan and the United States itself.

Even as the Japanese government raised barriers to IBM's competitiveness in Japan in the 1950s, the American government required that IBM license all its patents on reasonable terms to all comers throughout the world. In view of the government's unceasing antitrust suspicions, "reasonable" terms inevitably meant very cheaply. Since 1956, under the benign eye of the Justice Department, the fruits of IBM's vast research and development expenditures have been provided unilaterally to its global competitors on an essentially subsidized basis. AT&T was abused in the same way at the same time: it gave away its transistors and most of its other patents virtually for free, and was obliged, until 1982, to stay out of the computer industry.

Then in 1968, the Justice Department's antitrust division launched a thirteen-year vendetta that was extremely expensive to defend, consumed a disporportionate amount of executive time and attention, and created a legacy of competitive caution within IBM—particularly against smaller firms, some of which, like Microsoft, took full advantage of IBM's restraint.

The Japanese organized the full resources of their government and their electronic industries against IBM, competing by both fair means and foul. The Japanese assault on the semiconductor industry also greatly distorted IBM's competitive priorities. The world's leading producer of semiconductors itself, IBM devoted substantial attention to shoring up the nation's semiconductor manufacturing base, materially affecting its policies toward now-powerful competitors like Intel.

But while pressures from the Japanese and American governments were important elements in deflecting IBM from its successful course, at most they mitigate the responsibility of IBM's managers for their company's decline. The critical management misjudgments were well within Armonk's control.

THE GRAPH OF DISASTER

If one were to graph the downward slope of IBM's fortunes, certain key episodes would stand out in bold type.

The modern IBM was defined by the System/360. The project that created the 360 was big, enormously ambitious, and centrally managed. With only minor exceptions, the 360 was a total IBM computing solution. The 360 was the only computer the marketing force had to know how to sell. Once they had sized a customer's problem, there would be a 360 solution that would fit it.

When the second-generation 360, the 370, got off to a slow start, IBM attempted another 360-scale technical leap with the F/S project. F/S was self-consciously in the 360 mold: big, expensive, ambitious, centrally driven. It failed badly; because of F/S, there was no new generation of 360/370 machines in the mid-1970s, giving Japanese 370 clone-makers five years of breathing space to catch up.

The psychological costs were even heavier. F/S was IBM's Vietnam. It shook top management's confidence, and created a wariness and hostility toward centrally driven solutions on the part of the product divisions. During the bitter withdrawal from F/S, Opel construed criticism as disloyalty. Candor became risky. After F/S, political skills weighed more heavily in promotion decisions.

Even before F/S was officially killed, Cary and Opel began rapidly to push product, systems, and software development down to the divisions. There was a proliferation of successful niche products, including several quite different minicomputers and the PC. Revenues grew strongly, but by the early 1980s IBM found itself faced once again with the problem the 360 was originally supposed to solve—multiple incompatible architectures, exploding development costs (good solutions weren't portable from one product to the next), and a confused sales force and customer base.

But Armonk could never decide whether to enforce architectural coherence on the product divisions or to give them true independence. As management waffled, IBM lost its old hard-charging, forward-looking élan; slowly it became a status quo company. From time to time Armonk would try, very uncertainly, to impose a central logic, or minimum coherence, on the proliferating development efforts, but it met a general spirit of noncooperation on the part of the product divisions. So management fell back on process tools—committees, planning exercises, consensus building, consultative rules. Nobody was willing to dictate priorities; in fact, perhaps nobody could. Nobody could order a division to start cannibalizing its good products in the interests of the company's long-term health. IBM needed *either* strong central direction from the top *or* divisions that were free to compete. It got neither.

By the late 1970s, computer technology was moving very fast on many fronts. In the graduate schools and at technical conferences, the air was thick with excitement about VLSI and microprocessors. IBM managers, by and large, did not understand the changes that were afoot; most of them had gotten their jobs by being good at selling 360s.

The spirit of tooth-and-claw battling in the management suites that Watson had reveled in didn't die as the new process management slowly caked the company's arteries. But the battles subtly shifted away from issues of technology and markets to ones of status and turf. Outside activities—charities, social causes—began to count more heavily in promotions, a process that Watson himself had begun in his later years.

The process gridlock began to choke off promising technologies. RISC was the most expensive single casualty; neither the mainframe nor the PC division would hear of it. All forces converged to reinforce the status quo. The standard product offerings were very profitable. Managers moved from job to job quickly, and with no contrary mandate, readily slipped into a free rider mode. The PC division fought grimly against implementing superior in-house technologies in favor of increased reliance on inferior outside suppliers.

A Gresham's law of bureaucracy allowed only the most low-risk, low-profile solutions to emerge from the process maze. Gates easily bullied IBM down the path of least resistance on PC operating systems; the company repeatedly backed away from opportunities to regain the microprocessor initiative from Intel. IBM's product development cycles are now very slow, twice that of competitors like Compaq, Sun, or even DEC.

Vaguely aware of its growing peril, Armonk tried initiating centrally coordinated—but never quite mandated—design solutions. None was pursued with either confidence or conviction, coming to life more as a series of spastic lurches than as coordinated projects. After F/S, no one ever attempted to interfere with a comfortable divisional product barony. All the central initiatives were expensive, ungainly failures. Olympiad managed to pervert RISC sufficiently to produce a slow, dull, and expensive workstation that nobody bought. Fort Knox tried to bridge the minicomputer and workstation architectures under RISC; the coordinative process buried it under a mass of conflicting imperatives, and it was quickly put out of its misery. OfficeVision was a misconceived effort to create a comprehensive, mainframe-driven, OS/2-compatible IBM office environment, including application software. SAA is a complex, companywide software overlay intended to link a wide range of fundamentally incompatible system architectures. It lives on as a kind of software zombie's curse, a drag on the most critical development programs.

The disintegration became public in 1991. Akers started blaming lazy and complacent workers for the company's problems. Mid-level people are outraged. "Akers could fix IBM if he'd fire himself and the rest of the top two hundred managers" is a typical comment from an upper-middle-rank employee. High-quality staff have been offered early severance; many have grabbed it and moved to the competition. A sudden flurry of anxious partnering with a long list of other computer and semiconductor companies has an air of desperation. Akers has also decided that IBM can't be managed centrally. A new set of divisions will be almost completely independent companies; some may even issue their own securities someday. For the time being, the emphasis is on the "almost" and "someday"; as of mid-1992, there is much confusion.

Apologists point out that the downturn in IBM's fortunes is very recent. The company was its old dominant self as late as 1986. Profits in 1990 were very good. But the apparent suddenness of the decline is deceiving. The same pattern has recently been seen at DEC and Wang. Computer architectures can stabilize and survive for a decade or even more after they have stopped evolving. Mid-life and maturing product lines are often very profitable. Continued software, services, and maintenance revenues make business look healthy. Then one day customers start moving to a newer, faster, cheaper architecture. The old vendor is no longer a player, sales spin into a stomach-jagging plunge, and managers realize too late that their business is sliding swiftly away beneath them. The pattern at IBM is dishearteningly similar to that at DEC and Wang.

IBM's defenders also point to the industrial research laboratories, the greatest in the world, and the semiconductor manufacturing and development centers in Burlington and East Fishkill, New York, both national resources. Significantly, however, both are highly technical operations that readily lend themselves to centralized management. The weapons research and development centers in the Soviet Union may be an apt analogy. With a prior claim on resources, superb facilities, and a clear mission—be the first to build each new generation of DRAMs—top-flight people can work wonders. In fact, IBM is still always first with each new generation of DRAMs. The Soviets also built outstanding missiles until the very end.

The Megaproject Style

Like so many other American high-technology companies, IBM's development was powerfully influenced by its participation in huge and complex 1950s defense projects. IBM was much more effective than other electronics firms in not letting its defense work dull its competitive, private sector instincts. Indeed, the systems planning and management skills IBM developed as a defense contractor were no less important than its electronics technologies in the success of its flagship 360/370 product line. A megaproject mentality, however, is still deeply ingrained within IBM—witness the BMEWS and SAGE projects in the 1950s, the System/360, F/S, later failures like Fort Knox and SAA. IBM's standard problem-solving reflex is a big, complex, thoroughly engineered solution, often extending far beyond an immediate market need.

There is nothing fundamentally wrong with the megaproject paradigm. (We will have much more to say about this in Chapter 12.) It is the secret of Boeing's great success in commercial jetliners, for instance. But a business strategy—whether organized around the megaproject paradigm or any other—that is not matched to its market will fail. The rapid decentralization of computing in the 1970s and 1980s called for fundamentally new approaches; but IBM stuck with the tried and true.

The initial OS/2 strategy is a good example. Both Gates and the CP/X86 team favored a simpler solution, a multitasking overlay on DOS with a graphical interface, effectively what Gates later accomplished with Windows. Such an interim DOS fix could have been available relatively quickly at much less cost than OS/2, and later migrated toward a more capable network and server operating system. Instead, IBM chose an elaborate OS/2 development plan, heavily influenced by corporationwide mainframe-oriented software guidelines. The final product overstretched the effective capabilities of the processor it was designed for, and based on its market reception, filled no immediately pressing market demand. The burden of fixing OS/2 was then an albatross around the company's neck for another five years. Gates, of course, bears much of the responsibility for OS/2, but the IBM megaproject reflex allowed it to happen.

One characteristic of the megaproject style is to assume that the first product iteration will be a completely engineered, completely comprehensive solution built for a long life cycle. Ease of use is always a secondary consideration to technical elegance and comprehensiveness. Elaborate control systems ensure formally correct development solutions at the expense of brilliance. Since IBM has been so long accustomed to its role as architectural standard-setter, development cycle times were never its primary concern; customers are expected to wait for the new IBM standard. IBM's complete dominance of the mainframe world also reduced its sensitivity to competitive forces. For decades, no competitor was an industry pacesetter; IBM managers lost the habit of looking over their shoulders. With the exception of Boca Raton, which went to the other extreme, IBM until recently rarely looked outside for computer solutions; if a technology didn't exist in-house, it probably didn't exist at all. Particularly in personal systems and workstations, IBM's products were consistently late and consistently mismatched against a rapidly moving market standard.

A company's management is its nervous system. Like any neural network, it embodies hard-wired problem solutions built up over many years. The most costly legacy of an outmoded megaproject management style, such as IBM's, is a set of bureaucratic synapses wholly inappropriate to the challenges it is facing in the 1990s. And as might be expected, as the mismatch between IBM's management reflexes and real competitive problems grew, the quality of management deteriorated—the best defected, while the worst retreated into stubborn denial.

THE PROBLEM OF SIZE

Success sometimes presents the most difficult problems of all. Through the 1970s and 1980s, well over half of all American employees of computer vendors worked for IBM. IBM became the very symbol of excellence, solidity, stability. It is hard to keep running scared in a company earning $7 billion a year after taxes. When you hire almost everybody in the industry, it is hard to stay above average.

IBM was proud of its commitment to lifetime employment. It was proud of its sensitive handling of employee issues, its appeal processes, tribunals, educational and recreational opportunities. It made its employees feel comfortable and secure, and was much praised for that. But there is no doubt that by the early 1980s, the company was losing its edge. Managers could keep very busy their entire lives without doing anything to help IBM compete. These things can't be quantified, but all of the IBM employers whom we interviewed agree that gaming the system—abusing health benefits, vacations, educational leave—was widespread in the 1980s.

As a very rich company, IBM could afford all the business school nostrums that were fashionable in the 1970s and early 1980s: elaborate strategic planning exercises; big, centralized management information systems that collected and processed reams of data, most of it meaningless, like body counts in Vietnam. Generalist managers were in vogue, usually with financial or marketing backgrounds; technology was left to the boys in the white coats. In IBM's internal management development programs, MBA tracks predominated over computer science. Making presentations became the critical skill; the slide shows grew slicker and ever more professional. Almost all of IBM's top managers are ex-360 salesmen; they were constantly faced with technical judgments they could not have understood. "He didn't know what he didn't know" was a senior technologist's comment on a division president. "But he made really good presentations. The guy above him knew even less, but his presentations were even better."

IBM became a bureaucracy, almost a civil service. The substance of management gradually became absorbed in process, and process is easily self-perpetuating, its own cause and effect. Process became what managers did.

THE *NOMENKLATURA*

One of the persistent themes playing through our interviews with senior IBM technical managers is the steady decline in the quality of leadership in the company. Cary still is remembered fondly and is unanimously considered the best of Watson's successors. But the decay began under him after the failure of F/S, and got much worse under Opel and Akers. Under Opel, dissent was dangerous; under Akers, impossible—"fostering a cult of personality" was one former division president's judgment.

A steady politicization crept over the management bureaucracy. Even after all the decentralization moves of the 1970s, IBM in many ways still behaved like a highly centralized company. Major decisions were made consensually; the elaborate consultative process meant that any important decision flowed to the top—there was no other way to manage a consultative process. The higher a manager, the more presentations encroached on his time, and so presentations inevitably became shorter, punchier, more hermetically designed, served up at senior management meetings like canapés—crisp, bite-sized, bland. Selling a presentation defined success; the rotation policy made it almost impossible to pin blame later. By that point, process was pure cost.

The judgment on Jack Kuehler, president for Akers's entire tenure, is very harsh. Except for the official technologists, like the chief scientist and the director of research, Kuehler is virtually the only technologist in the senior management ranks. Fairly or not, the technical staff looked to him as their court of last resort, their emissary to the salesmen. The consensus of more than half a dozen senior IBM technologists interviewed was that Kuehler became utterly politicized—a "complete betrayal" was a mild comment.

In the former Soviet Union, years of Communist Party dominance created a privileged class of placeholders, the *nomenklatura*, people who flourished in the fetid intraparty intrigues of the totalitarian years. Overthrowing the party has not released the country from their grip; they sit protectively and defensively on every critical choke point. With only slight exaggeration, IBM's problem is similar. It still has tens of thousands of employees with energy, vision, and great technical competence. But it suffers from a management trained in a different era, who have done almost everything wrong for at least fifteen years. Now the Armonk *nomenklatura* sits like a dead weight on the company's soul. Akers's decentralization plans smack of Mikhail Gorbachev's obsessive shufflings of the Soviet ministries. Only a scourge of self-cleansing can save the company from a bleak and constricted future. At companies like General Motors and DEC, the board, or institutional shareholders, united to enforce changes. At IBM, however, at least for the moment, no radical change agent is in sight.

In the course of the previous chapters, we have highlighted a number of turning points for IBM. Conceivably, if different decisions had been made, different paths pursued, different people placed in the top slots, IBM's recent history and its immediate prospects would have been very different. Such speculation, however, is usually fruitless; the question for the present is whether IBM can survive. From our analysis thus far, it is clear that we think its prospects are very bleak. But we will reserve discussion of its new technical and market strategies until Part III, after we have set out our model for understanding information technology strategies in the 1990s.

PART II

WINNING IN A POST-IBM WORLD

7

THREE CONTENDERS

The computer wars of the 1990s will have three main classes of contenders. The first group comprises the big American, and to a much lesser extent, European, companies that dominated the first decades of mainframe computing. The second group is the integrated Japanese electronics companies—like Fujitsu, Hitachi, Toshiba, and NEC—that made such massive inroads into Western semiconductor, consumer electronics, and computer markets during the 1970s and 1980s. And the third we call the Third Force. These are smaller companies, virtually all of them American, many of them clustered in California's Silicon Valley. Each of these contenders represents a different strategic approach to winning the computer wars. None of them, we feel, has it exactly right, although the Silicon Valley competitive model fits best with the changing shape of computer technology in the 1990s. None of the other contenders, however, is compelled to stick with the strategy it has pursued so far. The ones that first get the right strategic blend will be the ones who win the computer wars of the 1990s.

101

THE DOWNFALL OF THE TRADITIONAL COMPUTER COMPANIES

Despite the painful story of IBM's decline told in Part I, it is arguably still by far the strongest of the traditional Western computer companies. Other large American computer companies fared much worse. The nature of their failures is instructive; in every case, as with IBM, it was not a lack of technology, but a failure to exploit it, either intentionally, as at DEC, for fear of cannibalizing an older successful product line, or more frequently, through sheer inadvertence or bureaucratic inertia. These companies have by no means passed from the scene. Taken together, the Western companies that we call the traditional computer companies still control the lion's share of world mainframe and minicomputer sales. With the exception of IBM, however, few of them have significant positions in personal systems.

DEC, still the world's second-largest computer company, was founded in 1957 by Kenneth Olsen, an MIT professor and former IBM researcher. DEC's PDP line of computers were low-cost, high-performance machines targeted at the academic and sophisticated industrial market—users who didn't need or want to pay for the extensive software and support services that came bundled with IBM products. The PDP-6, introduced in 1964, beat IBM to the market with time-sharing—a single main computer could support multiple simultaneous users. DEC followed up with a steady stream of improved PDPs; their relatively low cost—about a fifth of the cost of an IBM mainframe—and the time-sharing features made PDPs the almost universal choice for school and university computing. These were the machines that Bill Gates, Steve Wozniak, and the other young 1970s hackers first cut their teeth on. Then in the late 1970s, DEC broke with its PDP architecture and introduced its powerful VAX line of minicomputers, which made serious inroads at the low end of IBM's commercial mainframe business.

The operating system for the VAX was called VMS; it was

proprietary DEC software written by Dave Cutler to run only on VAX processors. Although DEC was slow to recognize it, VMS had a competitor in the academic community, UNIX from AT&T. UNIX was written in C, and could be compiled for, or ported to, any processor. Partly because of the antitrust pressure from the Justice Department, AT&T gave away UNIX licenses virtually for free to academia. A team at Berkeley under Bill Joy received a grant to develop an improved UNIX. Joy is a genius hacker-entrepreneur, who became one of the cofounders of Sun; he and Dave Patterson designed the Sun SPARC RISC processor. The UNIX grant came from DARPA, the research arm of the Defense Department, whose fecundity and disregard of bureaucracy is remarkable—Joy was in Berkeley's MIS organization, and had no formal affiliation with its computer science department when he got the grant. His team produced the so-called Berkeley UNIX, which passed quickly from hand to hand through the scientific and university communities. By the early 1980s, almost a quarter of the DEC VAXs were running under UNIX rather than VMS. Almost all university VAXs used UNIX rather than VMS, as did AT&T, a major DEC customer.

In the late 1970s, DEC began to think about faster processors. Patterson spent a sabbatical stint there in 1979; he was impressed with the complexity of the VAX's microcode and began to formulate his concept of a RISC microprocessor. Patterson had also been consulting with the computer researchers at Xerox's Palo Alto Research Center, or PARC, and introduced them to his RISC concepts as well. Shortly thereafter the entire PARC processor team, led by Forrest Basket, defected to DEC, where they developed a RISC processor, called the Titan, which tripled the VAX's performance. The Titan would run under UNIX, but not VMS. Titan was considered a research effort, but a commercial project called Prism quickly got under way.

Politics played a big part in the history of RISC at DEC. The Prism team had not been involved in Titan and insisted on starting over. But under the direction of Dave Cutler, VMS's creator, they designed a new family of very fast RISC processors, together with a new portable operating system that would run on either the VAX or the Prism RISC machines. Prism gathered powerful momentum within the company. The opportunity was to create a new architectural standard that would run from high-end desktop RISC workstations through a new, high-speed, RISC-based VAX computer line that would encroach well into IBM's mainframe territory. The Prism project was killed in 1988, in favor of simply buying RISC processors from MIPS to put into a new line of DEC workstations. Because of the clean-slate start, Prism was behind schedule when it was killed; but the implications of the decision was that RISC would continue to be a sideline at DEC, while VAX-VMS would remain the company's anchor. Olsen, especially, apparently felt that DEC was about VAX-VMS machines, and he wasn't about to meddle with a successful formula.

DEC's VAX machines, since they were so prominently positioned in the mid-sized market, received the full brunt of the onslaught by RISC-based workstations from Sun, MIPS, and others. With VAX-VMS suddenly looking like old technology, Olsen countered by trying to move the VAX architecture upstream into the heart of the 370 market, an expensive failure. DEC suddenly found its entire market sliding away beneath it; in 1992, the company almost imploded. After DEC posted the biggest quarterly loss in computer industry history, $2.8 billion, Olsen, under heavy pressure, resigned. DEC is now trying to re-create itself around the Alpha RISC processor—yet another clean-slate start—that will run under either VMS or UNIX, and soon as a Microsoft NT platform. The Alpha is currently the fastest RISC processor, although as of mid-1992 it was still not available in production quantities. Whether it is too late for DEC remains to be seen.

Cases of companies failing to exploit technologies through sheer inattention are much more common. IBM, for example, never commercialized its internal semiconductor manufacturing and testing technologies or some outstanding computerized semiconductor design tools. A number of companies—such as LSI Logic, Cadence, and Mentor—did turn similar technologies into profitable products that they now sell to IBM. The hard-disk drive in the personal computer—the so-called Winchester disk drive—was invented at IBM, as was the floppy drive, but almost all of them are sold by other companies. Relational data bases—crucially important software that allows a user to go almost instantly to any piece of information in a big data base—is another IBM-invented technology in which it has only a limited market position. The list can go on almost indefinitely—FORTRAN, microcode, semiconductor main memory, many peripheral devices, etc.

Other large American technology companies had records as bad. AT&T's Bell Labs invented the powerful computer language called C, now the basis for all leading personal computer software, without any commercial participation by AT&T. The invention of C was linked to AT&T's development of UNIX. Licensing UNIX cheaply was motivated by antitrust concerns, but AT&T never effectively maintained and improved the standard, allowing it to be captured by entrepreneurs like Bill Joy, who made it a key factor in Sun's success. AT&T bought 15 percent of Sun and has tried to take back control of the UNIX world by tightening licensing terms; it also spent billions in a hostile takeover of NCR, which has established a quiet UNIX position of its own.

The story of Xerox is almost a Keystone Kops saga. In the mid-1960s, conscious that its basic copying patents would begin to expire, Xerox decided that the commercial computer business offered a high-growth, high-technology market opportunity that would be the perfect complement to its position in copying. After buying a computer subsidiary, they set up a Xerox research facility, the Palo Alto Research Center, or PARC. Its charge was to create the "information architecture" of the future.

The information strategy never quite got off the ground. The acquisition, Scientific Data Systems, was a poor fit, and quickly turned unprofitable. The copier marketing force never adapted well to other products, and throughout the 1970s and early 1980s, the company repeatedly shifted its basic strategies. The people at PARC were isolated from the rest of the company, and when there was contact, too often managed to present themselves as arrogant and boorish.

But in the meantime, the researchers at PARC, with some assists from maverick researchers at other Xerox facilities, built a full-blown modern personal computer, the Alto, at least two years before hobbyist catalogs began selling the Altair in 1975. It had a modern display screen and an icon-based graphical interface program. (Apparently, Xerox's patent lawyers clearly recommended protecting the technology; the PARC researchers, however, never took the time to prepare the required documentation.) Steve Jobs appropriated the graphical interface for his Lisa and Macintosh machines, and it is still a major factor in Apple's success. The Alto also had the first WYSIWYG word processing software. (WYSIWYG, or "What You See Is What You Get"—pronounced wiseewig—means that the shape and arrangement of the characters on the screen exactly represent the final printed output.) The PARC researchers linked their Altos with the first PC Local Area Network, or LAN, incidentally inventing the Ethernet technology, now the most common office LAN standard. PARC also invented the Wide Area Network, the key to Novell's success. (Xerox's in-house WAN may be the best in the world, but it has never commercialized it.) Alto also came equipped with the world's first laser printer, sporting a higher level of resolution than today's standard printers. Naturally, the Alto came with a mouse, the little roller device favored by today's Apple and Microsoft Windows users, allowing one, for instance, to "click" and insert text.

The work at PARC was mostly ignored by Xerox management, who were financial specialists, salesmen, or copying engineers; for all practical purposes, save a belated and star-crossed office computer attempt in the 1980s, Xerox never did anything with the technology. A full four years after PARC built the Alto, and shortly before An Wang took the office market by storm with his electronic word processor, Xerox put its money on a traditional electromechanical typewriter that included a new daisy-wheel print head. It called the print head "the most important introduction of technology to the office in the last decade by Xerox." PARC technologists left in droves; most of them got rich. Bob Metcalfe founded 3Com and commercialized Ethernet. John Warnock and Bob Geshke founded Adobe, the standard-setter for printer software. Dave Liddle founded Metaphor, a graphical user interface company. Charles Simonyi is a top designer at Microsoft.

Disappointing as was the performance of the big American companies, the plight of European computer companies in the 1980s was almost pathetic. In contrast to American companies, the European companies had little technology to waste; instead, they concentrated on aggressively nationalistic, and usually quite wrongheaded, political strategies. Europe's national flag bearers, Siemens/Nixdorf in Germany, Groupe Bull in France, and Olivetti in Italy arguably do not have a leadership position in any computer technology. England's ICL has been sold off to Fujitsu. For the most part, European companies act as marketing/distribution arms for Japanese or American companies or occasionally as manufacturing subcontractors, under the guise of "partnerships," with DEC or IBM.

THE JAPANESE ASSAULT

The inroads made by the Japanese companies in computers and business electronics during the 1970s and 1980s were not nearly so visible at first as their assault on Western automobile and consumer electronics markets, partly because standard market-share statistics concealed the problem. American world market share in computers was about 70 percent in 1980; by 1990, it was still about 60 percent, while Japanese market share had risen from about 10 percent to only about 20 percent—not much to worry about there, it might seem. But the market share statistics are measured by gross revenues from final products—in other words, whichever company's name was on the label of the box that was delivered to the customer got all the credit for the sale. A huge portion of those revenues were being recycled back to Japanese electronics companies who were supplying more and more of the parts that were inside the machines with the American labels on them. Beneath the glossy market-share data, the American position was deteriorating rapidly. In 1980, America had a small computer trade surplus with Japan; by 1991, that had deteriorated to a $5 billion deficit. The total electronics deficit, including consumer electronics, is about $10 billion.

Semiconductors offer a good illustration of this changing relationship. Early in the 1980s, semiconductor manufacturing was basically an American handcrafted industry. With a few exceptions, such as IBM, AT&T, and Texas Instruments, semiconductor-makers were small-scale, artisanlike companies in California's fabled Silicon Valley—the center of American computer creativity that stretches along Route 101 between San Jose and San Francisco. Semiconductors were expensive—about $10 per thousand bits of memory. By today's standards, quantities were relatively small and yields were low.

In the 1980s, computer sales took off like a rocket, semiconductors began showing up in a host of consumer products, such as cars and microwave ovens, and the demand for chips became insatiable. The Japanese brought a thoroughness to making semiconductors that astonished Westerners. Each new product generation was introduced only after the production process was completely tested in a brand-new pilot factory. Japanese semiconductor pilot factories were major $50-to-$100-million installations, so every detail of the process technology had been worked out in a realistic production environment. The Japanese readiness to commit to the long term was also demonstrated by the deliberate policy of concentrating production of new devices in green-field factories, even when retooled older sites would have been perfectly suitable. The new sites concentrated on high-performance computer markets, while the previous generation of factories went down-market to consumer chips. New factories ensured that every detail of the equipment and tooling, of the layout, plant organization, and work flow, could be precisely adapted to maximum productivity on the new chip.

Big semiconductor factories are very expensive. The tiniest vibration, on the order of millionths of an inch, can cause a circuit-etching beam to skew wildly off its path, so buildings are suspended on huge concrete pillars to dampen any intrusive motion from the outside world. A speck of dust too small to be seen by the naked eye can crash across a chip circuit like a boulder on a highway, so workers in the interior clean rooms are muffled in astronaut-style bunny suits, and the air must be changed some five hundred times an hour. The world uses billions of standard memory chips, or DRAMs, annually. A run-of-the-mill DRAM factory costs about $200 to $300 million, and by the end of the decade, state-of-the-art plants will cost more than $1 billion.

Throughout the 1980s, with export earnings soaring, and the highest savings rate in the world, the Japanese invested massively in semiconductor capacity, building dozens of huge new factories with astonishingly high productivity and yields. In just a few years, the price of semiconductor memory dropped a thousandfold, from $10 per thousand bits to less than a penny—almost certainly the greatest single productivity improvement in industrial history. Smaller American companies lost billions of dollars trying to compete, until they either folded completely, or, like Intel, quit making DRAMs to concentrate on other chips.

By the end of the 1980s, the semiconductor industry was dominated by an oligopoly of huge companies. Six producers, four of them Japanese, held 40 percent of the market. In DRAMs, the most ubiquitous of all chips, Japanese market share had risen from about 25 percent in the late 1970s to more than 80 percent by 1990; American market share figures were exactly the reverse, from more than 70 percent in the late 1970s to only about 10 percent in 1990. For at least three years, from about 1987 to 1990, the Japanese ran a global DRAM cartel, extracting billions of surplus profits from the West. (The cartel was finally broken by the entrance of the Koreans into the DRAM market in a major way.) Andrew Grove, the chairman of Intel Corporation, America's most successful chip-maker, predicted in 1990 that Silicon Valley was about to become a "techno-colony" of Japan. "Computers," said Grove, "are just like cars, or machine tools, or consumer electronics. American market share is trending down and Japan's is going up. I call it the X-curve. It would depress a cow."

The investment requirements for keeping pace in semi-conductors keep going up. Since the mid-1970s, every technology generation has seen more than a doubling in the scale of research and development and capital investment required to compete. Technology progresses so rapidly that each new generation of DRAM, or other standard chip, lasts only about four years or even less. The useful life of the capital equipment in a factory is only about five years. Current technology requires, on average, $200 million to $1 billion for each generation of manufacturing process development, $250 to $400 million for each factory, and $10 to $100 million for each device design. These costs are all expected to double by the late 1990s, when the world semiconductor market should exceed $100 billion.

The same cost trend is apparent in other high-performance components. The kind of flat panel screens that are standard devices in laptop computers may gradually replace all computer screens, and eventually even the standard cathode-ray tubes on home television sets, presenting pictures with strikingly vivid color and filmlike quality. Flat-screen factories cost about $100 to $300 million, and the newest ones might cost double that. All of those factories are in Japan. And the more high-performance component manufacture became concentrated in Japan, the more the Japanese tightened their grip on semiconductor-manufacturing equipment; during the 1980s, they tripled their market share from 15 percent to about 45 percent, and almost completely control photolithography (light-etching) equipment. American and Japanese equipment market share stabilized at about the 50–50 level in 1991 and 1992, partly because the world is moving away from the lens-based technologies in which the Japanese excel. The Europeans have only a minuscule position in the equipment market.

At the end of this decade, current methods of producing semiconductors by etching the circuits with light will be too crude for the superdense components that the industry will require. Many experts think that circuit-etching will have to be carried out with X-rays, a vastly more expensive process. There is one experimental X-ray installation in America; there is one in Europe. There are ten in Japan.

THE THIRD FORCE

The decline of the big computer companies is not the whole story of American competitiveness. There is another side to the story; to see it, drive the forty miles or so along Route 101 between San Jose and San Francisco, through Milpitas, Mountainview, Cupertino, Palo Alto—California's fabled Silicon Valley. The nervous tension, the sheer intellectual megawattage, that radiates from the mile after mile of low-slung buildings, most of them with science-jargon Greek names, is astonishing and exhilarating. Whatever the problems of the American computer industry, and there are many, in these companies they are not ones of slothful managers, slipshod workers, or decaying standards.

These are the companies that we call the industry's Third Force. Strikingly, none of them makes the kind of traditional mainframe computers that were for so many years the bread-and-butter of IBM and the BUNCH, or their Japanese competitors, such as Fujitsu and Hitachi, or the 1960s generation of start-ups such as DEC, Data General, Prime, and Wang. Instead, the new companies are exploiting the new technology of very small, very high powered, and very dense integrated circuits (called "VLSI," for Very Large Scale Integration) to create a new world of *radically decentralized* computing. By using arrays of microprocessors, they can often match or exceed the processing power of the traditional mainframe. They are parleying quick reactions and innovative technologies— many purloined from larger American companies—into strong competitive positions. So far, they have been impervious to the attacks of either the Asian or the Western giants. And while the newer companies, even taken together, are too small to offset the loss of market share by the larger Western firms, many of them are growing to quite respectable size.

Microsoft, which has succeeded brilliantly in gaining a

near stranglehold over a large segment of the personal computer software market, has profits that exceed the personal computer earnings of Compaq and IBM combined. With sales and earnings both growing more than 50 percent a year, Microsoft's earnings could well exceed IBM's in the foreseeable future. Intel parlayed its control over its xx86 family of microprocessors and related chips into earnings of about $1 billion on $5 billion of sales and holds $3 billion in cash, although its position has recently come under much greater pressure. Apple has sales of nearly $7 billion. Novell, which has established its network operating systems as the industry standard, enjoys a P/E ratio in the 35 to 50 range. Sun Microsystems, which has the leading position in high-speed desktop workstations, has sales of nearly $4 billion, while Adobe, which has established the standard for graphics-based software, has topped the $250 million sales mark. Motorola and Hewlett-Packard are two more traditional, engineering-oriented companies that are, somewhat anomalously, in the same camp as our Third Force companies, although more through sheer excellence in engineering and manufacturing than through typical Third Force company strategies.

The secret to the success of the best Third Force companies is that they have managed to establish some form of proprietary control over a critical and fast-moving competitive space, typically one that is software-dominated or that speeds the transition to low-cost, microprocessor-based decentralized systems. Strikingly, for all of their globe-spanning success and financial power, the Japanese giants are distinctly uncomfortable in the competitive arena staked out by the American start-ups.

The Japanese—and Asian companies generally, it turns out—have fallen into a trap of their own. Consider again products where Japanese companies dominate, such as facsimile machines. All fax machines the world over conform to a transmission standard, called the CCITT standard, which is set by an international electronics standards-setting agency based in Paris, and all send and receive data the same way. The dot density of a fax printer, for example, is 200 x 100 dots per inch, a fairly low level of resolution to the modern eye, which is one of the reasons why fax pages look so bad.

The strategy for leading the world in faxes is straightforward: learn the standard and engineer multiple products that provide a range of features within the single standard; be sure they look nice, are well made, and can be turned out in high volume very cheaply. Then manufacture zillions of them to drive down unit costs and keep price pressure on your competition. Plow your earnings back into improving manufacturing and tinkering with the product's features, so the cost keeps moving down. But never challenge, or even enhance, the basic standard; for it is your skill in meeting it that is the secret of your success. This is a good description of the fundamental strategy that has kept Japanese companies on top in so many of the world's manufacturing industries.

The Japanese strategy in fax machines is precisely the same as the strategy that won them world dominance in television sets. Television standards are set by the government regulatory bodies that allocate airwave frequencies. The prevailing standards, the NTSC standard in the United States and Japan, and PAL and SECAM in Europe, were established in the 1940s and 1950s, and the Japanese have been superbly successful in engineering high-quality products that meet them at a very attractive price.

Even DRAMs fit this same basic pattern. They are, of course, extraordinarily difficult to manufacture, and the generational cycle is only about four years. But, in contrast to microprocessors, the basic design of DRAMs has been conserved from generation to generation, and future design directions are clear. Making better DRAMs has been primarily an issue of incremental design, process, and manufacturing improvements to reduce the size of devices and circuits and increase the memory capacity of a chip. For all their staggering challenges, competitive strategy in DRAMs is very much like that in televisions or faxes.

Japanese companies, and Asian companies generally, have succeeded, by and large, by being superb *commodity implementers* within well-defined, stable, open, nonproprietary standards—standards, that is, that are defined by regulatory agencies, other government bodies, industry standards-setting organizations, or very slow-moving incumbents, such as IBM has been in mainframes in recent years. Nonproprietary standard products, such as memory chips, printers, VCRs, CD players, or facsimile machines, are brutally competitive businesses, with high investment requirements and razor-thin margins.

But industries that are fast-moving, where standards are constantly evolving, and where the standards themselves are within the proprietary control of an individual company, are hostile environments for commodity implementers. And the computer industry in the 1990s, under the technological impetus and creative impulse of the American start-ups, has been transmuting into just such an industry, shifting the ground out from under *both* the slow-moving Western giants and the commodity manufacturing–oriented Japanese giants.

Silicon Valley–style firms are too small by themselves to make up for the declining position of the big American companies. To a great degree, they have depended on the big companies to supply the technical innovations that they have been able to exploit so successfully. But their strategies are much more closely aligned to the realities of technology in the 1990s and point the way toward a strategic recovery by the larger firms.

8

COMPETING IN RADICALLY
DECENTRALIZED SYSTEMS

Walk into a big Wall Street trading operation. On the traders'
desks, you will see powerful workstations or PCs from companies like Sun Microsystems, IBM, or Hewlett-Packard with
processing power comparable to that of most mainframe computers. Ten years ago, you would have seen machines on the
traders' desks that looked very similar. But they were "dumb"
computer terminals. Back then, all the processing power, and
all the data, resided in the back office in a big mainframe
computer. When a trader asked for some data, a message was
sent to the mainframe. The mainframe had to queue the requests coming in, look for the data, call up the program required to process it, do whatever calculations were required,
then send the information back to the trader's terminal.

Technically, the centralized mainframe environment with
remote data entry and retrieval was very impressive. But it had
many limitations. If the mainframe went down for any reason,
the entire system collapsed. (Virtually everyone has been vic-
timized by this phenomenon in dealing with banks or utilities

that typically still have older centralized systems.) Ten years ago, mainframe processing power was considerably less than that of a run-of-the-mill workstation today, so delays when terminals were all contending for the mainframe's processing power could be substantial. And mainframes were relatively inflexible. If the trader needed some special calculations or data formats, he had to request the program from the central computer staff. Frustratingly often, depending on how the files were organized, solving simple problems could be quite time-consuming and sometimes almost impossible. Finally, the system was very expensive and was organized around a single vendor standard, usually IBM or DEC.

The system sitting on today's trading desks could not be more different. First of all, the microprocessors in the newer standard workstations run at about 50 mips, or millions of instructions per second, much faster than the average mainframe of ten years ago. Since there is very little processing that today's workstations can't handle themselves, traders run their own programs and do their own analyses without having to beg the central computer staff to write programs for them.

More important, the workstations are connected to each other in a network. In contrast to the dumb terminals, which could talk only to the mainframe, modern networks are inherently decentralized; all the workstations can talk to each other, or to several others at a time. Companies are working on software that will let a number of workstations work together, in parallel, on the same problem. Harness a network of tens, or even hundreds, of 50-mips workstations to attack a single problem, and you have truly formidable computing power.

The network will still be backed up by a mainframe or devices called servers. Workstations are better at processing data than storing it. And some applications, like a model of bond price fluctuations over the past ten years, require enormous quantities of data. Servers are special-purpose machines, much smaller and less expensive than a mainframe, that can store large files of data, perform special computations very efficiently, and hand data to and from the workstations on the network. If the data base is very large, there will still be a traditional mainframe backing up the network, but much of the time it will be relegated only to very routine, data-intensive tasks—such as processing daily account statements in a bank or computing and mailing utility customer bills.

Now take apart the network. The workstation display screens are made by Japanese companies, probably Sony or NEC. The microprocessors will come from American companies. The Sun microprocessors are made by Texas Instruments or LSI Logic; IBM and Hewlett-Packard make their own. (If instead of workstations, the traders have IBM-compatible PCs, the microprocessors are made by Intel or one of their clones, like AMD or Cyrix; if they are Apple Macintoshes, by Motorola.) The memory chips come from Japan, Taiwan, or Korea. The disk drives are made by American companies, like Conner Peripherals or Seagate. The rest of the workstation, like the keyboard and ancillary chips, come from Asia, although the workstations are assembled into units in America. The same list of companies supply the components for the servers.

The network printers probably have American names on them, like Hewlett-Packard or QMS, but the laser marking engines—a complex arrangement of mirrors, lenses, laser diode, photosensitive roller, and toner cartridge—are mostly made in Japan, probably by Canon. Printers also have substantial memory requirements, and those chips, too, come from Asia. If they are graphics printers, they also need powerful microprocessors, which are made by American companies, probably AMD, Intel, or Motorola.

Underneath the visible system are a variety of other components—accelerator boards, coprocessors, network interface boards, modems, and so on—that improve the functioning of the basic equipment for specialized tasks, transmit data from point to point, or help manage the complicated process of transferring data around the network in an orderly way. These plug-in components come from a variety of manufacturers both in America and Asia. Items like the modems, which "*mo*dulate and *dem*odulate" computer data so they can be transmitted over telephone lines and vice versa, come from Asia, probably Taiwan, Singapore, or Korea. Accelerator boards and chips most likely come from smaller American companies, like Weitek, or Chips & Technologies.

And finally there is the software. It is almost all "shrink-wrapped"—meaning it is bought off-the-shelf. Ten years ago, most of the applications software in the mainframe system was written by the user's data-processing department and was therefore totally customized. Now easy-to-use shrink-wrapped software is available to solve almost any generic problem—doing complex bond calculations, analyzing customer accounts, or doing home bookkeeping or taxes. It is designed for people who are not computer professionals and who have never learned to program. And if a trader is at all technically sophisticated, most of the software vendors will provide tool kits that let a user custom-tailor the software to her own particular application.

There are many layers of software, and all of the vendors are American. There is the operating system, or the software that directs the computer's operations and interacts with the application-specific software programs. In a workstation group, the operating system will be a version of UNIX, but in a flavor provided by the workstation manufacturer. In all likelihood, the workstations will also have DOS from Microsoft, so the traders can run popular IBM PC programs, although the most popular applications, such as Lotus and WordPerfect, have been ported to UNIX machines like Sun's. There will be special hardware and software to run the network itself—for instance, to decide priorities when two chunks of data from different workstations collide in mid-flight. More likely than not, the network software comes from Novell, another American company, although there are several other American contenders, including Microsoft. The printers have their own software to convert computer data into marking instructions for the laser engines; the printer software comes from Hewlett-Packard or from a third party such as Adobe, the world's leading printer and font software company, or from any of a host of sharp-witted, quick-footed little companies that sell clones of the Hewlett-Packard and Adobe software. And there is much more; each of the plug-in devices, like a modem, will require its own software, which is probably supplied from someone other than the modem-maker.

Architectures

Look again at the network environment we have just described. Several features stand out. In the first place, the entire system exists in several layers. There is the network itself; there are the computers and peripherals, such as printers, in the network; and there are the components and subsystems in the computers and peripherals. Taken together, there are probably a hundred companies supplying major or minor components for the system, and most of them didn't even exist ten years ago.

This overall system is one we call *open* and *componentized.* By an open system, we mean there are published standards and interface protocols that provide sufficient information so other hardware and software vendors can develop components to plug into the system. If the vendor sells modems, for instance, he knows that data will come from the computer in certain formats, with certain standard wordlengths, at certain frame-rates, and so forth. A laser engine–maker knows that marking instructions will be transferred in a certain way and at a certain rate. The decision on *how* open a system should be is a complicated one, however, as we saw in the history of IBM's management of its PC franchise.

By a componentized system, we mean that the overall system will be designed to be built from a multiplicity of products from standards-complying hardware and software vendors. In such a system, most of the suppliers—particularly but not solely the hardware-makers—will be in the position of commodity implementers, and as we saw, most of those commodity components come from Asian companies.

But a few of the vendors will define the standards and protocols the others must meet. These are the ones that enjoy some element of architectural control over the system, or more accurately, their portion of a certain system space. In contrast to facsimile machines or television sets, the critical standards of these architectures are not defined by international or government standards-setting bodies, but instead are defined and controlled by private companies—the key software vendors or the microprocessor designers. They are therefore *proprietary* standards. Any complicated system or network will be organized around a complex of such standards, some of them proprietary and some not. They define how programs and commands will work and data will move around the system— the communication protocols that hardware components must follow, the rules for exchanging data between application software packages and the operating system, the allowable font descriptions that can be communicated to a printer, and so forth. *This complex of standards and rules is what we call an architecture.*

Architectures are not the same as products. In a network such as the one described above, typically four or five companies will control the proprietary architectural standards that define the overall functioning of the network. In the normal case, they also supply the key products that implement those architectures. As we will see in some detail, there is a constant struggle between the architectural standard-setter and other companies over the product revenues and profits that flow from the architectural standard, on the one hand; and a battle with companies trying to supplant the architectural standard on the other.

In the PC world, Microsoft, which supplies the DOS operating system and Intel, which supplies most of the xx86 microprocessors, control two major architectural standards. In the workstation world, Sun is still the standard setter, although its position is bitterly contested. In printers, Hewlett-Packard, Adobe, and now Microsoft are vying for control. In network software architecture, Novell and Microsoft are the main contenders. Controlling a proprietary standard is a very good place to be; and most of these companies are quite profitable.

For many years, computer users and even industry experts have argued that nonproprietary standards are in the best interest of users. That is emphatically not true. We have already discussed typical nonproprietary standards such as the CCITT fax standard or the television standard. They took a long time to establish and have been frozen in place for years. Because they were set by committees, they fixed technology at a lowest-common-denominator level and have stifled continued technological development. And because they are freighted with bureaucratic process, they are very hard to change; committees have been squabbling over an improved fax standard for years. To take another example, the FOR-TRAN computer language took ten years to establish (by an industry group called ANSI) after IBM created the language. It has been revised only twice since then, and is typically at least five years behind the evolving requirements of a good scientific programming language.

Imagine what would have happened if a decade ago, a government body—the FCC, say—had set standards for personal computers. The technology would never have progressed beyond the early Apples and first IBM PCs. And it would have played directly into the hands of the Asian commodity implementers. The great revolution in personal computer power might never have happened, and today we would all be using cheap, attractive, low-performance little computers from Japan, probably standardized at about the technical level of fax machines. But since proprietary architectures, by contrast, are such valuable franchises, they are constantly under competitive attack and vigorously defended, generating a very rapid pace of technological improvement, and producing an endless stream of additional benefits for users.

THE ROLE OF SOFTWARE AND DESIGN

The reader will certainly have noticed that all the companies mentioned in the preceding section who control or are fighting for the control of proprietary architectural standards are American companies. Outside of mainframes, in fact, they are almost all new companies—the American start-ups, the Third Force as we called them. Japanese companies have not been comfortable playing in an architectural arena; the set of skills developed as the world's best commodity implementers is simply not well adapted to architectural contests. The only Japanese companies we can identify that have successfully established a proprietary architectural standard comparable to, say, Microsoft's, are Nintendo and Sega, who are vying to control the standard in games. (Nintendo is at least partly an acculturated American company. It even owns an American baseball team.)

The American advantage in architectural contests is based on a massive advantange in rapid innovation, conceptualization, and flexible design, rather than detailed engineering. The phenomenon is most evident in software and microprocessors. Over the past decade microprocessor speeds have been roughly doubling every twelve to eighteen months, with no end in sight. The 386 microprocessor, the current workhorse of the PC industry, was introduced in 1986, and runs at about 3 mips, or close to the speed of a normal 1980 mainframe. In 1986, Sun's new RISC chip could hit 10 mips; 50 to 75 mips chips are the workstation standard in 1992. DEC plans volume production of its 100 to 200 mips Alpha microprocessor in early 1993, and a number of companies expect to introduce 1,000-mips chips within the near future. This enormous processing power of silicon chips that cost only hundreds of dollars is the root of the radical decentralization of computer systems.

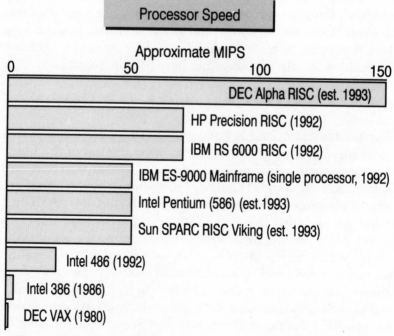

The ES-9000 mainframe processor in the middle of the chart costs from 25 to several hundred times as much as the other processors.

The speed breakthrough did not depend primarily on process or manufacturing breakthroughs. Rather, each new generation of technology opened up new possibilities for thinking about what a processor should do and how it could do it. It is the design of the new RISC microprocessors, today's speed champs (the real "screamers" in the argot), that makes them so fast. They are actually simpler chips than conventional microprocessors. As it turns out, only a fraction of the circuitry of conventional microprocessors is in use under normal processing conditions. By efficiently tuning the processor's stored instructions sets to match the processor clock cycle and keeping the instructions as small and simple as possible, the RISC designers picked up stupendous speed increases. The newest chips pile on more and more intricate tricks—like forecasting a sequence of operations so no time is lost reaching out for the next bits of data, or breaking up operations so they can be performed in parallel on the chip, and so on.

Perhaps the most elegant example of small-company mind-over-matter alchemy is the massively parallel computer from companies such as Maspar, Intel, and NCube. The Connection Machine, made by Thinking Machines Corporation, a fast-growing Massachusetts supercomputer company, is a good example. It is the brainchild of an MIT graduate student named J. Daniel Hillis, and represents a whole other world of computing. Its speed is measured in tens of billions of "flops" (or floating point operations—basically additions or multiplications—per second). In supercomputer contests to crown the world's fastest computer, the Connection Machine routinely racks up victories over traditional supercomputers from America's Cray Research and Japan's Fujitsu and Hitachi.

Supercomputers deal with problems that would take big conventional computers years to solve. But until recently, they have been designed fundamentally like other computers. Making supercomputers has therefore been a virtuoso exercise in wringing out higher and higher speeds by squeezing circuits more and more tightly together, without the whole collapsing into a melted jumble of wires and silicon. But most interesting supercomputer problems are really data intensive, not computation intensive. For example, the computations required to simulate the path of an air molecule over an airplane wing are fairly easy. But the simulation is only useful if it is carried our for millions or even billions of separate air molecules. It is the huge mass of data, not the complexity of the computations, that defeats conventional computers. Computing molecular interactions to simulate a pharmaceutical reaction is similarly a massive, data-intensive task, as are random text searches or discovering statistically interesting groupings—say, by buying patterns—from a large customer data base. (Calculating pi to a million decimal places, on the other hand is a computation-intensive exercise; but that is a problem form atypical of scientific or business applications.)

Massively parallel computers are designed to fit around data-intensive problems. Instead of trying to stream millions of separate calculations through a single stupendously fast processor, the Connection Machine has more than sixty-five thousand fairly unexciting processors. But by assigning a relatively small group of data points, or air molecules, to each processor, the Connection Machine carries out millions of calculations in a blink. Piranhas consume their prey much faster than do lions.

The secret of the Connection Machine is in the parallel architecture and software that assigns tasks among processors, manages the data flow among processors, and ties all the separate results together. And as the software improves, it opens the door to unimaginable speeds. By introducing superfast RISC processors into the network (not as trivial as it may sound), parallel computer designers can bump up their speeds enormously before hitting any important physical constraints. There is currently a hot intramural race between massively parallel companies to be the first to hit a "teraflop"—a trillion floating point operations per second, or about 50 to 100 times faster than today's world records. A number of other companies, like Kendall Square Research, Sequent, and Teradata are building machines that are less spectacularly fast, but also much better suited to commercial problems. They are a real threat to traditional mainframe regimes.

The American lead in chip design and software is based

on more than decade's investment and research and may be as entrenched as the Japanese advantage in DRAMs. Intel has become arguably the most successful, and possibly the most profitable, semiconductor company in the world by pouring out an almost endless series of high-performing new chips. It is the intellectual content of Intel's chips that distinguishes it from the pack. And since each new breakthrough lays the ground for the next, Japanese companies have had a tough time playing catch-up. Japanese companies have also embarked on relatively few architectural, design, and software initiatives of their own. Aside from Nintendo and Sega in games, there is perhaps only the NEC V-series of microprocessors, which have no market outside Japan, and ill-fated government-industry initiatives like the TRON family of processors and the so-called fifth-generation computer.

The lack of a deep research base in Japan may be a fundamental handicap. Japan graduates only about fifty computer science Ph.D.s a year, most of them second-rate by American standards. Sony has recently created an advanced research facility on the Xerox PARC model, under Mario Tokaro, a professor at Kao University. Sony is not a typical Japanese company; neither is Kao part of the Japanese university establishment. If any company could break from the more traditional monolithic Japanese competitive pattern, it would be Sony. Marrying their formidable product development skills with American-style innovative research could turn them into a truly dangerous competitor. But the low quality of Japanese universities—ironically inconsistent with the very high level of Japanese secondary education—remains a problem, and the Japanese lack the long tradition of basic laboratory research that is the glory of America's elite institutions.

The Shape of Opportunity

It should now be clear why, despite the extraordinary manufacturing achievements in Japan and elsewhere in Asia and the precipitate decline of large American bellwether technology companies, Japan has not run away with the computer industry. Computers are not the same as television sets or cars. And the basic forces that opened opportunity for the American start-ups will only accelerate through the remainder of the decade. A powerful global software industry dominated by vendors like Microsoft will grow to rival the traditional computer and consumer electronic industries in size and profitability. Personal systems already constitute almost half of the world hardware market; when consumer electronics is fully digitized and the software industry matures, that fraction will rise to two thirds or more. It is the decentralized, mass-produced, software-intensive, turbulent low end of the industry, in short, that will be the strategic high ground of the 1990s.

We do not believe, however, that the American advantages in architecture, design, innovation, and software will be sufficient to win the computer wars of the next decade, although they will be extremely helpful. Nor, for reasons that now should be clear, do we believe that the Asian manufacturing advantage is enough to control the industry or even necessarily to succeed. Both sets of skills will be crucial, to somewhat different degrees in different segments of the industry.

During the 1990s, the critical competitive battles for technological leadership will center on the struggle for control of proprietary architectures. The American Third Force companies, the Silicon Valley–style, intellectual content–based firms, have so far exhibited the greatest understanding of the dynamics of architectural contests. But a broader grasp of architectural strategies is essential if American firms are to dominate the future information environment. We will explore those strategies in detail in the next three chapters.

9

WINNING:
THE BASIC ARGUMENT

WHERE WE ARE

The fundamental reality of the global information technology industry is the radical, ten-year-long shift in cost structures as a result of inexpensive, extremely high performance microprocessors, VLSI (Very Large Scale Integration) generally; cheap, very high speed fiber optic networks; and related technologies. Measured purely in terms of raw processing power, the price/performance ratio of newer RISC microprocessors is already a hundred times better than that of standard mainframe computers and within just a few years will be a thousand times better.

With the wide availability of cheap, high-performance components, the typical business systems configuration is shifting rapidly away from traditional, centralized, tightly bundled, hardware-vendor-specific solutions. Essentially all new information processing architectures, ranging from consumer electronics to supercomputers, are open, modular, VLSI- and usually microprocessor-based, using mass-produced components and subsystems from multiple vendors, scalable across a wide range of performance levels. There are already 100 million personal computers in use, and another 25 million are sold each year.

The three main groups of contenders in the computer wars have exhibited quite different competitive strategies in the face of the industry's transformation.

The traditional Western mainframe computer companies, led by IBM and DEC, invented many of the technologies driving the radical decentralization of systems. But their established franchises of traditionally configured computers were so profitable, and their stakes in maintaining the established technologies so great, that they mostly tried standing pat. They couldn't resist the trend toward decentralization, but lost the opportunity to lead it. Despite their powerful entrenched positions, their profitable franchises were invaded from below by open, componentized, microprocessor-based systems, and their architectural leadership positions were lost to software- and design-oriented companies like Microsoft, Intel, and Sun. We have documented this process in considerable detail at IBM, traditionally the Western technology leader. All large computer companies are currently struggling to redefine themselves and adapt to the rapidly changing world of a decentralized, distributed system. Few, if any, have yet done so successfully.

The second contending group, Japanese and Asian companies generally, that had honed their process technologies in consumer electronics, like VCRs, at first did extremely well in a componentized, modularized systems industry. The global market share of Japanese companies in high-volume, cost-sensitive components like DRAMs, facsimile machines, and display screens rose to 90 percent or even higher, at the same time as Asian clone-makers drastically undercut the pricing assumptions of Western makers of desktop computers and peripherals. But competing as a commodity implementer of nonproprietary standard products such as memory chips or facsimile machines is a brutally difficult business strategy, requiring enormous investment and producing only razor-thin margins. Over the long term, such a strategy can be successful only within a stable technology regime, as is the case with television sets and facsimile machines, the paradigmatic Asian success stories.

Trends in consumer electronics illustrate both the strategic problem and the strategic opportunity facing Asian commodity manufacturers. In the near future, television sets, a staple of Asian electronic manufacturing, will become completely digital products. As such, they will require large numbers of electronic components like memory chips, and extremely responsive, reliable, very high resolution digital display screens. Those are all technologies in which Asia excels. But inside each television set will be one or more very powerful microprocessors, and some very complex software that will control the compression and decompression of digital transmissions, reconstruct and manipulate the color images on the screen, and manage the interface with other systems, such as movie libraries or electronic shopping catalogs. Those are all technologies in which American companies excel. About half of computer industry revenues come from high-volume, cost-sensitive components. To the degree that Asian companies can push the industry toward commoditization under stable architectural regimes, the greater their advantage. To the degree that American companies can maintain the pace of architectural innovation, and extend it into consumer electronics, the more they undercut the Japanese position.

The third group of contenders, and recently the most successful, are the Third Force companies, American firms typically created within the past fifteen years, who seized the lead in exploiting the technologies neglected by the traditional companies. The successful start-ups have almost uniformly succeeded in establishing some form of proprietary control over a critical and fast-moving competitive space, typically one that is architecture-, design-, or software-dominated or that speeds the transition to low-cost open systems. With intelligent strategies, these can be the most profitable systems opportunities of all, and it is a strategic arena where Asian companies are distinctly uncomfortable.

But in the same way that the commodity manufacturing skills of Asian companies are not sufficient to control the computer industry, the great design skills of the smaller American companies do not by themselves make up for the loss of market leadership by major Western companies. Traditional companies were much more labor-intensive and vertically integrated; small companies source their components throughout the world much more than larger companies did. The pending employment reductions at IBM and DEC—some seventy-five thousand people, if analysts' guesses are correct—is about a *quarter* of American computer vendor employment. Small companies are also fragile—witness the recent collapse of MIPS, one of America's outstanding design houses. (It was acquired by Silicon Graphics, a leading RISC workstation-maker.) They also tend to be capital short, and have often been a major conduit of technology leakage to cash-rich Japanese electronics giants. With the exception of companies like Intel, they often lack the detailed implementation skills that in some components can be the difference between success and failure. Finally, even the biggest and most powerful of the newer firms, such as Microsoft and Intel, have yet to make the commitment to fundamental research and development that has been the often uncommercialized glory of an IBM, an AT&T, or a Xerox.

Neither taking on the Japanese at their own game, in short, nor placing all our hopes on California's covens of magicians, is a sensible strategy for American companies in the 1990s. Recovery of market leadership by the major information technology firms—or, alternatively, the growth of the strongest of the 1980s start-ups into truly powerful global competitors—will be essential to Western success. It is time now to turn to the outlines of the strategy that Western firms must follow to win the high ground in this most critical and competitive of all industries.

A NEW STRATEGIC SYNTHESIS: THE BASIC ARGUMENT

In the global information technology industry of the 1990s— that is, in the new era of open, modularized, inexpensive, extremely high performance systems—market dominance and corporate profitability will flow to the companies that succeed in converting an innovative technology into a broader, longer-term, proprietary architectural franchise. Access to outstanding manufacturing skills will often be extremely helpful, and sometimes essential, to establishing an architectural franchise, but will rarely be sufficient. Outstanding software and design skills will similarly be extremely helpful, and more often essential, to establishing an industry standard proprietary position. But as Lotus and WordPerfect have learned to their grief, good products are not the same as an architecture. Architectures are emphatically not products; an architecture creates the environment in which products operate. The rules of an architecture are embodied in products; products, in turn, become an architecture's means of distribution and proliferation.

Architectural franchises are built upon successful products. The usual route is that a special-purpose product, usually incorporating a proprietary technology, is transformed into a general-purpose platform that serves as the base for a radiating family of products providing an increasingly powerful, proprietary solution to a specific space of information technology problems. The franchise is won when a proprietary architecture becomes the de facto industry standard, when, for instance, commodity component-makers and third-party software developers implicitly recognize it as the standard they must design to.

The textbook case of a successful strategy in information technology, the prototype that contains almost all the essential lessons, is IBM's management of its franchise in mainframe computers. Even today—after two decades of hostile, even malign, American and Japanese government policy, after decades of massive intellectual property theft, after twenty years of concerted assaults by European and Japanese companies backed by the full resources of their national governments— IBM is still by far the dominant company in the IBM-compatible mainframe market and holds a disproportionate share of its profits, not only for the mainframes themselves, but also for disk drives, systems software, and after-market products, such as expanded memory.

IBM did not win by always having the best products, although its products were always very good. The secret to its success in mainframes was that it created an architecture, which only it controlled, that defined the environment for mainframe computing. The architecture was proprietary, but over time, relatively open—other manufacturers could make equipment that plugged into IBM systems. Paradoxically, the proliferation of plug-compatible manufacturers, particularly of peripheral equipment, only reinforced IBM's grip on the mainframe industry. The ready availability of third-party support and equipment made the IBM architecture the more natural choice for a mainframe computing enviroment. But since IBM could always control how its mainframes interacted with the rest of the world, it could make life very unpleasant for the peripheral manufacturer who attempted to migrate into technological spaces IBM had reserved for itself. Therefore, competitors were always reacting to IBM, reverse-engineering its products, entering the market late, usually after IBM had already harvested the most attractive profit opportunities and was moving on to the next generation of machines.

In stunning contrast, IBM's management of its franchise in PCs was marked by a grotesque series of blunders that violated all the strategic principles that it had taught the world in mainframes. Its first impulse, to create a solid, business-oriented desktop computer, and to use predominantly externally supplied, well-proven technologies in order to move quickly, was both sound and highly innovative for IBM. The wisdom of the strategy was demonstrated when IBM quickly accounted for more than half of world PC sales. But, inexplicably, IBM never grasped, until very late, that selling a good PC product was emphatically not the same as controlling the desktop computing architecture for the 1980s and 1990s. That failure is the more astonishing in the light of the experience with the System/360, whose very genesis was grounded in the recognition that software was more important than hardware in defining a computing architecture. In any event, IBM simply handed control of the software architecture to Microsoft, not even insisting on the rights to the source code. And since DOS was written in Intel assembler, the primary hardware architecture for the PC was defaulted to Intel.

Misjudgments in the early days, when the PC team was under the cruel pressure of a twelve-month design and production deadline, are understandable. But even very early in the market cycle, particularly after cloning had started, the weakness of IBM's PC architectural position should have been apparent—indeed, it was to many people in the company. With the dominant world position that it enjoyed in desktop computers in the early 1980s, IBM could surely have enforced its own architecture, enticing its customers with technologies far superior to those available from Microsoft and Intel. And yet, as we have seen in painful detail, the company repeatedly passed up opportunities to do so.

There is as much learning to be derived, we believe, from IBM's failures in the 1980s as from its successes in the 1960s and 1970s, and the lessons are very much the same. The lesson is that the big winners in computers are companies that establish long-term, proprietary, general-purpose, expandable, industry-standard architectures. Only a few companies have demonstrated, over any extended period, that they understand this principle—IBM in earlier days; Microsoft and Intel, the big winners of the 1980s; and perhaps a handful of others. Once a company establishes control over a specific architectural space, it can enjoy a highly profitable franchise whether or not its products are by themselves the best that the market can offer; whether or not its manufacturing is the best in the world; and whether or not its software is the most outstanding. Its products, its manufacturing, and its software must all be very good, of course—that is the price of entry— but it is the strategic knitting together of those capabilities into a proprietary architectural franchise that is the consistent difference between the big winners and the also-rans.

Struggles to control computer architectures can be extremely complex, and have become more so with the advent of networked, open, componentized systems. Several architectural layers can coexist within the same product—the game, that is, is more like Go than like chess. The IBM PC contest, for example, includes at least four important, partially independent, layers: the processor/CPU architecture; the system architecture (including the system bus, BIOS, glue logic); the operating system; and the applications software. A system may be dominated by a single standard (DOS/Windows) or multiple incompatible ones (the various flavors of UNIX). The standard may be proprietary (DOS/Windows), multivendor (Open Systems Foundation) or completely nonproprietary (fax, SCSI). It may be fully open (IBM PCs at the system hardware level); selectively open (Microsoft, Intel, Sun, Apple); or completely closed (Japanese palmtops, Xerox Star, and Wang word processors). There may or may not be a bundled implementation leader (like IBM in the 360/370 world and Sun in workstations); and there may or may not be widespread licensing of intellectual property (Sun in SPARC as opposed to Apple in Macintosh). There may be wide or limited cloning, and widely varying rates of technological change and generational product improvements. All of these conditions can, and do, coexist in almost any conceivable combination.

Launching a competitively successful architecture is therefore an extremely complex challenge. The strategies and pitfalls of architectural struggles will become clearer from specific cases.

Launching an Architecture: From Star to Mac

We have already seen how Xerox PARC produced some of the most outstanding innovations of the entire computer era. Years before there was a personal computer industry, the PARC researchers actually built a network of personal computers, with an advanced word processing program, a Windows-like user interface, a laser printer, and a local area network linking it all together. The inventions were not wasted; almost all of them were eventually commercialized with great success by companies other than Xerox.

Xerox did, however, make one major attempt to create a business out of the fruits of PARC's research. In 1981, it introduced the Xerox Star, a network of desktop workstations that attempted to capture all of PARC's most important innovations in a single system. The target was the business professional "whose main job is to create, interpret, and manage information and distribute the results to others in a convenient form." The Star system, by common consent, was a truly impressive piece of engineering. The buyer got a network of workstations, with user interfaces that made them genuinely easy to learn. Most people could master a Star workstation in about an hour. But despite the stunning technology, the Xerox Star was a failure. A number of reasons have been adduced for the Star's lack of success. Analysts have tended to blame Xerox's marketing force, and they are at least partly right; Xerox salesmen were trained to sell copiers and probably never completely understood the Star's power and potential. But the problems were much more fundamental than that.

The Star was a closed, tightly integrated system—for example, the software that came with first Star workstations did not include a spreadsheet such as Visicalc. Normally, that should have been an easy problem to fix. There were innumerable garage-shop hackers who could have quickly turned out what passed for a respectable spreadsheet program at that stage of the market. But Xerox had made that impossible. The Star operating system was idiosyncratic and difficult to use to start with but, most important, it was a Xerox secret. Hoping to exert total control over the office environment, Xerox purposely shut out independent software vendors from writing Star programs: if customers wanted a spreadsheet program, they would have to wait for Xerox to provide one.

There were other rigidities. The Star's hardware configuration was very inflexible. Xerox assumed that the only desktop computer buyers would be large offices. So the Star could be purchased only in a large-office package: the workstations worked much more effectively as part of the network, and the peripherals, like the laser printer, were much too expensive to be paired off with a single workstation. Each workstation cost more than $16,000, a hefty price to begin with, but the minimum cost-effective package ran about $250,000.

The designers of the Star, brilliant as they were, did not perceive that personal computers were a democratic technology. The great insight of IBM's Boca Raton team—the more startling because it so ran against the grain of the IBM tradition—was that personal computer customers should have maximum freedom in choosing software and the maximum flexibility in deciding to work either with single machines or with linked systems. Xerox tried to impose its own concept of office computing on its customers, one that was rigid and closed, and was therefore summarily rejected by the market.

The next chapter in the saga of the Star is the Lisa, the forerunner of the Apple Macintosh. Xerox had a brief business flirtation with Apple in the late 1970s and gave Steven Jobs, Apple's cofounder, a demonstration of Star's technology. Jobs was much impressed and, when a deal with Xerox fizzled, recruited some key PARC researchers and introduced the Lisa in 1983. Ever since the Lisa, the outstanding feature of Apple computers has been their friendly Star-like user interface, making them easy to learn and easy to use. At almost $10,000, the Lisa was a pricey machine, although not nearly so forbidding as the Star. But it, too, was a commercial failure. The Lisa offered a poor development environment for outside software developers. Apple was not quite as rigid as Xerox in this respect, but still tried to supply most of the Lisa's software, and so drastically limited its market appeal.

Apple got it more nearly right with the Macintosh, introduced in 1984 and still the Apple flagship product line. The Macintosh had an even better Lisa-like interface for the user, was much cheaper, and Apple went all-out to make sure there was a wide selection of top-notch software available. The Macintosh has a fanatically loyal following. Macs are much easier to learn to use than IBM-compatible machines, and until the advent of Windows, were far superior to IBM-compatible machines in any application requiring graphics, such as desktop publishing or business presentations. But even the Mac has never commanded more than about a 10 percent market share and must be rated a disappointment given the qualities of the machine and the enthusiasm of its users.

Because Mac software can run only on the Mac, it is still too closed a system to be a truly pervasive computing solution. The Mac's hardware has never been its outstanding feature. The screen on the earlier machines was small and cramped, and the Mac was very late to offer a hard drive. For a long time Apple illogically insisted on a completely closed hardware system. Customers could not add better monitors or disk drives, for example. Apple seemed never to understand, until very recently, that its customers were loyal not to the Mac box but to Apple software, and were merely tolerating the second-rate hardware they were forced to buy with it. By misconceiving the computer business as fundamentally a hardware business, Apple missed a once-in-a-lifetime opportunity to create a dominant Mac/Motorola PC architecture. PC software vendors almost always release products for the IBM-compatible world first, because it's so much bigger. If Apple had licensed the Mac operating system to clone-makers to increase the base of Apple machines, Mac and Mac clones would have had far more attention from third-party software developers. And if Apple had succeeded in making its architecture pervasive early, Mac-compatible PCs could have had a real shot at unseating the Microsoft-Intel-IBM standard. The misconceived strategy of hardware-software bundling condemned Apple to be merely a moderately successful niche player. Apple's mistakes were at the opposite extreme from IBM's. IBM failed by giving away the PC architectural opportunity to Microsoft and Intel; Apple failed by trying to control its architecture too closely.

How might either company, Apple or IBM, have managed the PC architecture if it had made the right decisions early? First of all, of course, it would have ensured that it controlled the licensing rights to the bundled operating system/microprocessor environment (as IBM did not). Then it would have selectively opened the standard to clone-makers and software developers to ensure the broadest possible base of installed machines and the widest possible availability of software (as Apple did not). But it would have kept careful control over the cloning. Presumably, it would have reserved the manufacture of each new machine generation to itself for some reasonable period—say, a year or so—and then released it for cloning when the technology was ready to move on. The precise period of reserved manufacturing before the opening to cloning would vary from product to product. The trick, which would require some skill, would be to strike a balance between the market's demand for broad product availability at falling prices and the market leader's fair claim to first-product profits. It would have required artful, consistent management over an extended period—precisely the kind of management that IBM applied to its mainframe franchise for so long. And the prize—say, a 50 to 60 percent share of the 120-million-unit global desktop computer market—would have been of comparable value.

Products and Architectures

Architectures, as the case of the Mac illustrates clearly, are not the same as products. But it takes a good product to launch an architecture. There were many other entries in the personal computer market in the late 1970s and early 1980s—the Altair, Osborne, Commodore, Atari, and many others. Most fell by the wayside, while the better products, such as the Star, the Lisa, the Mac, and the IBM PC, rose to the top. The first lesson, therefore, is that only good products, which can gain a significant toehold in the market, can distribute architectures. Once an architecture has been established as an industry standard, however, it will help sell more products. But architectures always begin with products.

Which products make promising architectural platforms? There are no hard and fast rules, but experience points to a few basic principles.

General-purpose systems almost always win out over special-purpose products. Wang Laboratories made its word processors into one of the most successful growth businesses of the 1970s; it virtually created the market for office computers by acclimating a generation of clerical workers to working with a display screen and computer keyboard. But Wang never successfully converted its word processors into stand-alone computers. The IBM PC offered the same capabilities as a Wang word processor, but gave users a wide choice of word-processing packages and, even better, could also run many other applications, such as spreadsheets. But at that point, just as the market was on the cusp of a boom, Wang had begun to diversify into minicomputers, effectively walking away from its desktop franchise—a truly disastrous decision.

The same story can be seen in engineering workstations. Computer-assisted design, or CAD, was becoming an important new market at roughly the same time as the emergence of desktop computing. CAD has great advantages over hand drafting, but graphics is very processing intensive, so early CAD applications were run on minicomputers. Minicomputer CAD products were displaced in the early 1980s by special-purpose, free-standing workstations from companies such as Daisy, Calma and Applicon.

But special-purpose workstations are quickly going the way of the Wang. The most successful workstation vendors, like Sun and Silicon Graphics, have converted their machines into general-purpose platforms that can be used in a broad range of applications, including financial analysis, medical imaging, and typesetting and publishing, in addition to their original scientific and engineering roles. Sun, indeed, has gone much further than any other workstation-maker in establishing its own UNIX-based operating system and Sun applications software as a challenger to the prevailing Microsoft-Intel standard for general-purpose office computing during the 1990s. It will be an uphill battle, to be sure, for the Sun-installed base, although the largest of the workstation-makers is still comparatively small; but the DOS/ Windows versus UNIX versus OS/2 versus NT operating systems battle is looming as one the more interesting of the mid-1990s. There are many other examples of the persistent migration from specific to generalized: traditional fax machines, for instance, are now being absorbed by multifunctional networked laser printers/copiers.

The evolution from special-purpose to general-purpose platform is probably an inherent feature of computer technology. When a new application like word processing or CAD first comes within range of current computer power, it usually requires specially optimized hardware. But the rate of improvement in microprocessor power is so great that general-purpose hardware almost always absorbs the new function within just a few years. The same phenomenon has been evident from the earliest days of computing, although the pace of change was slower. The first computers were typically optimized as scientific, business, or military machines; but general-purpose mainframes, particularly the 360/370 family, gradually absorbed most of the specialty applications.

The lesson is simply that a niche, special-purpose product that cannot be expanded into a more general-purpose computing solution as technology evolves will be a dead end. Nintendo may now be facing this challenge. Its game consoles are vulnerable to attack by more general-purpose, architected home computers. If Nintendo can move up to a more general-purpose position itself, it may be in a strong position; if it does not, it may die.

It is a common error to sacrifice an architectural opportunity for short-term product profitability—usually by adopting a design path that gets a product to market quickly but impedes its longer-term development. Correct strategic decision-making in the early period is, unfortunately, as difficult as it is important, particularly for smaller companies. There is great pressure to bring a product to market; cash is often short; investors or underwriters are clamoring for results. The first MS-DOS and Intel 8088 products were no exemplars of architectural beauty. But both companies realized their mistakes very soon thereafter and worked hard for a long time to reengineer their offerings into respectably robust architectural platforms. For large companies—companies, presumably, with resources, experience, and a long-term view—there is much less excuse for fumbling the early-period architectural opportunity, an expectation that, however, is lamentably short of empirical support.

THE CHALLENGE AND RISKS OF DIFFUSION

Proprietary franchises that are kept narrow and closed can enjoy only narrow successes. As we have seen, a closed architecture will rarely succeed in establishing itself as the industry standard, particularly in the current era of democratic technology markets. Secondly, since niche, special-purpose products almost always get swept away by general-purpose solutions, it is imperative that an initial product have the potential for developing into a general-purpose platform that can support a radiating family of products over a broad computing space.

Assuming, however, that a company has introduced a product with architectural promise and that it has gained a market foothold, the next challenge is to diffuse the fledgling architecture throughout the relevant competitive space. Without broad diffusion, there is no possibility of a promising architecture becoming the industry standard; successful diffusion, on the other hand, leads to very attractive positions. Consider again the cases of the Xerox, Apple, and Microsoft operating systems. Microsoft made almost all the right decisions to ensure maximum diffusion of its system. Microsoft's Windows/DOS is the least expensive operating system, the most open, and the least bundled to any vendor's hardware, although it is still tied to the Intel microprocessor. Star and Lisa each sold about 100,000 units in their lifetimes. The Mac has sold several million units. But DOS sales are well in excess of 100 million copies, and the new Windows software sold 15 million copies its first two years and another 10 million in the first quarter of 1992; it will almost certainly top the 50 million mark before 1995. Microsoft enjoys one of the highest rates of profit of any company of its size in the world. Windows/DOS is now facing a new challenge in the pen-based and palmtop computers, which have unusual internal requirements and limited memory space, matching up poorly against Windows/DOS.

IBM is strenuously contesting the Windows/DOS lock on PC operating systems with its newest version of OS/2. Although OS/2 is technically superior to Windows/DOS, it requires more expensive hardware and is not well supported by applications and alliances. In a series of ads in the summer of 1992, Microsoft rubbed in the advantages of the more broadly diffused position, teasing IBM for being the only one of the top ten personal computer-makers not to include Windows in its basic offering. The technical capabilities of OS/2 will assure it a market, but we expect that it will remain a niche product, restricted to perhaps the 10 percent or so of the most demanding users.

Examples of successful and unsuccessful diffusers can be easily multiplied. Running a printer requires special software called a page description language, or PDL, that translates the digital representation of a page in computer memory into instructions for the printer. Xerox's PARC, as usual, invented the first PDL, called Interpress, generally regarded as an outstanding piece of software engineering. But Interpress is bundled tightly to Xerox printers, which have a significant market presence only at the very high end, typically in mainframe computer centers. Adobe, one of the many companies formed by PARC refugees, developed its own Interpress-like PDL, PostScript, and diffused it aggressively. PostScript has problems of its own, however—it is very complex and requires very fast processors to run efficiently—and is under constant competitive attack. But with $250 million in annual sales and very high profits, Adobe is closer than any of its competitors to establishing PostScript as the industry standard PDL.

Diffusion is a risky game. Apple understood that it needed broad application support from outside software developers to diffuse the Mac architecture, so it enlisted the support of Microsoft. Microsoft insisted it could not develop programs that fit the Mac's user-friendly, icon-based interface unless Apple licensed some of its software secrets. Years later, when Apple sued Microsoft for allegedly stealing its user interface concepts for Windows, that license was fatal to Apple's case. Apple, of course, had originally copied the concept from Xerox, which was not lost on the court. (To add to the incestuousness, the chief designer of Windows, Charles Simonyi, also came from PARC.) Apple wouldn't have had to sue at all, of course, if it had unbundled and diffused its Mac operating system in the first place, since it would have foreclosed the market opportunity to Microsoft.

Intel similarly licensed its xx86 architecture broadly in the early days to ensure that it had broad market coverage. The initial licensing was under duress; IBM insisted on second-sourcing as a condition for adopting the Intel chip for the PC.

Intel licensed more than twenty sources for the 8088/8086 and a half dozen for the 286. Its licensing was so aggressive that at one point Intel held less than a third of the market for its own microprocessors; and for a while AMD held a larger share of the 286 market than Intel did, and had faster parts. But once Intel had established its microprocessors as the desktop standard, it sharply limited licensing. It held a lucrative, almost a monopoly, position in the 386 for many years; IBM was the only licensee, and that for its own use only.

Diffusion decisions are never costless. Recently, a number of companies—AMD, Cyrix, and others—have begun selling competitive 386 and 486 microprocessors, making a substantial dent in Intel's profits. Intel is suing for patent infringement, but the wide licensing of Intel's patents and earlier xx86 designs may protect the cloners. But the different positions of Intel and, say, that of Motorola, who did not diffuse a technically superior processor, speak for themselves. Diffusion almost always involves a risk of being ambushed by partners. Philips brought in Sony to help manufacture its CD audio technology, and Sony took half the market. But the lesson is to manage intellectual property carefully during the diffusion stage, not to avoid diffusion. At the end of the day, the choice is usually stark: one can own all of a narrow, short-term franchise or bet on winning proprietary (if less than total) control over a franchise that is broad, expanding, and long-lived.

Aggressive architectural diffusion is a game that only technologically confident companies can play. Diffusion makes no sense unless the architecture is one that is continually moving. Licensing away a static architecture is merely giving the business away to clones, but static architectures aren't worth very much in the first place. To be successful, diffusers must follow up the initial product set with a continuing stream of innovations and enhancements. Intel's 186 was faster than its unimpressive 8086; the 286 added memory protection; the 386 brought a new 32-bit architecture, but one that was backward compatible. The 486 bundles in Intel coprocessors, the Pentium, originally the 586, has a much faster 64-bit internal bus, and the next generation will add Intel's video processor, giving it a jump-start on a potentially major new market. This is a game that IBM taught the world how to play with the System/360/370. By the mid-1970s, the system was almost totally unbundled; the American and Japanese governments had forced the broad licensing of most of its technologies; Hitachi and Fujitsu had stolen what they couldn't license; and much of what couldn't be stolen had been acquired by Fujitsu through Amdahl. But IBM still controlled the global mainframe market by always being first with the *next* generation of technology, leaving the clones and copiers to squabble over the shrinking profits from last year's product line.

Winning architectural strategies require both technical virtuosity and strategic subtlety. But because of their rich tradition of rapid innovation and far superior base of R&D talent, it is a strategic challenge that American companies are uniquely qualified to meet.

Initial winning positions, however, are always open to attack. The challenge for the early winner is to lock in its position over the long term.

10

Locking In a Winning Position

The endgame of an architectural strategy is always to create and own the proprietary industry standard, to achieve, in our language, architectural lock-in. To be more precise, the goal is to achieve *proprietary* lock-in. The fax standard and the NTSC television standard, to name just two, are utterly locked-in architectures, but since nobody owns them, they are valueless.

Some readers may recoil at the notion of "lock-in," with its sinister monopolistic overtones. But as we stressed earlier in the book, proprietary architectures are in the best interest of users. Nonproprietary or publicly owned architectural standards, like those for faxes and television transmissions, are almost always technologically retrograde. The basic television standard was set more than half a century ago and has been updated just once, almost forty years ago, for color—this in an industry, electronic communications, that has seen some of the most rapid technological advances in history. The basic fax standard is now more than twenty years old. Contrast that experience with computers or printers, where the standards are controlled by private companies and the profits from winning a standards battle are very high. Because the profit opportunities are so alluring, the leader's architectural position is under constant attack from all sides, generating a steady stream of technological advances, wide product distribution, and rapidly falling prices.

There are many paths to lock-in, and the best players usually follow multiple paths, depending on the nature of their product and the stage of their architecture's life cycle. In this chapter, we will focus on three primary ways to win standards battles. The most basic is sheer, consistent price/performance over an extended period of time. Second, and closely related, is the development of an extensive supporting infrastructure that increases customer dependence and increases their switching costs. And third, and a persistent prob-

---

ATTACKING, OR LIVING WITH, AN
ARCHITECTURAL LEADER

I. **Bundled, Niche Architectures**. Optimized for a minority, specialized market. Example: Apple Mac vs. IBM PCs in publishing.

II. **Clones**. Unlicensed imitation of the leader's architecture and/or products. Example: AMD vs. Intel; Fujitsu and Hitachi vs. IBM in mainframes; Borland vs. Lotus in spreadsheets.

III. **Standard Stealers**. Beginning with licensing or cloning, a competitor enhances and diffuses the leader's architecture and steals the franchise. Example: Sun vs. AT&T in UNIX.

IV. **Neighbor Franchises**. A competitor develops a franchise in an adjacent competitive space. Example: Novell vs. Microsoft.

V. **Point Product Vendors**. A firm contents itself with selling products inside of the leader's architecture. Example: almost all PC applications vendors vs. Microsoft.

VI. **Radical Innovators**. A new entrant leapfrogs an aging architecture. Example: parallel processors vs. traditional mainframes.

lem for American companies, is the development and management of strong intellectual property positions.

OVERWHELMING PRICE/PERFORMANCE

Architectural battles are truly won in the hearts and minds of customers. Lock-in is secured when customers believe that one company will almost always beat its competitors with a continual stream of product improvements; it is then in the customers' self-interest to stay loyal and not risk breaking architectures. In the early days of mainframe computer competition, a large number of competing architectures waged war against each other. IBM gained the upper hand in the architectural battle when the market accepted its System/360 as the preferred solution for an extensive space of mainframe computer applications. But the race was not really conceded until the 1970s, after the success of the System/370. That was when competition shifted wholesale to IBM-compatible products or to mainframe solutions that promised, even if they frequently did not deliver, painless emulation of the IBM operating environment. Cloning was a backhanded acknowledgment that customers believed IBM would always lead the market in innovation and new product development. Changing architectures for the sake of a temporary cost or performance improvement would risk being shut out of the next generation of solutions. When competitors begin to adapt their products to the leading architecture, the struggle, at least temporarily, will be over.

By the end of the 1980s at least, Intel achieved a similar position in PC microprocessors. When NEC introduced its own technically solid V-series processors in the mid-1980s, it made sure they were compatible with the 8086. But in subsequent releases, NEC tried to plant its own architectural stake with a series of chips that were functionally excellent but intentionally incompatible with the xx86 standard. The chips bombed on the market. Intel had so convincingly demonstrated its commitment to continued improvement in the price and performance of its chips that customers were not willing to risk losing access to them. Microsoft is in a similar position with respect to operating system software. IBM had to make sure that its new versions of OS/2 would run DOS and Windows. Microsoft's DOS replacement, NT, due this year, will have to fail badly, we expect, before customers will be willing to risk shifting away from the Microsoft standard.

The best lock-in players are almost always enthusiastic cannibalizers of their own product lines. Good architectures facilitate graceful cannibalization. The fatal temptation is to try to milk an existing profitable product: IBM stuck with its 286-based PCs while Compaq stole their thunder with the 386.

Cannibalizing one's own architecture is a once-a-decade decision, and much tougher than deciding to cannibalize products. IBM cannibalized a string of successful architectures with its 360, but dithered with its superior RISC technologies for years rather than disturb either its profitable minicomputer position or the apparent success of its Intel/PC franchise. The DEC VAX is perhaps the clearest example of losing for failure to cannibalize. In the early 1980s, DEC had one of the most advanced RISC capabilities in the industry and a microprocessor that was several times faster than the processor unit in its VAX machines. But moving to RISC technology would have meant dropping its VMS operating system, and the DEC VMS-VAX had achieved a highly profitable position contending for the minicomputer standard. The risk was that if DEC shifted to a more open RISC-UNIX architecture, it might weaken its grip in minicomputers; in return, it would have a shot at a greatly expanded competitive space both above and below minicomputers. DEC made the fateful decision to stand pat; and in computers to stand pat is to die. Within a few years DEC's position was swallowed up by RISC-UNIX workstations moving up from the low end. DEC has experienced huge losses in the early 1990s, $1.85 billion in the first quarter of 1992 alone, and is now desperately trying to reconstitute itself as a RISC-UNIX company.

Nintendo is arguably the first Japanese company to display a sophisticated understanding of architectural contests. From the very first, it understood that the popularity of its games would sell its game machines, and it enlisted a broad stable of software writers. When games such as Super Mario swept the world, Nintendo was established as the architectural leader and began to devote its energies to fending off clones and unlicensed software. But it sat too complacently on its 8-bit architecture and found itself suddenly vulnerable when Sega introduced a superior 16-bit console. Nintendo then compounded the error by responding with its own 16-bit product, but one that was not backward-compatible with its large established software base. Sega and Nintendo have now formed partnerships with Sony and Matsushita to supply games software and are squaring off for another round. This is a serious industry. By the end of 1991, there were more than 30 million Nintendo sets in American homes—this represents 70 percent of all homes with a child between the ages of eight and twelve.

Nintendo will survive because it played an architectural game well enough in earlier stages that it has room to make mistakes, although as we have suggested, it may soon face competition from more general-purpose products. Sun is another company that survived mistakes because of its earlier good strategies. Once it shifted its workstations to its SPARC RISC architecture, it licensed the SPARC widely and secured the broadest base of software support of any workstation-maker. Over the past several years, however, it has suffered a series of technical hiccups. Its SPARC architecture is now the slowest of the major workstation microprocessors, and its newest generation chip, the Viking from Texas Instruments, was late to market because of manufacturing problems and runs much slower than expected. Intel's Pentium, a conventional microprocessor, due soon as the follow-on to the 486, may have performance comparable to the Viking's, and Sun will have to improve its performance sharply to survive. Computer markets are extremely unforgiving, but an architectural leader can survive technical reverses that would sink another company because of its well-earned reputation and base of customer investment.

The computer industry moves much too fast and is far too competitive for any proprietary architecture to hold sway for an extended period unless it is constantly refreshed and renewed. Customers will ride with leaders through short-term stumbles; most customers will have made big investments in an architectural leader's continued success. But if the leader allows its technology to stagnate, or the stumbles persist too long, the market's retribution will be harsh and irreversible. The PC software industry is remarkably clearheaded in this respect, and the leaders are constantly striving to reinforce their positions. Witness Novell's purchase of DR-DOS as at least a minimal restraint on Microsoft; Borland's purchase of Ashton-Tate to control the data base franchise; and Microsoft's virtually instant response in buying Fox, an Ashton-Tate dBase clone. In short, just as it takes aggressive technology to gain a leadership position, it takes a continued stream of improvements to maintain it. The locked-in leader will be in the far superior position with each new round of competition, but each new round must still be won on the merits.

INCREASING SWITCHING COSTS

Aggressive enhancement and expansion of the basic product family is essential to architectural lock-in in the computer industry. Expanding customers' infrastructure investment in the basic architecture deepens and tightens the lock-in.

IBM, once again, is the exemplar. It first unbundled its System/360 in 1969. Initially, the unbundling was in reaction to the Justice Department's antitrust action. But IBM soon learned that selectively opening its architecture actually increased its effective presence in customer back offices. As computer peripherals proliferated, no one company, not even IBM, had the ingenuity or the capability to supply every need. The more that peripheral manufacturers supplied additional IBM-compatible products to support and enhance the IBM architecture, the more committed IBM customers necessarily became. Over time, IBM came to understand that selectively opening its architecture was not only good politics but strategically wise. Part of the motivation for selling its mainframe MVS operating system to purchasers of Amdahl hardware was to ensure coverage of the entire competitive arena with IBM-compatible machines.

Architectural lock-in can happen at many different levels. Autodesk sells desktop computer CAD software that has a particularly strong following among the (real) architectural community—that is, the people who design houses and buildings. Autodesk protects its core software from imitators, but has provided independent software developers with tool kits to facilitate add-on special-purpose packages—a kitchen design package, for example, that runs inside of Autodesk's basic CAD programs. The availability of add-on software for Autodesk products is now many times greater than for its competitors. At the same time, Autodesk has made substantial investments to assure that it will run on as many different platforms and operating systems as possible. Therefore, it has achieved a certain architectural control over a relatively small but very lucrative competitive space, within other people's overall operating software environments. As the infrastructure of Autodesk-compatible software products steadily increases, so do customer switching costs. And as the product becomes more pervasive and customers routinely exchange Autodesk files, the lock-in can become very strong.

It is important to distinguish between architectures and point products, even the very best ones. As we have seen when we unraveled a modern computer network, hundreds of companies will typically supply network hardware and software. Only a few of them will be architectural leaders; the rest will be supplying point products. Most point products are commodities like memory chips or modems, but not all of them are. WordPerfect, for example, sells a point product, word-processing software, within the PC software architecture controlled by Microsoft. WordPerfect software is not a commodity; it is expensive and loaded with special file management, printing, and other office-oriented functions. But it is still a point product within someone else's architecture. Just like a peripheral manufacturer selling into an IBM mainframe environment, WordPerfect must continually adapt itself to the Microsoft architecture, not the other way around, and is increasingly vulnerable to Microsoft's Word. Autodesk's CAD

programs, on the other hand, because of their relative platform independence and the company's success in encourag-
ing a large supporting software infrastructure, may have
transcended point product status and established its own, albeit restricted, architectural space.

Lotus seems never to have understood the difference between a point product and an architecture. The history of the
company is a veritable bestiary of architectural misjudgments.
To begin with, the first several versions of Lotus were written
in Intel assembler, rather than a more portable language like
C. Lotus took years to produce its first C version, much too
late to establish any useful independence from the Intel-DOS
standard. In the meantime, it haphazardly acquired, or developed, a broad family of products—Jazz, Manuscript, AmiPro,
Notes, Freelance, Improv. Some of them were excellent, but
they had no architectural commonality and established no
franchise. So Lotus ended up with a grab bag of unrelated PC
point products instead of a consistent and reinforcing software
architecture. The breadth of Lotus's market penetration—it
has an installed base of more than 16 million 1-2-3 users—
once made it seem almost unassailable. Gates said recently
that Lotus was the only serious competitive threat to Microsoft
in the mid-1980s. If Lotus had produced a Lotus-compatible
general purpose user interface, it could have forestalled Windows and left DOS's vulnerabilities very exposed. But Lotus
missed the opportunity, and the fragility of its position became evident when competitors attacked with seamless conversion programs, effectively eliminating switching costs. Now
Lotus is under assault from the architectural leader (Microsoft) and the rising tide of clones. Its future looks very
bleak.

No competitor has played the architectural game more
shrewdly and subtly, or with more strategic insight, than Bill
Gates's Microsoft. Very early on, when his bargaining position
was absurdly weak compared to IBM's, Gates managed to
protect his independent control of DOS, even though IBM
played a major role in developing it into a capable operating
system. He understood the importance of gaining a licensed
position for the use of Apple's advanced user interfaces, and

he was quick to extricate himself when the OS/2 development program bogged down within IBM—indeed, he may have let it happen. A successful Windows offering took years longer than Gates hoped, but it clearly struck a chord with users. Instead of gouging the market on price, Gates kept Windows very cheap in order to gain the broadest possible distribution. His control over Windows is now a major advantage in producing application programs. Microsoft's Word for Windows is cutting heavily into WordPerfect's leading word processing position, just as Microsoft Excel for Windows is doing serious damage to Lotus. Microsoft's advance knowledge of each new Windows release confers a massive advantage over other applications software companies, who are always playing catch-up.

Microsoft has always insisted that its Windows team and applications team are kept hermetically isolated from each other to avoid creating an unfair advantage for applications programs like Word and Excel. Recently, however, both operating and applications systems have been placed under the same executive, former IBMer Mike Maples, creating considerable consternation among applications software vendors. More tellingly, it was disclosed in 1992 that Windows contains a large number of undocumented "calls"—these are the handles that third-party software writers use to adapt their software to an operating system environment. Microsoft applications programmers, of course, had the complete list of calls and so presumably had shortcuts available to them that competitive vendors did not have.

Gates and Microsoft have made a number of false starts and run into many technical dead ends, but they have pursued a clear strategic objective with remarkable single-mindedness: to make Microsoft the pervasive architectural standard-setter for the entire software environment for desktop computers. With Windows now well entrenched as the user interface of choice, Microsoft is steadily expanding its offerings to cover the entire competitive space—not only word processors and spreadsheets but also data bases, publishing packages, printer page description languages (run under Windows on the PC, not in the printer), and many others. NT, the forthcoming

DOS replacement, will move Microsoft into the UNIX and multiprocessing world and begin to reduce the dependence on Intel. Overall, it is an extraordinary lesson in strategy, executed with extraordinary skill and persistence. As of mid-1992, Microsoft's market capitalization was greater than General Motors', and its revenues and profits were growing at compound annual rates in excess of 50 percent. Microsoft is also the first of the newer companies to begin investing in fundamental research and has begun an interesting pattern of investment aimed at controlling content—stored images of art, encyclopedias, and other texts and images.

One of the most critical of all strategic challenges is managing the subtle tension between the two objectives of being very aggressive technically while, at the same time, protecting customer investment in the infrastructure that supports the basic architecture. For example, Intel's microprocessors are known for their complexity or, less charitably, the clunkiness of their designs. The new Pentium will have three million transistors, for instance, several times more than better-performing RISC chips. But a large part of that complexity is devoted to assuring compatibility with the entire previous xx86 family. There is an unavoidable trade-off between compatibility and performance, but Intel has shrewdly walked a fine line between customers' constant demand for more power and their need to protect the growing base of Intel-compatible software investment. Microsoft has managed the same trade-off with great skill. Windows/DOS has never been admired for its elegance, but it is an effective and technically advanced user interface that has managed to maintain compatibility with ten years of previous DOS releases, no mean accomplishment.

MANAGING INTELLECTUAL PROPERTY

Intellectual property issues loom large in protecting a proprietary position, although very occasionally it is possible, as the IBM mainframe case demonstrates, to exercise proprietary control with trade secrets that are an open book—it is just much harder. In general, Western companies have been extremely casual in enforcing intellectual property rights, an attitude that was reinforced by the confused state of patent and copyright protection in computer technology during most of the 1960s and 1970s and by a generally hostile antitrust and regulatory environment. Xerox, as we have seen, simply gave away virtually all the leading edge technologies developed at PARC during the 1970s, while the Justice Department forced both IBM and AT&T, and later even Xerox, to license their technologies to all comers. The American practice of broad technology cross-licensing agreements frequently undercut potentially valuable patent positions. AT&T did not exploit its UNIX operating system, Apple allowed Microsoft access to its operating system technology, and Intel's broad licenses to companies like Texas Instruments opened the door to widespread cloning of its most advanced chips.

The licensing strategies of the larger American companies, and the casualness of patent policing, is an outgrowth of the strong American technology position in the 1950s amd 1960s. The industry was divided among a few major players, such as AT&T, IBM, and RCA, each with strong research laboratories. Broad cross-licensing was simply an efficient way to avoid patent battles. The rise of the Japanese and Silicon Valley competitors upset that reasoning, because the direction of licensing was unilateral. It took a full decade for the larger companies to adjust to the changed circumstances.

The Japanese were always quick to exploit American intellectual property naïveté and subjected all the larger American firms to massive intellectual property theft. The sordid dark-of-night stealing from IBM by Hitachi and Mitsubishi is only the most egregious example. MITI forced American firms seeking entrance to Japan to form manufacturing alliances with Japanese partners, who almost invariably stole the Americans' patented technologies. In an extraordinary exercise in cynicism, in 1984, after the exposure of widespread Japanese intellectual property theft, MITI introduced legislation that effectively legalized stealing from foreigners. The law would have extended copyright protection to software only if it was developed entirely within Japan and would have permitted "nonconsensual second scoring" of software. It was ultimately withdrawn after strong protests from the United States.

There have been some recent improvements in intellectual property enforcement in Japan, primarily as the result of the relentless pursuit of redress by companies like Texas Instruments; TI won Japanese recognition of its integrated circuit patents in 1989, *twenty-nine years* after the initial filing. American companies participating in the recent wave of cross-Pacific technology partnerships generally report much improved Japanese behavior, and Americans are certainly much more vigilant than they once were. The patent thefts, however, have left a residue of suspicion and ill will that will color technological relations between the two countries for years to come.

The first imperative in protecting intellectual property is to ensure that a patent position is a strong one from the outset. One quite legal Japanese maneuver that has repeatedly burned Western companies is the tactic of "encircle and negotiate." When a Western company files a promising new patent, Japanese firms almost immediately file a flurry of new patents covering almost any conceivable application of the technology; they will then sue for infringement when the Western company tries to sell applications of its technology. Typically, the Western company has no choice but to license its technology to the Japanese at a favorable price since it is suddenly negotiating from a position of weakness. (This is not a specifically anti-Western strategy; business is rough in Japan, and Japanese companies behave the same way toward each other.) The only antidote is solid early patent documentation, careful searches, the broadest and strongest possible patent claims, and continual monitoring to ensure that rights are being respected. (Japanese patent tactics, it should be pointed out, also suggest that assessments of national research prowess based on raw patent counts should be regarded with some skepticism.)

American companies are now generally much more aware that licensing practices are a key element of a technological strategy. Licenses must be managed with a careful eye on the future, and whenever possible, be both specific and modular, in contrast to the broad cross-licenses of the past. One patent expert, commenting on Intel's current attempts to defend against widespread cloning of its leading edge microprocessors, remarked that past cross-licensing may have made it impossible to defend any microprocessor design based on current technology. That is hardly a tribute to American companies' foresight and a sobering admonition for future intellectual property management.

PRECARIOUS WINNERS

There is no such thing, unfortunately, as a stable lock-in; information technology moves too fast. Just as lock-in appears secure, a new challenge will arise from some unexpected quarter. Hewlett-Packard's standard-setting laser printers are an excellent example. Almost all desktop laser printers use Canon engines. The engine includes the laser diode itself, the paper handler, the mirror and lens systems, the toner cartridge, and the photosensitive roller. HP supplies the complex processing circuitry and the page description software that directs the engine's laser pulses to form a wide range of fonts and graphics, and is responsible for overall product design and marketing and distribution strategy.

For years, HP has more or less successfully fought off assaults from two directions. Canon and other Japanese engine-makers have for many years tried to establish their own printer brands, although they are weak in the necessary processing and software skills. From the other direction, American companies can package Japanese engines, software from Adobe or the innumerable HP cloners, and circuitry from American chip houses to produce quite formidable printers. HP has managed to maintain the upper hand by skillfully managing a powerful distribution network, being consistently first on each new product design cycle, and aggressively undercutting its competition on price. It has been a grim and constant battle, and HP has waged it with remarkable skill. HP currently holds about a 60 percent share of the global low-end desktop printer market.

HP is now facing an entirely new and possibly a much more formidable threat. First Sun, and now Microsoft, have introduced page description software that will run under their operating systems. That is, instead of having the printer process the digital representation of a page into control signals for the print engine, the host computer will do it. The great advantage of host-based page processing is the assurance that the output from the printer, fonts and all, will be exactly the same as the image on the screen. Until recently, PC processors did not have enough power to bring graphics and font processing into the host, but the newest generations of chips certainly do. Especially if Microsoft succeeds in bringing page processing into the Windows environment, as it clearly intends, desktop printers will need to be only "dumb" laser engines, and the entire basis of HP's printer business will disappear. HP might still head off the Microsoft threat by packaging its PCL page description software and licensing it to other software vendors.

The continued instability of any proprietary position suggests that excellent strategists must adjust their tactics continually over the long term. In the next chapter, we will consider how successful strategies are modulated over an architecture's natural life cycle.

11

LIFE CYCLE STRATEGIES

All competitive architectural struggles have a natural life cycle. Like products or technologies, architectures are created, struggle for dominance, flourish, and die. Different challenges and different strategies apply to each stage of this inevitable cycle.

EARLY-STAGE CHAOS

The early days of a technology are marked by struggles for market share among special-purpose products from companies who may have only the vaguest inkling that an architectural opportunity is shaping up. The first mainframes were highly customized machines. With a thousand installed units, the IBM 650, the first popular business computer of the 1950s, became the first mass-produced computer. IBM seems to have been the first computer company to understand that general-purpose, noncustomized machines would offer a massive market opportunity. Its System/360 was the first thoroughly architected computer solution.

Similarly, in the early days of desktop computing, there were quite separate product battles between problem- and market-specific machines. Wang word processors, Xerox's electronic typewriters, and IBM's Displaywriter fought it out for the electronic office text market. The IBM 5100 and a host of machines from companies such as Texas Instruments and Hewlett-Packard provided scientific computing and calculating capabilities. The Altair, the Apple I, and many other kit-based products targeted the home hacker, the competent programmer who wanted a computer all his own. Apple may have been the first to realize the opportunity to sweep all three markets into the same general-purpose architectural space, and its Apple II was the first machine with a clear chance of dominating the desktop computer market. But Apple muffed its chance, and IBM grabbed the ring with its IBM PC.

The first requirement for a successful computer strategy, therefore, is to understand that one is *in* an architectural contest in the first place. If the initial product is not a good platform for future development, as Wang's word processors were not, short-term success is likely to be followed by crashing failure. Inevitably and understandably, many mistakes are made in rushing the initial product to market. If the initial product is successful, there is usually time for redesign to broaden capabilities and increase its generality. Microsoft and Intel plowed back their early earnings into repairing their deficiencies.

Intel showed its early appreciation of the architectural implications of its processors in a contest with Zilog, at the very outset of the personal computer industry. Intel's 8080 chip, the one used in the Altair, gained the leading market share in the late 1970s. Zilog produced a more capable 8080 clone, the Z80, and rapidly took share from Intel. Intel countered with the 8088, its first processor with 16-bit internal architecture; it was backward-compatible with the 8080, but pointedly not with the Z80. At that point, Zilog's R&D stumbled. When it could not quickly trump the 8088, it was effectively out of the running, and the Intel 8088 was chosen for the first IBM PC. Firms without the strategic vision to perceive an architectural opportunity stick with their initial technologies and see their markets disappear beneath them. The shocking event of the 1980s is that IBM could make such a critical error.

THE ARCHITECTURAL LIFE CYCLE

I. **Early-Stage Chaos**. Technology opens a new market space; early entrants probe for niches.

II. **The Diffusion Race**. The opportunity takes shape, architectural contenders appear, fight for market coverage through alliances, licensing, and early architected products.

III. **A Winner Emerges**. The market chooses a de facto standard. The standard accumulates supporting infrastructure and third-party point products.

IV. **Harvesting and Extension**. The winner expands and enhances its architectural coverage, favoring its own and its allies' products. Proprietary control tightens, but the architecture remains open and available.

V. **Obsolescence and Migration**. As the architecture ages, the sponsor develops new layers to facilitate migration of its users and products to a new architecture, giving it a jump-start on a new diffusion cycle.

Of course, there is nothing dishonorable about eschewing architectural contests completely and setting out to produce point products, commodities, or clones. But surviving within someone else's architecture is a very tough business. A few companies have flourished with such a strategy. Storage Technologies, for example, has built an outstanding, albeit still small, business producing advanced disk units for mainframes. Autodesk, as we have seen, may have built a point product position in CAD software into a small architectural franchise of its own. But as the squeeze that Microsoft is steadily exerting on Lotus and WordPerfect demonstrates, the point product maker is always vulnerable when the architectural leader starts to expand its reach.

Commodity and clone positions—that is, producing a low-cost or feature-enhanced product within a proprietary, or worse, a competitor's architecture—are particularly unattractive, especially for Western companies. Since competition almost always turns on price, operations must be very lean and costs kept very tight; even for the best firms, absent collusion or government market-rigging, profits are usually very low. Commodity and clone competition is most often undertaken by companies—and as often as not by countries—seeking to enter electronics markets for the first time; this strategy, pioneered by Japan, is being emulated by other rapidly growing Asian economies. American companies have carved out successful niches in lower-volume, very fast moving, higher-margin components; Chips & Technologies is probably the best example, although it has been hit hard by the computer recession of the early 1990s. Japan's great failure is that it has yet to move beyond its initial commodity/cloning strategy, despite its extraordinary manufacturing prowess (perhaps because of it), its high rate of investment, and more than twenty years of experience in global computer markets.

The absolute worst outcome is to engage in an architectural contest and lose. The loser ends up playing the brutal game of the clone-maker, but usually with the overhead costs and research burden of an architectural leader. IBM ended up in this position when it lost control of the PC architecture. Compaq is another interesting example. At first, it assumed that IBM would control PC architectures and mapped out a cloning strategy beneath the IBM pricing umbrella. When IBM faltered in the mid-1980s, Compaq stole a march with the 386, and for a time looked to become the architectural leader. But Compaq no more controlled the PC DOS-Intel architecture than IBM did, and almost went down in flames when cost-cutters like Dell challenged its clone position. As of mid-1992, Compaq seems to have recovered smartly, but with profit margins more befitting its clone position.

DIFFUSION AND ARCHITECTURAL PROLIFERATION

Once the chaos of point products shakes down into a clear architectural contest, the initial struggle is usually resolved when one of the technically superior contenders achieves sufficient market presence to become the de facto industry standard. This is the stage of aggressive diffusion.

We have already seen many examples of companies who

missed their opportunity by keeping their architectures too closely controlled. Apple failed to license its operating system, leaving the architectural opportunity to be snapped up by Microsoft. Many companies also made the opposite mistake. IBM failed to control the PC opportunity when it had the chance to, and Xerox gave away winning technologies prodigally. A clear sense of strategic direction and careful intellectual property protection are a must. Luck also plays a part. Neither Microsoft nor Intel expected the IBM PC to be such a dominant product, but once they landed in such attractive positions, they exploited their opportunities shrewdly.

Once the initial architectural standard is established, however, the contest is far from over; in complex systems, there are often many layers of architectural struggles. In the PC system, the tight link between DOS and the Intel architectures is merely fortuitous, and they are now breaking into quite separate contests. The newest versions of UNIX will be compatible with either Intel or RISC processors, and both Microsoft and IBM are taking pains to make sure that their competing operating systems will be portable to a variety of processors. And there is no guarantee that the creator of the winning architecture will end up controlling it. IBM passed up several opportunities to take over the Intel standard with superior, backward-compatible processors. Widespread cloning once again raises that possibility; the company that produces a superior microprocessor that integrates video/graphics capability, but is backward-compatible with the Intel architecture, would have a real shot at taking over the standard.

Deeper inside the PC, there was a contest over the bus architecture in the late 1980s (the bus is the device that transfers data between peripherals and the microprocessor). In 1986, with its PS/2 series, IBM introduced a 32-bit bus, called the MicroChannel architecture. The bigger bus was necessary for speed, but MicroChannel was not compatible with most add-on circuit cards, which represented a considerable investment for many business users. Led by Compaq, the clone community responded with EISA, a new bus of its own, that maintained compatibility. IBM claimed its bus was superior, and may have been right, but it had lost the ability to dictate to the market. Customers voted to stick with the clones and keep their circuit cards; a few years later, IBM, while still clinging to MicroChannel, began producing machines that used the old bus.

As systems, peripherals, and networks have grown in complexity, a variety of other contests have ensued. Adobe and HP contest the printer software standard, both among themselves and with their clones. And now Microsoft has entered the fray. Novell is the architectural leader for network software, apparently having won out over Microsoft and Banyan. With about $640 million in revenues, Novell has almost two thirds of the market, and Compuserve, a leading on-line information data base company, has recently begun to advertise seamless connections to Novell networks. Begrudgingly, and without announcement, the newest release of Microsoft LAN software will connect to Novell, a sure sign of Novell's emergence as the leader. In another arena, Apple, Intel, and a variety of RISC-makers are girding for an important contest over the video/graphics multimedia standard. If consumer applications boom as some analysts expect, the multimedia standard could be one of the most important architectural contests of the mid-1990s.

Finally, there is an emerging architectural battle over data base software. Data bases have some characteristics of point products, like word processors, since they live within an outside architecture like DOS-Intel or UNIX-RISC. But they are also development platforms and provide power users with sophisticated customizing tools. Borland, owner of the two leading packages, dBase and Paradox, has by far the strongest position. There are other data bases from companies such as Oracle, Sybase, and Ingres that dominate the mainframe/minicomputer market, with Oracle as the market leader. Borland has hopes of spanning the desktop-to-mainframe market with a software package called Interbase that would provide user-invisible linkages between desktop and mainframe data bases. Oracle professes not to be worried, but as workstation networks spread, customers are likely to insist on the data base formats they are accustomed to using on their desktop machines. The mainframe data base vendors may well find themselves adapting their software to a Borland architecture and getting steadily squeezed out of their most lucrative markets. If history is any guide, the low-end vendor moving up the power curve always has an advantage over the high-end vendor defending a position. The reason is simple: the price/performance of low-end components is improving hundreds of times faster than that for mainframes or minicomputers, so low-end systems inevitably swallow more and more of any competitive space. The emerging opportunity in data bases, of course, has not been lost on Microsoft, which has recently taken an ownership position in Sybase.

HARVESTING, ARCHITECTURAL OBSOLESCENCE, MIGRATION

The happy result of lock-in is that the successful player can finally begin to harvest the fruit of its long-term efforts. We have seen how Intel managed its licensing strategy as its franchised position gained a more secure lock-in: there was widespread second sourcing for the 8088/8086; only limited licensing of the 286; and only one restricted license to IBM for the 386. Sales of the xx86 family account for less than half of Intel's sales but well over 100 percent of its profits. In Intel's best year to date, 1991, *after*-tax profits, at $1 billion, were more than 20 percent of sales, which suggests that xx86 profits were in the 40 to 50 percent range after taxes. There is always a risk of moving to a harvest mode too soon. Intel's huge margins on the 386 have drawn a formidable list of cloners into the fray, placed its intellectual property positions in some jeopardy and forced it to cut prices sharply.

A fatal mistake is to shift to a harvest mode when it is time for a major architectural break. DEC is the clearest example. Its VMS/VAX minicomputer standard was superb but vulnerable to attack from RISC-UNIX machines moving up from the low end. Instead of attacking its own franchise with its outstanding RISC-UNIX technology, DEC chose to sit tight with its current technology, counting on continued profits from its strong established position, with disastrous results.

When a company has a large installed base, as DEC did, continued earnings from service and support can mask a sudden loss of market leadership. The turndown at DEC appeared to hit very quickly, but the rot had started years before. It is also clear that the IBM mainframe division has been content for much too long with its extraordinarily successful, but now superannuated, 370 architecture.

Since no architecture lasts forever, it is therefore necessary, every decade or so, to start from a clean sheet—to develop a new architecture and play the game again. Nothing is harder for the holder of a powerful franchise than cannibalizing its successful, enduring asset, but nothing is more critical. If the problem is confronted squarely, the incumbent usually has powerful advantages over new challengers, such as the opportunity to migrate its own installed base to the new architecture. But all too often, incumbents let their opportunity slip away, as IBM has repeatedly done.

The best architectures are layered well enough to permit a relatively painless migration from one systems and technology level to the next. When, sooner or later, an architectural leader is faced with the painful necessity of breaking with an established architecture, it can at least bring along the most desirable layers of the old one. For example, IBM is finally making its most important mainframe transaction processing system, CICS, available on its RS6000 workstations, but the move comes very late. Even better, IBM should package both CICS and the RS6000 operating system for other hardware vendors to attempt to establish an industrywide standard. There is no sign that it is yet thinking in such radical terms.

Microsoft again provides contrast. It is aggressively expanding its operating system franchise into the workstation, server, and multiprocessor world with its new NT operating system, reaching for minicomputer and mainframe territory. Microsoft is porting its Windows GUI to the NT system, which will greatly ease both migration and broad diffusion. Microsoft's NT system is an excellent example of how a layered architecture can support strategy, including the problem of migrating an old franchise to a new one.

When an architecture is reaching end of life, complacency and resistance to change are fatal. Although defeat can be postponed for several years, it will be sure and brutal. There is nothing more painful than losing an architectural contest after a long successful run. Ask Wang, Control Data, and DEC.

The same technological instability that undermines architectures affects the position of nations. As we have seen, Japan grounded its computer position on its great implementation skills, primarily targeted against IBM's mainframe position, inadvertently relegating itself to the position of commodity implementer within foreign-owned architectures. The strength of the current American position is grounded on American skills in software and innovative design. Developments in software technology, however, such as object-oriented programming and Computer-Assisted Software Engineering (CASE), could ultimately undercut the American advantage.

Object-oriented programming is another of the many technologies that Xerox PARC bequeathed to the world. The basic idea is to increase the standardization of software by breaking programs into "objects," or small packages of code that can be mixed freely with other objects—removing or adding one object will not affect the performance of any of the others. Each of the many objects must be very carefully engineered, of course, but once a critical mass of objects has been achieved, writing new software should be very fast and much more adaptable to CASE tools. The premium on innovation and creativity, therefore, might be considerably reduced, at least for standard program development. Although American companies currently have the lead in object-oriented programming, the great Japanese skill in managing detailed complexity should adapt very well to just such an environment. Americans have only recently shaken the misperception that Asian manufacturing skills inevitably mean Asian domination of computer technology. A misperception that the American lead in software is invulnerable, however, would be a much more serious mistake. Bill Gates once suggested that his entire industry would disappear in twenty years, when computers will write software better than people can. If there is any lesson from the computer wars, it is that the complacent die unpleasant deaths.

THE ELEMENTS OF STRATEGY

The computer industry is the most competitive that ever was. The profits to the winners can be very large, but investment requirements are enormous, customers sophisticated and unforgiving, product life cycles nasty, brutish, and short. From the cases discussed thus far, however, we can distill certain overall strategic rules that distinguish the successful architectural players, the companies that have managed to achieve a sustained competitive advantage. It is axiomatic, of course, that strategy cannot substitute for technology. But the converse is true as well: superior technology uninformed by strategy is a dead end, as demonstrated by the dry bones of companies with outstanding technology that are piled up in the graveyard of systems solutions past. We set out the basic elements of successful computer strategies below. We make no claim that they are easy; merely that they are fundamental.

1. Architectures are distributed through products. Particularly when dealing with start-ups, users are interested in present capabilities, not visions of the future. Only superb products—and "superb," as technologists sometimes forget, is defined by users, not by other technologists—can gain a sufficient market foothold to serve as the base for a broad architecture. Later, when an architecture is established, it will in turn be a distribution vehicle for additional products.

2. The architecture must be robust and open-ended enough to be extended from the initial niche into a general-purpose platform. The objective is to achieve an architected product line, not a series of point products. In the early days of an architecture, competition can be extremely subtle; the danger is always that an architectural contestant winds up locked into someone else's architecture.

3. Fundamental technology trends imply that the price performance of the lowest-cost systems will continue to improve faster than expensive systems. Low-end personal systems will continue to swallow higher-end systems. Starting from the low end offers the most promising path to system expansion; there is rarely a realistic growth path for systems that start from the high end.

4. Aggressive diffusion is essential, but managing the tension between diffusion and control is one of the most difficult architectural challenges. The best defense is a good offense. That requires a selectively open design; smooth compatibility with supporting point products and commodity components; and wide, carefully managed licensing. For a viselike lock-in, an architecture must be refreshed by a steady stream of new products that are compatible throughout the product family. Static architectures are devoured by clones.

5. Careful development of a broad, complex supporting infrastructure increases customer switching costs. The lock-in player encourages second sourcing and third-party development when it broadens an architecture's reach. The leader can usually pick and choose which parts of the market to leave to clones.

6. Sophisticated intellectual property management is essential at every stage of the architecture's life cycle—at its creation and through diffusion and licensing. Careful patent preparation and constant monitoring and enforcement are critical.

7. The more mass-produced the product and the closer to consumer markets, the more important manufacturing skills will be to maintaining the locked-in position.

8. Winners can harvest rich profits, but complacency is always punished. Lock-in is never complete. Architectures that are not continually rejuvenated and expanded do not survive.

12

MANAGEMENT STRATEGIES
IN HIGH TECHNOLOGY

MANAGEMENT PARADIGMS

The fierce competition between architectural contenders in the computer industry is giving rise to a new management paradigm, which we believe may be of profound importance. By a management paradigm, we mean a comprehensive model for the strategic ordering of a firm or an industry that determines its formal organization; its investment priorities; its relations with suppliers, customers, and employees; its operational work flow; and virtually all other important activities.

By way of illustrative background, we distinguish four other paradigms of recent importance. There may well be others.

• *The American Mass Production Model.* Characterized by long production runs of identical units, it became the dominant production mode in the United States, and derivately in Europe, after World War II. America was a huge, homogeneous country, with lots of money, and two decades' backlog of unmet consumer needs dating from the onset of the Great Depression. The mass production model, built from the ideas of Henry Ford, was well suited to the problem of putting an identical black phone, a radio, a modern kitchen, and a washing machine in every household. The leading companies were highly vertically integrated and functionally organized (that is, "Manufacturing" and "Engineering" would be autonomous organizations covering all products and markets). Relations with suppliers tended to be adversarial, with much whipsawing on price.

The mass production model proved galumphingly inadequate once most of the West's basic consumer needs were satisfied by about the early 1960s and the basis for competition shifted to product variety and quality. Mass production factory scheduling was rigid and inflexible; tooling and model changes were time-consuming and expensive; the deep gulf between functional organizations meant constant mismatches of markets, products, and factory capabilities. It took more than fifteen years for America to shed a generation of executives trained in the old paradigm. The model's last crumbling bastion is in Eastern Europe and the former Soviet Union, aping the West of the 1950s to the very end.

• *The Japanese Lean Manufacturing Model.* The lean manufacturing model, the prevailing mode of business organization in Japan, was created largely by one man, Taiichi Ohno of Toyota. The model evolved to meet the need for many car and truck models in a small country lacking the capital to develop large-scale mass production model industries. It is characterized by rapid model and tooling changes, beautifully orchestrated supplier relationships, and choreographed plant flows.

Lean manufacturing quickly spread from its base in automobiles to all Japanese consumer product and mechanical manufacturing industries, including mid-range capital goods, such as commodity machine tools. Its great flexibility is fundamental to the basic Japanese competitive strategy—achieving total coverage of a relatively commoditized space with many variations on a small number of product platforms. Multifunctional product teams engineer a constant stream of

incremental improvements to generate very rapid product cycles. For the past ten years, the West has been evolving its
own version of lean manufacturing usually involving greater
reliance on computer-assisted design and manufacturing and
less on inherent work force disciplines than the original Japanese model. Ford and Motorola are leaders in the Western
lean manufacturing movement.

• *The American Megaproject Model.* The megaproject paradigm was created by the American military in the 1950s, no-
tably by Admiral Hyman Rickover, when the Cold War shifted
to a contest of high-tech weaponry. It is characterized by very
large, highly engineered projects, involving large numbers of
specialist suppliers, extremely complex systems integration requirements, and handcrafted production. Its fundamental assumptions are very low volumes, very high unit costs, and a
community of expert users. The user friendliness that is critical in consumer industries is a minor consideration in the
megaproject model.

Rickover's Polaris-class nuclear submarines, the IBM Sys-
tem/360, and the Boeing 747 are among the model's signal
accomplishments. Applied to the right competitive space, the
paradigm can be formidably effective and is an important
source of continuing American success in, for instance, large
communication systems and major construction projects such
as hydroelectric plants and ocean-based oil rigs. Airbus In-
dustrie may be the most successful European attempt at competing globally in a megaproject industry. The Japanese and
Koreans have been successful in shipbuilding and oil rig construction, and the Japanese have been attempting for many
years to move into airframes. The success of American megaproject companies was a distraction for American mass production executives, however; in the late 1960s and 1970s,
many companies, abetted by business schools and consulting
firms, attempted to apply the megaproject model's highly centralized control systems and project organization to consumer
product industries with little success.

• *The Monolithic Model.* Developed independently at IBM in
the 1970s and at Toshiba in the early 1980s, the monolothic

model is the industrial approach that has won the Japanese a dominant position in commodity semiconductors and related components. (IBM does not compete in merchant semiconductor markets.) It is characterized by extremely careful, extremely long-range planning and investment horizons; it is enormously capital intensive, and investment is continuous. A brand-new generation of semiconductor plants is built every four or five years with state-of-the-art process and manufacturing technology. The system assumes a natural progression of technology layers from high-performance computing down to low-end consumer products. As each new generation of plants comes on line, it absorbs the highest-technology production; each lower layer bumps up to a newer generation of plant, and the oldest plants are discarded. The same model is now being applied to flat panel displays, although so far less successfully, since basic designs and process technologies are still far from stabilized.

The logic of the monolithic model inherently presses toward cartelization and/or government market-management. Investment requirements are so high, and the marginal unit cost of production is so low—it costs about 25 cents to make each additional DRAM—that overproduction is the norm. Government administered average-cost, antidumping provisions tend to be self-defeating since they raise costs in the purchasing country and help absorb the cartelizing country's overhead costs. The Japanese cartelized the DRAM industry in the late 1980s, but lost control when the Koreans entered in force.

The creation of the monolithic model coincided with a period of extraordinarily low capital costs in Japan; it remains to be seen whether it can be sustained as the cost of Japanese capital approaches world levels. The recent spate of transnational partnerships in commodity semiconductors may be a sign that the Japanese are losing their appetite for monolithic model investment demands, but at the moment such a conclusion would be decidedly premature.

We call the fifth, and entirely new, management paradigm that is evolving in the United States the Silicon Valley model. It is a response to the requirements of a high-intellectual-content industry, involving very rapid, and frequently unpredictable, technological change, where dominance is always based on architectural control as we have defined it, usually involving system design and software and selected implementations. In contrast to the megaproject and lean manufacturing models, where base technologies are centrally managed and assumed to be stable over one, and usually several, development and production cycles, the Silicon Valley model evolved to accommodate very rapid, open-ended, asymmetric, and unpredictable technological change at any level in the system. The characteristic product evolves from a small, open-ended core into a highly complex system that can tolerate widely differing rates of technological change among system layers and individual components.

The model is still in its early stages of development and is far from being standardized. There is no firm that is organized completely in accord with the model we sketch in this chapter, although a number are evolving toward it. Perhaps the form has been brought to its furthest point of development at Microsoft. The outline of the system we provide here, therefore, is both tentative and idealized, a composite portrait drawn from dozens of partial examples. One of the great questions for future American competitiveness is how well the Silicon Valley model can be wedded to the emerging American lean manufacturing base to recontour the competitive landscape in areas like consumer electronics.

THE SILICON VALLEY MODEL

We have described the nature of architectural contests in information technology in the preceding chapters. The Silicon Valley management model is the organizational and strategic management reflection of an architecturally based business.

To understand how the model works, consider first an idealized architected product like an operating system. The system will have a compact central core that will establish the basic parameters of the system's capabilities and provide clean, or in the jargon, "orthogonal"—handoffs to other system components. Radiating out from the core, for example, there will be a GUI, or graphical user interface, and a shell with a built-in system command structure that will enable, say, connection to a network. Each of these, in turn, will have its own set of handoffs. The GUI, for example, will hand off to applications software, to "help" files, to a variety of interface files, such as screen painting and so on. The shell will hand off to network software, to a variety of input/output files, and to various device driver files. And each of these, in turn, may have its own set of handoffs and interfaces. A well-designed system, that is, has a fractal-like structure. The central core hands off to a set of satellite system components; each of those serves as the core for its own series of satellites; each of those, in turn, can serve as a new core, and so on.

The logic of a well-architected developmental system pervades every aspect of the Silicon Valley model firm—its formal organization and personnel policies; its "make or buy" decisions and management of suppliers; its relations with competitors and the formation of alliances.

The fundamental organizational node in the Silicon Valley model is the core design and development group. The group that is defining and controlling the architectural standard, in other words, is the center of the organization. Both the group and the architectural core are kept as small as possible. And just as the central system core is a platform for other layers of systems functions and applications, there will be a radiating series of development groups surrounding the core group, that is, a shell group, a GUI group, and further subsidiary groups, such as a device driver group and so on. If the handoffs have been well architected, each of these groups will have fairly complete control over its own space. Thus, the device driver group should be able to accommodate a wide array of device driver types with no changes in the core and only minimum interactions with the core group. Well-designed systems are modular, hierarchical, and evolutionary, and so is the development organization. The cleaner the handoffs from the core group, the larger the number of satellite groups that can work in parallel without confusion, and the broader the development space that can be accommodated. Properly applied, the fractal-like structure of the Silicon Valley model becomes an extraordinarily powerful, flexible, and efficient mode of organization. Systems projects can become quite large and complex and still run efficiently with a minimum of central management overlay.

Silicon Valley model firms are the most unbuffered meritocracies imaginable. The core development group sits at the top of a natural hierarchy, while the remaining development groups fill out the pyramid, or fractal cascade, based on their importance and performance. The remaining employees, of which there is usually a bare minimum, exist primarily to facilitate the development work. Everything is subordinated to performance: rank, tenure, age, status, prestige are fundamentally irrelevant. Compensation is closely tied to profitability or stock performance—as many as a thousand Microsoft employees are paper millionaires. Personnel management at Microsoft is instructive: every six months the members of each development group rate each other, and the lowest 5 percent are fired. Contrast that with the elaborate, bureaucratic personnel evaluation systems that exist at IBM and other Fortune 500 firms. There are not many slots for traditional generalist managers at Silicon Valley model firms; these are companies where the rubber is very close to the road. One of the major sources of confusion at IBM in the 1980s was that it was attempting to compete in Silicon Valley model businesses with a megaproject management style derived from its System/360 experience. The implicit management assumptions that had proved so successful a decade before were confusing and disruptive when paradigms shifted.

Supplier relations follow the same pervasive logic. In the traditional firm, the classic "make or buy" decision is usually decided on cost or similar grounds. The sole question in a Silicon Valley model firm, however, is whether there is any critical component of its architecture where control over implementation is a significant source of advantage. In microprocessors, for example, a good implementation can improve performance by a factor of two. It follows, therefore, that companies whose architectures are heavily dependent on microprocessors or other logic devices will control their own implementations, as Intel, Motorola, and Hewlett-Packard do. Lack of control over implementation was a fatal deficiency at MIPS, appears to be an increasingly serious problem at Sun, and always has been a major weakness at Apple. The evolving manufacturing partnership of Apple, IBM, and Motorola in microprocessors is the first clear recognition of the importance of microprocessor implementations at both Apple and IBM. By the same argument, there is no advantage in vertical integration where components are not architecturally significant, as, for example, DRAMs rarely are. Thus the purchasing and/or manufacturing function of the Silicon Valley model firm will be architected to match up against the basic competitive architectural strategy. It is the nature of the architectural contest that determines the firm's detailed implementation and production strategy, not the other way around.

Silicon Valley model firms pay careful attention to commoditization forces. It is usually in the firm's interest to *increase* commoditization of components that are not directly architecturally relevant. Adobe, for example, has long distributed without charge microprocessor designs for chips optimized to process its PostScript language. The more high-speed clone printers are on the market, the more the printer architectural standard shifts to the printer software and, by implication, to Adobe. Microsoft's DOS strategy had the similar objective of commoditizing PC hardware. Traditionally organized companies such as IBM or the vertically integrated Japanese giants frequently seem to pursue vertical integration merely to capture additional margins, without distinguishing carefully between components where implementation is crucial to an architecture's success. The history of the PC at IBM evinced little discrimination in this regard. Few architecturally oriented firms have demonstrated commodity manufacturing skills and vice versa.

Alliance strategies and implementations will follow the same pervasive logic. In a merger between traditional firms, great emphasis and attention is placed on merging governance structures, realigning management responsibilities, establishing common functional groups, such as purchasing and finance, and so forth. To Silicon Valley model firms such issues are, or should be, irrelevant. Alliances tend to be completely empirical, focused, ad hoc, and easily shed when their purposes have been served. They are organized around precise substantive issues—designs, implementations, service or distribution arrangements, and the like. The inherent open-endedness of a well-architected system can accommodate multiple alliances at different times at different points in a system.

Such an alliance pattern is now becoming quite common. Witness the multiple new alliances IBM has formed with Apple, Motorola, Thinking Machines, Go, etc. Each is organized around a specific product or a specific architecture and will last as long as the effort is fruitful. Intel's recent alliance with VLSI Technologies to develop a low-power family of Intel designs for the palmtop market is in the same mode. The network of invisible alliances is actually much broader than that of the visible ones. Architected software commonly now incorporates "engines" from other companies, such as software for text search and retrieval, spreadsheet analysis, or facsimile services, in networked word-processing packages. Oracle's data base software is the invisible engine for many special-purpose inventory, manufacturing control, or purchasing software.

It should be no surprise that the life cycle of many Silicon Valley model firms is so short. Firms structured in the way we have described will typically self-destruct when their architecture or product life cycle has run its course. Point product firms will self-destruct the fastest. Firms that establish robust architectural franchises, however, should be able to sustain growth over several development cycles. Even at today's rapid pace of technological development, well-managed architectural franchises can enjoy relatively long life spans and finance the move to new architectural generations. Microsoft's NT is an attempt to occupy a greatly expanded architectural space, as is Intel's Pentium (586) processor, with its RISC core.

Even the short life span of so many firms is no tragedy; the best talent simply moves on to other groups and other firms.

An infrastructure has sprung up in California and elsewhere to support the stripped-down style and short life spans of the smaller firms—short-run silicon foundries and contract manufacturers can get a new product out the door quickly while minimizing overhead requirements. Newer companies are also getting increasingly skilled at using external suppliers and partners for the product elements that are not central to their architectural concept. Eo, for example, a palmtop computer start-up company, plans to compete on the basis of a superior system design. Its first products will incorporate AT&T's fast, but very low power, "Hobbit" RISC microprocessor (AT&T is an equity investor), other AT&T communication chips, and an operating system from Go. The San Mateo Software Group has a similar relation with Toshiba, HAL with Fujitsu, and SSI with IBM.

The AT&T/Eo style of equity investment and manufacturing/supply relationship between a big company and a start-up solves problems for both sides. The start-up gets a stable financing base, while the big company keeps a window open to new developments and the opportunity to participate in new high-growth markets. Tensions invariably arise if the small company is very successful, since the large company will often wish to extend its participation and control. Strategic financial planning (contractual puts for the small company's management, the right to go public) and arm's length contracting procedures can protect both sides. Start-up veterans and big-company managements are getting quite sophisticated in negotiating such contracts. A similar pattern is also becoming routine in biotechnology-based pharmaceuticals, which has somewhat similar technological dynamics. In pharmaceuticals and computers, the equity flow from large companies may gradually supplant the venture industry.

The Silicon Valley model firm is obviously not one for the fainthearted, nor is it suited for every industry. To date, however, America is the only country that has mastered it. We expect Taiwan to be the second; its population has a strong entrepreneurial tradition and close relations with the California business and educational system. The model has been the source of much of the American recovery in computers after

the poor performance of IBM and the other American electronic giants, and may prove very powerful in the right consumer electronics environment. The model also has obvious
limitations. There would seem, for instance, to be some inherent upper bound on the size of a company organized in the
Silicon Valley mode. Microsoft, however, now has thirteen
thousand employees, and Gates apparently still has the company running scared. How long he can keep up the pressure
will be interesting to watch, particularly with so much wealth
walking the halls. Nor has the model yet been fully globalized.
Silicon Valley firms' supply networks are almost always global, and their sales frequently so; but they usually have little
direct operational presence in other major markets outside
America, possibly because of their relative newness.

A potential near-term danger is increased aggressiveness
of larger companies in enforcing intellectual property rights.
Small companies, for the most part, have enjoyed a free ride
on large-company technology. Xerox's PARC, for example,
has spawned an almost uncountable number of companies, as
have IBM, AT&T, Texas Instruments, and many university
research departments. In the days when a few big players
dominated the industry, they habitually cross-licensed all
their patents, avoiding delicate pricing issues and nasty legal
battles. The avidity with which the Japanese and Silicon Valley start-ups mined American big-company patent portfolios
has finally changed big-company behavior and may reduce
the flow of innovative technologies to smaller firms.

The habit of living off other people's research may be a
hard one to break. Even the most successful of the newer
companies, such as Microsoft and Intel, whose profits are
enormous, spend relatively little on basic research. (Their
R&D spending rate is high, but it is almost entirely focused on
the next generation's product development.) Both can clearly
afford to do better. Basic research is surprisingly inexpensive.
Xerox's PARC never had more than about two hundred professionals or a budget of more than $50 million a year. Mi-
crosoft has recently exhibited signs of becoming a serious
basic research investor, a very positive development. Silicon
Valley firms will find they need their own substantial intel-

lectual property portfolios to trade with larger American and Japanese firms. We also expect that the Silicon Valley model firms will be more successful in commercializing basic research than traditional companies because of their fundamentally entrepreneurial, antibureaucratic business approach.

The unwillingness to invest highlights the generational issue that is now facing many successful Silicon Valley firms. Few such firms have managed to survive over multiple generations of technology. Now, however, the industry leaders with near-dominant positions command great power and resources. Both Microsoft and Intel have managed to keep aggressively expanding their space and their areas of architectural control. Perhaps significantly, both are still under the control of their founders, Gordon Moore and Andrew Grove at Intel and, of course, Gates at Microsoft. It is far too soon, therefore, to say whether either company has become a self-sustaining institution that will outlive its original architectural franchise and founding management. The way the two companies make the transition to a new generation of technology and leadership will make a fascinating new chapter in technology management.

All the companies we have used as illustrations of the Silicon Valley model have been relatively recent start-ups. Intel, which dates from the late 1960s, is the granddaddy of them all. Can incumbent firms with large established businesses adopt a Silicon Valley model? Put more negatively, are all large incumbent firms condemned to be manufacturing partners or commodity suppliers to Silicon Valley model firms?

The question is a pressing one, for the same digital, microprocessor-based technologies are now encroaching on the traditional space of many other companies outside the computer industry, such as Kodak, Xerox, and most other information and communication companies. Forewarned should be forearmed. Large incumbent firms burdened with traditional organizational models and traditional thinking have clearly had a hard time adapting to the new fast-moving technological environment that the Silicon Valley model firms thrive in. But if they recognize their danger in time, apply common sense and sound strategic principles, the best firms should be able to manage the transition successfully.

THE PERILS OF INCUMBENCY

Based on the experience of the last fifteen years, incumbents in information technology cling to very precarious perches. No American incumbent has emerged unscathed, and the vast majority, if they have survived at all, have been severely battered. IBM, DEC, Wang, Unisys, Honeywell, Data General, Prime—the list goes on and on. Even brand-new incumbents like Compaq have learned to their grief how unforgiving the competition in information technology can be. In Europe, all the native computer companies have been wheezing on life-support systems for years. Even the Japanese electronic giants confront an uncertain future, facing the necessity to commoditize almost all of an extraordinarily fast-moving industry or risk being locked into high-cost, low-profit commodity positions as the industry's leading edge moves rapidly away from their established skill base.

We have chosen to explore IBM's recent history in such detail because it has always been the best of the incumbents, with a much broader range of technologies and opportunities at its disposal than any other company. The fact that IBM is in such serious trouble may be cause for despair among incumbents everywhere. We believe, however, that our analysis suggests important lessons for the incumbent companies' management and boards—the most important of which, perhaps, is that the fierce competitive cycle in computers and information technology is like no other, so managers must behave differently from their peers in other industries.

WARNING SIGNALS

There are at least two primary warning signs of a dangerous incumbency position. The first is when a company becomes accustomed to living within a stable architectural regime, and the second is when the refreshment rate of a company's management ranks is slower than the underlying technology replacement cycle. Understanding the sources of incumbent vulnerability can lead to action steps to cure the disease before it becomes life-threatening.

When an architectural regime begins stabilizing, it is ripe for replacement. The discriminations required are subtle; new products are not the same as new architectures. Indeed, a rapid pace of product development can conceal a drift into an underlying stability. Neither IBM nor DEC would have admitted living within stable technology regimes in the 1980s. DEC was introducing a steady stream of new DEC VAX models, increasing their power and ease of use over a wide performance spectrum. IBM produced a series of major extensions to its mainframe architecture, including extended memory, its first multiprocessors, and improved data storage and handling technology. But while both companies were greatly improving their product offerings, their fundamental computer architectures were standing still. The top-of-the-line DEC VAXs are souped-up models of the basic VAX-VMS architecture that DEC defined in the late 1970s. IBM's powerful new ES-9000 mainframe is a 1990s version of the 370, an architecture that dates back to the mid-1960s. Nobody makes VAX-VMS machines better than DEC, or 370s better than IBM. The problem is that the market is moving on to fundamentally new architectures, and neither company has moved quickly enough with it.

Stable technology regimes can be extremely profitable and readily produce complacency. IBM's mainframes and mainframe support businesses still account for almost all the company's profitability. Wang's minicomputer-based office networks were likewise extremely profitable for ten years. Compaq carved out a highly profitable franchise in desktops, and Fujitsu and Hitachi in mainframes (but both depended on IBM controlling and stabilizing their base technology). Five years or so of consistently high profits in most companies suggests a job well done and a powerful competitive position. In computers, it is usually a sign that a company is harvesting a maturing architecture that is headed for a major upheaval.

The second major, and all too common, management failure in technology companies is to allow the cycle of managerial renewal to lag behind the cycle of technological change. In most industries, the basic technology cycle moves slowly enough so that the normal generational turnover rate of senior managers matches reasonably well against the turnover rate of the underlying technologies. Upheavals occur from time to time, but big-company managers typically do not become technologically obsolete within their own career span. That is not true in the computer industry. When the fundamental technology moves as fast as it does in computers, an established company will almost inevitably, sooner or later, find itself burdened with an obsolescing management team—which, of course, reinforces the tendency to settle within a stable technology regime.

When management develops a deep stake in sticking with an existing architecture, a computer company is in trouble. If there is any consistent causal theme in the batterings suffered by incumbent computer companies during the past decade, it has been that their managements instinctively resisted shifting away from once-successful technologies. The natural human instinct to stay with the known and the proven is a lethal trap.

ACTION STEPS

The challenge for incumbent managements and boards of incumbent computer companies is to institute an internal cycle of self-refreshment that matches the underlying pace of change in their technology. IBM did this until the 1980s but failed to keep pace when the rate of change accelerated. Few, if any, other companies have had even IBM's success. Companies could be excused for not recognizing the problem when the pace of change was slower; after the blistering experience of the 1980s, however, it should be at the top of every management agenda. What can companies do to stay technologically fresh? Some general principles suggest themselves.

Separate Old and New Businesses.

IBM got in trouble when its basic business required multiple management paradigms. The mainframe and minicomputer businesses—still two thirds of its revenues—fit comfortably within the old megaproject style. PCs have become a lean manufacturing challenge—which IBM could be quite good at, if freed from overhead burdens. The new technology-based businesses, innovations such as RISC, microprocessors, parallel processing, and architecturally innovative consumer electronic products that threaten established architectures, need a Silicon Valley style of organization and competencies. Indeed, IBM has recognized this to a considerable degree with its equity investments and partnerships with a large number of start-up companies, such as Steve Chen's parallel processing company, SSI, and Go, a pen-based computer operating system developer.

New-model businesses in an old-line company will need careful protection. The natural homeostatic mechanisms of an established business will resist nurturing potentially disruptive new technologies. To protect such architecture-breaking technologies from the incumbent management's self-protective instincts, the "new" business responsibility must be located as high up the management chain as possible, perhaps with close oversight from a special committee of the board.

Match Managers and Models.

In the normal case, it is impossible for megaproject-style managers to operate a Silicon Valley–style subsidiary or a Japanese-style commodity implementation business, and vice versa. The instinct to recruit from the inside can often be destructive; IBM's reluctance to reach out for microprocessor designers, for instance, was severely limiting. IBM's managers were also very late to understand the revolutionary implications of desktop computing; it ran counter to all of their learning from years in mainframes—the instinct for elaborately detailed development cycles, for centrally controlled programming guidelines, for maintaining "rational" pricing structures, for milking an existing standard, such as the 286, before moving on to a new one.

It is even more difficult to adjust personnel policies to fit the relevant styles. The lack of stock appreciation opportunities, for example, was always a severe handicap in Boca Raton. It takes a strong and confident CEO and board to break with long-standing internal social and political norms to move a new business along. But there is often no choice between that and stagnation.

CREATE INTERNAL CANNIBALIZATION MECHANISMS.
All computer technologies will be attacked and supplanted. The issue is not whether a company's technology will be supplanted, but by whom. Companies that resist internal cannibalization will die at the hands of outsiders. Almost uniformly, the leading computer companies of the 1970s and 1980s rejected disruptive internal technologies such as RISC and paid dearly for it. The problem in almost all cases was that the internal cannibalizers needed the approval of the managers of the incumbent regime—IBM's RISC advocates searched for a sponsor for more than a decade. The owners of a reigning technology invariably greet cannibalizers unenthusiastically; typically, the upstart technology is repressed or hedged by so many development constraints that its effectiveness is compromised. The necessity, therefore, is to institutionalize a cannibalization process beyond the control of the threatened sectors of the company.

EXTERNAL SOURCING.
An internal technology base developed to support an established architectural standard will usually match up poorly against the requirements of a new architectural contender. Substantial outside sourcing will usually be necessary to support an innovative start-up. The classic mold-breaking story is still the impressive early performance of IBM's Boca Raton unit in the first days of the PC. The shooting-star success of the PC eventually overwhelmed its managers, and they failed to make the transition from start-up to big company with the right mix of internal and external sourcing. But the initial steps were mostly all the right ones. The challenge is always to match sourcing against the requirements of the business's architectural strategy. That may mean forgoing internal sup-

pliers or creating new ones, as IBM should have done for PC microprocessors.

CREATE A TECHNOLOGICALLY INFORMED MANAGEMENT.

Traditional big companies were not run by technologists, although there have been exceptions, like DEC. (Ken Olsen was an MIT professor and a computer inventor.) One of IBM's major problems in the 1980s was that its top managers had trouble steering their way through complicated technological terrain. Not every company can be run by a Ph.D., but the hands-on technological involvement of the managers of, say, an Intel or a Microsoft is a clear advantage. Every big company has to develop the nontechnological side of its business, such as marketing, finance, and manufacturing; the tendency in America in recent decades has been to draw top executives from the marketing and finance sides of the house. But in an industry where technological upheaval will occur at least once a decade and probably sooner, a management not completely conversant with its own and competitive technologies is living dangerously.

Once again, a variety of mechanisms are possible—special technological committees of the board, active policies to ensure greater representation of technologists in top management, possibly even a shadow management structure of technological commissars to keep line managers honest. The key requirement is the simple recognition that slipping behind the technology curve is fatal in the computer industry. If management and the board are not alert to that danger every single day, a company will inevitably stumble.

Every business might envy the presence of Ben Rosen, the legendary venture capitalist, on Compaq's board. When he suspected Compaq's costs were getting out of line, he organized a secret internal team that designed and procured the parts for a quality PC that was much cheaper than the standard models. Confronted, Compaq's CEO, Rod Canion, claimed it couldn't be done, and was fired. Big company directors are far too often placeholders, political ticket-punchers, or "old boys" to supply the degree of vigilance that a Rosen provided.

It is much easier to recommend self-cannibalization and

self-renewal mechanisms than to implement them. In many big companies, the task may be impossible, simply because natural homeostatic mechanisms can be so strong. In the final analysis, the only solution may be simply to spin off promising new businesses to shareholders. IBM's printer division, for example, appears to be performing much better as a separate company (Lexmark) than it did within the IBM system. The PC division is in the process of being spun off as this book goes to press. As a separate company, presumably, it will have a much better chance to hone its cost structure, product cycles, and decision-making chain to be competitive with the standard of its industry. Instructively, since AT&T was broken up in 1982, the market value of the successor companies has almost tripled; over the same period, IBM's is up only 66 percent, a dismal performance.

Managing high technology businesses at the present headlong pace of technological change is one of the greatest management challenges in all of business history. The rewards and the pitfalls are equally large. Good strategy—competitive, managerial, organizational—does not supply all the answers; but bad strategies can make the job impossible.

PART III

PROSPECTS AND OPPORTUNITIES

13

THE NEXT DECADE'S MARKET OPPORTUNITY

Electronics will shortly be the world's first trillion-dollar industry. High-performance components, including hardware and software, now account for about a third of total sales. We expect that share to grow as computer technology extends its reach into ever-broader competitive space, as it is already doing in the automobile and television industry. The same technology trends that have dominated the evolution of the information industry in the 1980s will continue unabated, and at the same breakneck speed, for at least another decade and possibly much longer. Radical change, as always, will be extremely disruptive for incumbent firms, the established companies with big market shares built on a previous generation of technology. And as always, radical change will offer limitless opportunities to the quick thinking and the fast moving.

Four critical technologies drive the information industry:

1. The power and price/performance of *microprocessors* will continue to improve at roughly the current pace for the foreseeable future. Processors as powerful as today's best supercomputers will cost $10 well before the end of the decade.

2. Digital *storage* technology is improving just as fast. The music industry, for example, is well advanced in its conversion to digital formats; the video industry is not far behind. Business records have long since been digitized, and digital technologies are advancing rapidly in publishing. Because of its light weight and high-resolution display capabilities, paper is still the preferred information delivery medium. Its advantage will diminish rapidly, however, particularly when the environmental costs of paper-based communications are taken into account.

3. Digital *display* technologies currently lag well behind storage technology, but will improve very rapidly in the near-term future. The large consumer market opportunity in advanced television displays has led to the rapid development of a broad range of display technologies; we expect intense competitive struggles and a hyperrapid pace of change for at least the next five years.

4. Despite rapid improvements in *communications* technology the effective pace of change will be much slower because the industry is so heavily regulated. We expect communications to be the gaiting factor in information technology markets for the foreseeable future, especially in consumer markets. Established information businesses, such as newspapers and cable television companies, have become quite adept at using the regulatory process to frustrate innovative competitors.

THE CHANGING FACE OF BUSINESS COMPUTING

The well-established trends that have reshaped traditional business computing markets over the past decade will continue apace, while newer business technologies will provide a preview of widespread consumer computer applications toward the end of the decade.

In traditional computing markets, established mainframe technology will remain under severe cost/performance pressure. The very top of the IBM mainframe line, the ES-9000, released in mid-1992, runs at 400 mips with eight processors. It also bundles formidable data input/output subsystems that raise its effective processing power to the 1,000-mips range.

The mainframe has already lost its speed advantage to open, componentized systems, and its edge in data storage and handling is eroding quickly. Multiprocessor RISC- and Intel 486/Pentium–based computers can already match the sheer processing clout of an ES-9000 and are sold by a wide range of companies, including Sequent, Intel, Compaq, Dell, and AST. Massively parallel machines from Thinking Machines, HAL, NCube, Kendall Square Research, and Maspar are much faster. The data storage and input/output capabilities of the parallel, microprocessor-based machines are now catching up very rapidly to those of the mainframes. A variety of companies build big, fast memory and data handling systems from large arrays of inexpensive components, using technologies such as those meeting the RAID (Redundant Arrays of Inexpensive Disks) family of standards, just as parallel processors do. Contenders include Storage Technologies, NCR, and EMC. The inherent redundancy of multiprocessor and multidisk storage arrays can also be harnessed to greatly improve fault tolerance, a big selling point to customers like banks. Within the next two or three years, multiprocessor and multidisk configurations should match mainframe performance on every critical parameter for only 5 to 10 percent of the cost, and will far outstrip minicomputers. None of this is good news for IBM and DEC, nor for companies like Xerox, with high-margin product lines (such as Xerox's printers) that are closely tied to the IBM mainframe computing center standard.

The fall of the mainframe regime will open up very large markets for software vendors who have cut their teeth on desktop computing. That fall could come very fast, particularly as microprocessor-based competitors start emulating 370 instruction sets. We expect a pitched battle for the business operating system standard between Microsoft's NT and the two main versions of UNIX, the Sun/AT&T standard and that of the Open Software Foundation, led by IBM, DEC, and Hewlett-Packard. NT is not yet released, but is known to include substantial multiprocessing capabilities. There will also be an intense struggle for control of the business data base standard, with traditional mainframe vendors such as Oracle fending off the assaults of companies such as Borland/Ashton-Tate, the current PC data base leader. The mainframe data base vendors need much more professional maintenance and support than the microprocessor-oriented systems and are much less user-friendly, which are probably fatal disadvantages. Finally, Adobe has the inside track for the business print/publishing standard, but there are a number of contenders, including Microsoft and several from Europe.

All these trends, important as they are, are still operating within the currently established markets for business computing. Of potentially far greater import is the spread of computing technologies into a much broader span of business activities. The economic and social impact of the expanded reach of computing in the 1990s will be every bit as great as that of the spread of desktop computing in the 1980s.

The Advent of Ubiquitous Computing

One of the hottest new product categories is the tiny portable computer, dubbed variously the Personal Digital Assistant, the palmtop, or the personal communicator. The hardware contenders include Apple/Sharp, IBM, Hewlett-Packard, Motorola, Sony and the other Japanese consumer electronics companies, and some start-ups like the American Eo. Control of the palmtop operating system standard is currently being contested by Microsoft; Apple with its Newton operating system; and Go, 15 percent owned by IBM. Most palmtops run on low-power RISC chips. AT&T has introduced a very small, very fast (20 mips), but quite simple low-power microprocessor called the Hobbit, which could have a major impact on the palmtop standard.

Palmtop computers are still in their infancy, at the same stage roughly as personal computers were about 1980. Apple hopes that its new Personal Digital Assistant, or PDA, will be used by business people or consumers to store addresses and business notes, run spreadsheets, send and receive electronic mail, store travel maps for business trips, and help in route-finding in strange cities. John Sculley, Apple's CEO, expects the PDA to be "the mother of all markets." Others are more skeptical, at least in the short term, since the considerable technology infrastructure needed for PDAs and their progeny to reach maximum usefulness is still lacking. Andrew Grove, the CEO of Intel, who sometimes affects a constitutional gloominess, calls the PDA "a pipedream driven by greed." Revealingly, Intel has just partnered with VLSI Technologies to produce a very low powered processor suitable for palmtops.

Pen-based computers that use a pen or stylus to mark a screen are slightly larger than the palmtops and are becoming widely used in highly structured business applications, such as checking off an inventory list or delivery receipt from a remote location, with a minimum of free-form printing. With continued progress in character-recognition software, applications may spread rapidly. The newest models of machines are very easy to use, very small and lightweight, and incorporate voice/fax/data communications to a home location, any phone, or another computer. The emerging contenders are roughly the same as in palmtops.

Communications technologies will be much less of a hindrance to the spread of ubiquitous computing in business settings than in consumer applications. Proliferating dedicated private systems—fiber-optic, microwave, and satellite—are incorporating advanced technologies barred from the heavily regulated public access systems. Full-motion, high-resolution, two-way, interactive digital video and voice transmission will be available within the next five years in business settings for video-conferencing, technical presentations, medical diagnostics, and other video-intensive applications. Palm-tops, conceivably, will evolve into portable video phones. The business overhead investment requirement, however, is still quite high. The current generation of local area networks does not have the capacity to support fully interactive video; the necessary fiber and over-the-air technologies are available, but they are expensive.

As high-capacity business digital networks are put in place, business video and graphics applications should spread rapidly, much of it later filtering down into consumer markets. Big, high-resolution, flat-panel display screens for business conferencing, engineering work groups, education and training, along with the related data compression/decompression technologies, may be the testing ground for the next decade's high-definition consumer interactive television. The display industry is almost totally controlled by the Japanese, while compression/decompression technology and multimedia software are largely American. The Japanese have made enormous investments in liquid crystal display screens, but have still not succeeded in making commercially practical displays of the size, brightness, and responsiveness needed for advanced video applications. No American company competes directly in the high-volume display industry, although IBM and Toshiba have a laptop screen partnership, as do AT&T and Motorola. There are a number of American and Japanese technologies in developmental stages that could well leapfrog conventional liquid crystal.

The business video and graphics market will be much more lucrative over the near and medium term than consumer video applications. Over the longer term, however, consumer applications will be very important. The most publicized consumer technology issue, one that has become virtually a symbol of the future of competition in consumer electronics, is High-Definition Television, or HDTV.

We believe that the struggle over HDTV has been widely misunderstood. The question is not what kind of television pictures consumers will see, but whether there will be a market for *digital, interactive, multimedia* computer technologies in the home.

THE FUTURE OF TELEVISION

HDTV is a concept developed in the mid-1970s under the sponsorship of NHK, the Japanese government broadcasting monopoly, to improve the sharpness and clarity of television transmission to a level approximating that of movie films. Conventional television in Japan and the United States—the NTSC standard—traces 525 horizontal lines on a screen at a rate of 30 frames a second (625 lines at 25 frames per second in Europe). Consumers have been more or less satisfied with the NTSC standard for a half century, but it has obvious deficiencies. The 30-frame-per-second rate is slow, and is perceived by the human eye as an irritating flicker. While 525 lines of resolution looks reasonably sharp on very small screens, when screens are much larger than twenty-one inches diagonally, the loss of detail is apparent, and the pictures look dull and blurry. After extensive consumer testing, NHK set out to remedy these problems by creating a new television standard, called MUSE, with roughly twice the resolution—1,125 lines—at twice the frame rate and a screen horizontal-to-vertical ratio of 16:9—or more like a movie screen—rather than the current standard of 4:3.

After more than a decade's work, the Japanese announced in the late 1980s that they would proceed to implement MUSE, touching off near-hysteria in the United States and Europe. The American Electronics Association, a trade lobby group, calculated that HDTV would be a $100 billion annual market by the late 1990s and warned that the digital picture enhancement technologies necessary for HDTV would give the Japanese a commanding lead in computers and semiconductors as well. They demanded "a complete cocoon of federal aid and support," in *Newsweek*'s words—$1.3 billion in federal funds for research and manufacturing, protectionist measures against Japanese TVs, antitrust exemption, and even conversion assistance for broadcasters. The Japanese tended to be patronizing. As a ranking Sony official put it, "We've got a ten-year lead in HDTV technologies. There's no way you can catch us." The proposals of the electronics lobby never survived the Congress, despite much Sturm und Drang, but the European Community did adopt a similar set of measures, under the umbrella of a Community-wide organization called Eureka, involving some thirty companies, that has developed its own MUSE-like standard, or MAC, for "Multiplexed Analogue Components." Both the Europeans and the Japanese broadcast part of the 1992 summer Olympics in their HDTV formats.

There are serious problems with both MUSE and MAC. Both are fundamentally extensions of current NTSC-style technology. Both, for example, are primarily souped-up traditional analog systems. That is to say, the pattern of the broadcast radio wave mimics the pattern of the video and audio signals to be transmitted, much as the wiggle of the needle in a vinyl record mimics the sound pattern of the music. Digital transmission can provide much more detail, much more accurately than analog; just as important, it can be manipulated more easily at the receiver, in order to zoom in on a picture detail, for instance. Nor does a digital picture degrade. Since it is reconstructed by the receiver, it is either there in full clarity and crispness or—if the data didn't get through—there is nothing at all.

High-resolution analog signals are prone to interference and "artifacts," or picture anomalies, which require fiendishly complicated digital cleanup and therefore a complex analog-to-digital-to-analog conversion process. Doubling screen resolutions also requires much more broadcast information and therefore hogs a much greater share of the over-the-air radio spectrum, an awkward requirement in the face of increasing demands for cellular telephone and other over-the-air transmissions, and one which necessarily limits the number of channels that can be broadcast. Finally, the standard cathode-ray-tube technology in current televisions is severely strained with the large, thirty-inch and above screens that show off HDTV to its best advantage. Solving all those problems requires a very heavy, very expensive television set, and very expensive conversions of broadcasting studios. By the summer of 1992, the Japanese were producing eight hours of HDTV programming a day, but Sony, the industry leader, had sold only four hundred sets at $30,000 apiece.

Analog HDTV is a brilliant engineering achievement, a virtuoso challenge, rather like making an automobile that can fly. As technology, however, it is obsolete. When the Japanese began developing HDTV almost twenty years ago, there was no alternative; digital technology just wasn't yet up to speed. (It takes very fast microprocessors to process digital image data in movie-frame time; they were not available even five years ago.) The enormous, and continuing, commitment of resources to an analog solution, however, exposes a major weakness in the Japanese system. Mistakes are not easily admitted; the celebrated ability to commit to the long term can easily turn to mulishness. The Europeans, of course, have even less excuse. But both Japanese and Europeans are beginning to concede that the future belongs to digital transmission.

In the United States, the FCC is in the process of adopting a new television standard with a final decision expected in 1993. Although the MUSE standard is an official contender, there is almost no possibility of its being chosen. There are three other competing American and European digital systems sponsored by consortia involving AT&T and Zenith; MIT and General Instruments; and an alliance involving NBC, CBS, the Sarnoff Laboratories, Compression Labs, North American Philips (Holland), and Thomson (France). The key requirements are that the resulting transmissions be of HDTV-like quality, but that they use the current radio spectrum allocation, be compatible with current television receivers, and be sufficiently robust to withstand cable retransmission without degradation. Any digital solution will also be compatible with fiber optic transmission, holding out the ultimate possibility of video transmission over telephone lines.

Adoption of an American digital standard for HDTV does not, of course, guarantee that American, or Western, companies will win back consumer markets. A requirement of the FCC process will be that the winning standard be broadly licensed at a reasonable cost. At best, an FCC engineer has estimated, the owner of the winning standard will have less than a year's head start on the competition. One would expect the present market leaders in consumer electronics, like Sony and Matsushita, to get quickly up to speed in whatever standard is eventually adopted.

If the only consequence of HDTV is better television sets, it will hardly have been worth all the trouble. Television sets, compared to, say, computer workstations, are inexpensive products, with razor-thin margins. No one expects that the global HDTV market will amount to more than a few million sets by the end of the decade, a relatively small market. Nicholas Negroponte, the director of MIT's Media Labs, a leader in digital video technology, has commented that consumers' main complaint about television is that it's "dumb," not that it's not sharp.

Sharper conventional television may soon be available very cheaply anyway. For example, a small California company, Faroudja Laboratories, has demonstrated a remarkably HDTV-like television picture, from standard over-the-air signals, using modified conventional television receivers with VGA screens, the same as in most personal computers. The chip set that sharpens up the picture would sell for about $20 in volume production. A preliminary judgment by the FCC is that the concept requires no special regulatory approvals. A number of other companies are working on similar technologies. Low-cost advanced television could conceivably undermine the market expectations for HDTV. Selling $20 chip sets, even for most of the world's new televisions, is a nice medium-sized business, but hardly front-page news.

Multimedia Home Computing

The alternative vision that does merit genuine excitement foresees a transformation in home electronics comparable to that currently taking place in business. Under this scenario, television sets would be replaced by *interactive, multimedia* computers. A home multimedia station could receive digital input from any of a variety of sources—over-the-air signals, fiber optic or cable, CD-ROMs, or digital tapes. The entertainment uses of interactive, multimedia computing are obvious. The ability to interact with the source would permit the consumer to select from an enormous menu of television shows, movies, music, or video games. The regional telephone companies have shown intense interest in this market.

New technology would not be entirely restricted to entertainment. Interactive video/sound libraries, with instantaneous searching could be an educational boon. Home catalog shopping and price comparisons would become the norm. "Smart house" control functions—monitoring heat, light switches, security devices, and other home network applications—could be controlled from the computing center. Video telephones would be standard. Daily newspapers would be delivered electronically, with news always up-to-the-minute. Most people cannot envision replacing their morning paper, or a good book, with a session at a video terminal. But once a home display station was the size and weight of a magazine, with magazine-picture sharpness and complete, cordless portability, the objections should disappear.

Electronic delivery of data could have significant environmental implications. Despite the pro-"green" rhetoric of *The New York Times* and other major news organizations, newspapers are a major consumer of wood products and, along with telephone books, the single largest contributor by far to solid waste. Although newsprint is theoretically biodegradable, the process takes centuries. Newspapers, of course, have lobbied ferociously against regulatory proposals to permit the Bell companies and other carriers to enter electronic information distribution businesses.

Multimedia, interactive video/audio capability would also speed the transformation toward a decentralized organization of work. The advent of the personal computer has already had a major impact on traditional working arrangements. A less happy consequence of electronic data transmission would be continued pressure on low-skilled job availability. It takes a lot of people, for example, to deliver and dispose of newsprint and newspapers, and to service centralized office buildings.

For the foreseeable future, the lack of sufficiently high-capacity information channels to the home will be the major obstacle to the complete democratization of information technology. We will return to this issue in the last chapter.

GAMES

Over the near term, video games will continue to be the most financially attractive consumer opportunity. Nintendo is one of the most profitable companies in the world, more profitable even than Microsoft. With 30 million sets in American homes, Nintendo sets have already achieved the ubiquity John Sculley dreams of for Apple's PDAs.

Game technology is evolving very rapidly. Indeed, Nintendo was blindsided by its competitor Sega, when it sat too long on its 8-bit processor architecture. Thirty-two-bit games are already entering the market. Games incorporating virtual reality, with goggles and gloves that give the user the illusion of being inside the scene portrayed, realistic screen images, and complex "plot" developments, exist in prototypes. (Whether any of this represents a social advance is left to the reader; Aldous Huxley, doubtless, would wear a tight smile.)

Nintendo, indeed, may stand at a crossroad. Nintendo hardware is a tightly closed architecture with bundled software; only one hundred third-party companies are approved to develop Nintendo games, all of which are marketed only by Nintendo. The history of computing suggests that general-purpose computers absorb special-purpose solutions. Nintendo may be in danger of losing control of its software standard. A federal court has already ruled that the patents and copyrights of its look-alike competitor, Sega, do not prevent independent software houses reverse-engineering its operating system. If this decision stands, it will almost certainly apply to Nintendo as well. That will permit companies like the San Mateo Software Group to market Sega- or Nintendo-compatible games outside the controlled channels. The logical next step would be to clone the Nintendo operating system, opening the market to Nintendo clone manufacturers. To fight back, Nintendo will have to try to build on its strong position in games to define the architectural standard for portable home and recreational computing. No Japanese company has ever attempted such a strategy, and the costs of failure would be high. But Nintendo has demonstrated an understanding of architectural strategies in the past and may be facing a stark choice: either try to extend its reach broadly or stand pat and end up like Wang. Europeans do not compete in this market.

THE OPPORTUNITY

Computing has always been marked by constant technological discontinuity. Profits have tended to flow to American companies, once primarily IBM and DEC, and more recently, Microsoft, Intel, and other newer firms that have created proprietary technologies and constantly upgraded them. The challenge is always to keep rival standards, commodity implementers, and clones at bay by outmaneuvering them strategically and moving the market to ever-higher standards of expectation and performance. That same pattern of challenge and opportunity will continue to dominate the industry through the 1990s and beyond. The business multimedia market—graphics, animation, electronic publishing, videoconferencing—should grow robustly over the next decade, more than tripling from about $4 billion to $14 billion between 1991 and 1995, with continued acceleration through the remainder of the decade.

Consumer electronics markets, on the other hand, tend to be characterized by quite stable technology regimes. The black-and-white television standard is fifty years old, the color standard almost forty years old. For twenty-five years few changes occurred in "hi-fi" sets. Even a new technology such as compact music discs has been stable for ten years. As a stable technology becomes pervasive, competition inevitably degenerates into a commodity contest, ideally suited to the competitive strategies of Asian firms.

The promise of consumer electronics is that we may be on the threshold of an entirely new competitive environment, marked by the same kind of continuing technological discontinuity that has recently characterized business computing. The critical technologies—high-speed digital networks, improvements in compression algorithms, video-capable microprocessors—are being rapidly developed in business. American semiconductor, software, and computer firms have strong positions in all the relevant multimedia technologies. As they percolate down to consumer markets, American companies could be well positioned to win back substantial consumer electronics market shares. A decade of competition with Asian firms in commodity-like PC clone and printer markets may have restored at least some of the low-cost manufacturing skills Western firms will also need to succeed in consumer markets.

There are, however, major obstacles to such a consumer electronics transformation taking place rapidly—sheer consumer inertia, for instance. Early consumer electronics enthusiasms, such as educational computers in the home, have often proved a disappointment. Much more serious is the lack of an information delivery capacity to take full advantage of the available technologies. And finally, of course, there is the question of whether American companies can shape the market to their own strengths. To do so, they must create open, architecturally dominant design- and software-dominated consumer technology regimes; regain sufficient mass production skills to control the key implementation points within the architecture, even if the commodity components are off-loaded to Asia; and keep the technology moving fast enough that the commodity implementers are continually off balance.

Over the longer term, some such transformation as we have been describing is inevitable; the real question is not whether it will happen, but whether it will happen within current technology and investment planning cycles, and whether American firms will seize the opportunity when it arises.

14

THE FUTURE OF
COMPUTER COMPANIES

Computer companies have been condemned to live in interesting times. The 1990s will be more traumatic and tumultuous than even the 1980s. Assuming a continuation of the fundamental forces we have identified in the previous chapters, we can construct likely scenarios for the most important companies competing in computers and information technology. These are not forecasts or investment judgments, but rather projections of likely outcomes under current policy and technology regimes.

IBM

Regardless of its ultimate organization, IBM segments logically into several different business types. According to the management paradigms we set out in Chapter 12, IBM incorporates four quite different business models:

• A core megaproject-style business, comprising its mainframes and minicomputers and their related peripheral and other businesses, still the lion's share of its revenues and earnings

• A lean manufacturing-style business, in which we would categorize the PCs and workstations, pen-based and palmtop computers, as well as certain of its OEM manufacturing operations (making components for other branded original equipment manufacturers)

• A Japanese-style monolithic model business—IBM may still be the world's largest producer of advanced DRAMs

• Several Silicon Valley model businesses, which would include PC and RS6000 software, especially the OS/2 operating system, the Taligent and Kaleida partnerships with Apple, and the Power PC microprocessor partnership with Motorola

We are not proposing that IBM organize itself into four business lines; as of mid-1992, Akers is planning some thirteen decentralized divisions. Our argument is merely that different business models should not be mixed in the same division, and that the organization, the overhead structure, the business practices, and the incentive arrangements in each business should be consistent with its competitive paradigm. One of Armonk's fateful predilections in the past has been to inflict its accustomed megaproject management style on businesses where it is utterly inappropriate. Armonk's willingness to let go the reins and allow its subsidiary businesses to develop according to their own internal logics is still the great question facing the company.

MEGAPROJECT BUSINESSES.
About 70 percent of IBM's revenues are derived from megaproject-style businesses, including hardware sales of mainframes, minicomputers, and peripherals such as high-speed printers and disk drives; system maintenance; software; and systems integration services, heavily oriented toward mainframe applications. The revenue trends are shown in the

table below. (Software sales include software for PCs and workstations, but are dominated by mainframe software.)

IBM REVENUES IN BILLIONS				
	1986	1989	1991	Annual % Change
Mainframes	$14.4	$12.5	$9.1	-8.8%
Minicomputers	$3.0	$6.6	$5.9	14.5%
Peripherals	$11.3	$10.0	$10.3	-1.8%
Software & Services	$5.8	$9.5	$14.2	19.6%
Maintenance	$7.4	$7.0	$7.4	0.0%

This is not a bright picture. IBM's traditional revenue and profit flagship, the mainframe computer, is slipping badly. Minicomputers showed strong growth in the late 1980s, much of it related to the AS400, but have slipped recently. We also estimate that a substantial portion of AS400 sales were cannibalizing the more profitable mainframes. Maintenance and peripheral products are flat. Services and software sales have grown strongly, but they are tied very closely to the mainframe business. The steady decline in mainframe sales and flattening minicomputer sales are the leading indicators of future performance. The lag time before falling mainframe sales show up in reduced peripheral, software, and maintenance sales is probably about three to five years; the expectation, therefore, must be for sharp declines in all of those areas.

The bleak future for mainframes and minicomputers is made clear by looking at regional purchasing patterns. The only country where mainframe and minicomputer sales are growing strongly is Japan, whose businesses tend to be a full technology generation behind America's in data processing. And Japan, of course, is where IBM faces its most formidable national mainframe and minicomputer competitors. At $25 billion, world mainframe sales were basically flat between 1987 and 1991, but the American share of mainframe purchases fell from 53 percent to 37 percent, while the Japanese share grew from 6 percent to 24 percent. Minicomputer sales trends were almost identical. The market was also flat between 1987 and 1991, at just under $25 billion, but America's share of purchases fell even faster, from 54 percent to 33 percent, while Japan's rose from 5 percent to 22 percent.

There is no reason to expect Western mainframe and minicomputer sales to recover. Much of the remaining staying power of mainframes and minicomputers against networked PCs and workstations stems from a software base with industrial-market features, like strict security provisions, audit-oriented accounting trails, and similar functions. That is an ephemeral advantage, and legions of microprocessor-based system software developers are working diligently to make it disappear as rapidly as possible. About five years from now, if history is any guide, Japanese computer purchases will fall into the present American pattern and world mainframe and minicomputer markets will implode.

One of IBM's great recent successes has been increased sales of systems integration services, primarily a consulting business. That is the main factor in the rise of revenues in the "Software and Services" category. We presume those revenues could grow for some time, although it is a very competitive business, where companies like EDS and Andersen Consulting hold strong positions. However, since IBM's systems integration services are still closely tied to mainframe environments, in the long run they too will be dragged down by the continued shrinkage in the mainframe market.

IBM also has little presence in parallel processing, one of the major threats to the high-end computer line. Ironically, perhaps typically, IBM has long had outstanding in-house parallel processing computers that it has used for designing logic circuits—computerized design of complex logic circuits takes enormous processing power. A development group at Yorktown has also created formidable machines using RS6000 processors in a highly parallel mode. Neither capability has ever been converted into a commercializable family of products.

IBM now has several internal parallel processing development efforts under way and has recently invested in Thinking Machines Corporation, a leader in massively parallel machines. Its most advanced announced entry in parallel processing, however, for the moment at least, is an equity partnership with Steve Chen's SSI. (Chen was formerly one of Seymour Cray's top designers.) IBM owns a 15 percent stake in the venture, which has yet to announce a product in a fast-moving market. All the development efforts, with the sole exception of an internal project targeted at the scientific market, are 370-compatible, including those with Thinking Machines and SSI—that is, the parallel machine is either used as back-end high-speed processor in a 370 environment or 370 processors themselves are run in a parallel mode. The unwillingness to break with a favorite old dog of an architecture unnecessarily ties IBM's parallel processing efforts to a computing environment with a rapidly shrinking claim on the market, and gratuitously leaves a potentially much larger space to microprocessor-based multiprocessor technologies moving up from below.

Almost exactly the same comments can be made about IBM's disk drive business. It generates some $7 billion in annual revenues and is highly profitable. But again, it is heavily oriented toward mainframe and minicomputer data centers and is being supplanted by parallel arrays of inexpensive disks. IBM has developed its own high-end parallel disk array technology, but it is designed exclusively for a 370 environment. As a consequence, IBM is defaulting the parallel disk array opportunity to quasi-commoditized standards like the family of RAID (Redundant Arrays of Inexpensive Disks) standards. The AS400 and the RS6000 have adopted a RAID disk array standard, implicitly conceding the chance to set a new architectural standard in disk drives.

The long-term decline in mainframe and minicomputer sales at IBM, therefore, can mean only continued contraction of all its related revenue sources, the mainstay of IBM sales. IBM's megaproject businesses are high-overhead operations with a set of long-ingrained management assumptions of perpetual 15 percent per year revenue growth. High fixed costs and falling revenues will have a fierce downward ratchet effect on profit margins. These businesses, in short, are in serious trouble and will contract dramatically over the medium-term future. Declining businesses can be profitable, of course. One of Armonk's major challenges will be executing a graceful transition to a smaller mainframe and minicomputer business while protecting the financial health and morale of its growth businesses. As of mid-1992, we are not convinced that IBM management has yet recognized the seriousness of the problems it faces.

Lean Manufacturing.

The center of gravity for IBM's lean manufacturing businesses is the Personal Systems division, essentially a hardware manufacturing and sales company, which apparently is in the process of being spun off as a separate company under Bob Corrigan and Jim Cannavino. With more than $7 billion in sales, the new Personal Systems company will be the largest in the industry, bigger than Apple and as big as Compaq and Sun put together. While we do not believe it is any longer possible, at least within the current technology regime, for a pure hardware manufacturer to capture the standard-setting role in personal systems, we expect that the new company will be successful. IBM has formidable manufacturing skills; if the new company is freed from its existing overhead burden, it should have a good shot at achieving a low-cost, high-quality position with competitive product cycles. The apparent success of the Lexmark printer business is a good precedent, although it also suggests a painful period of layoffs and downsizing to achieve fully competitive operations. One glaring hole in the PC product line that should be filled quickly is the lack of a family of Intel-based multiprocessor servers. A host of companies, from Compaq, Dell, and AST, now offer such machines; we suspect that cannibalization issues may have prevented IBM from doing so. At the moment, IBM offers only a two-processor solution purchased from Parallan, a small start-up, and sells it with a marked lack of enthusiasm.

It is worth stressing once again that it was never necessary for PCs to become a commoditized, purely lean manufacturing business. IBM missed a golden opportunity to control the PC architectural standard and snookered itself into competing as just another clone. It seems to be following the same approach with palmtop and pen-based computers. While consumer-oriented businesses like palmtops will always have a lean manufacturing component, IBM appears not to be making any effort to establish an architectural standard in these new categories of machines.

IBM is also exploring whether there are opportunities for it to enter consumer-oriented businesses. It has an alliance with Rogers Cable, the leading Canadian cable television system, examining opportunities in interactive television, and has been holding discussions with Time Warner in the United States, apparently with similar objectives. Finally, IBM has aggressively pushed into OEM subsystems and components, apparently with considerable success. OEM sales in 1991 topped $3 billion, after starting virtually from scratch just three years ago.

We expect IBM to be a formidable lean manufacturing competitor once its manufacturing divisions are released from standard overhead controls. Profit margins in these businesses, however, will not approach IBM's historic norms. They are commodity or near-commodity businesses; profits are thin, product cycles are very short, and price wars are the norm. Being the architectural standard-setter is always a far more desirable position; competing merely as a clone is a second-best solution.

MONOLITHIC MODEL BUSINESSES.
Along with Toshiba, IBM is, and will doubtless continue to be, the world's leading producer of semiconductors. It is the world's process leader and for many years has consistently been first to reach the level of volume production of each new generation of memory chips, usually by about nine months over the closest Japanese competitors. IBM does not sell its chips on the open market. Since sales are at internal transfer prices, there are no reliable figures on sales and earnings. Based on estimated share of market by major semiconductor categories, however, if IBM competed at world prices, annual semiconductor sales would be approximately $5 billion.

IBM is known as a high-quality but high-cost producer, as might be expected of a captive foundry. Worse, IBM's main technology base is still in memory devices, possibly the most brutally cost-competitive industry in the world. With the exception of periods of government-inspired market rigging and/or cartel behavior by the largest producers, industry participants almost always lose money. There is currently a glut of even the most advanced memory chips that is likely to continue for some time. The strains of competing in the world merchant memory market has begun to tell even on the endlessly masochistic Japanese, who have been searching for partners to share investment costs. IBM has recently formed a number of cost-sharing and production alliances—with Toshiba in flash EPROMS (a memory device); with Toshiba and Siemens in DRAMs; and with Toshiba in advanced flat display screens, which have cost and investment dynamics much the same as those in DRAMs.

Because of the high fixed costs of semiconductor foundries, plants that run below capacity are certain money losers. IBM's own shrinking hardware sales and need for additional revenues will force the semiconductor businesses to enter the merchant market in force. We expect a difficult learning period adjusting to free-market cost disciplines and customer servicing requirements. We have no doubt that IBM's foundries can earn significant outside revenues, but there is little reason to expect them to be profitable anytime soon.

Silicon Valley Model Businesses.

Finally, IBM participates in a long list of new Silicon Valley model businesses, either as owner, partner, or investor. We discuss only some of the most important.

IBM's OS/2 2.0 personal systems operating systems software is a significant improvement over its predecessor, although it has not yet captured serious market share from Windows/DOS for single desktop users. The critical question is whether the long period of recovery from the initial OS/2 disaster has put it fatally behind the yet-to-be-released Microsoft NT in the networked industrial and office market. That market appears to be moving rapidly toward multiprocessor architectures. NT is designed as a multiprocessor system; OS/2 is not. We understand, however, that IBM is creating a new OS/2 release built on top of "Mach," a very powerful multiprocessor kernel developed at Carnegie-Mellon Institute with DARPA funding. Initial reports from third-party software developers have been quite positive. The company is apparently also working on RISC and palmtop

OS/2 versions. IBM has a lot of software talent, but is still badly hampered by its management and its inexperience in developing software in a Silicon Valley competitive environment. It is running out of time.

There are two software partnerships with Apple: Taligent, designed to produce a next-generation operating system; and Kaleida, aimed at next-generation multimedia systems and applications software. The two partnerships offer the hope of eventually leapfrogging over Microsoft. Taligent, in particular, could be crucial if OS/2 is completely defeated by Windows/DOS and NT. It is much too early in either venture to offer useful comment, although both appear very much in the two companies' interests. For Apple, it means finally entering the open systems world, while for IBM, it provides access to Apple's software skills, which have always been among the best in the business.

One other software venture deserves mention. IBM was a founding partner in the nonprofit Open Software Foundation (OSF), organized to develop a nonproprietary UNIX standard to compete with the AT&T/Sun standard and presumably now NT. The OSF-installed base is still small but is rising rapidly, and it could become a formidable competitor to Microsoft, particularly in multiprocessor-server markets. If OSF is successful, it will amount to a kind of scorched-earth attack on Microsoft, because it will commoditize the operating system standard. Commoditized architectural standards usually freeze at something less than an optimum level of development. That would be a heavy price to pay for the psychological pleasures of cutting Microsoft down to size.

Finally, IBM has several microprocessor businesses, both within the parent and in the new Power PC partnership with Motorola, designed to produce a leading-edge RISC-based processor for the newest generation of fast desktop machines. Microprocessors have never been a strong point of IBM's internal foundries. There is no doubt that IBM can make very high quality chips, but the business has been consistently hampered by being lodged within traditional, mostly commodity, semiconductor divisions. In fact, none of the monolithic model companies (including IBM's semiconductor divisions and most of the Japanese) has ever competed effectively in advanced microprocessors. If IBM intends to compete with Intel, it will need to set up an Intel-like company out from under the day-to-day control of Armonk.

The Power PC partnership with Motorola, however, appears quite promising. Motorola's microprocessor capabilities match those of any company in the industry, including Intel, while IBM has substantial RISC capabilities. In the same way as the Taligent partnership offers a new competitive angle against Microsoft, Power PC could develop into an engine for taking on Intel head-to-head. The assumption, of course, is that the partnership will function as a relatively freestanding business.

If IBM is prepared to manage through a major contraction in mainframe and minicomputer businesses, we believe it can survive and even prosper after a fashion, although the prize will be only a much smaller, sadder, less pretentious, and much more constrained IBM. We are not optimistic that IBM will negotiate the transition gracefully. The departure of the Armonk *nomenklatura,* for all of Akers's blustering, is proceeding very slowly, and there seems little urgent awareness at the board level of the need for change, as there was, for instance, at DEC and Compaq. External hiring is still not the norm—in sharp contrast to, say, Microsoft's eager scouting out of the leading lights in each new technology it targets. IBM's Silicon Valley–model businesses are still organized in the old way, with an incentive structure and hiring pattern matching up poorly against the competition; the exodus of good people continues. Finally, IBM is still extremely reluctant to cannibalize its mature product lines. It has recently ported its CICS mainframe transaction processing software to the RS6000 workstation, a positive sign. RS6000 emulations of the AS400's best-selling minicomputer software, however, remain locked up in an IBM safe, just as countless other breakthrough IBM products have been.

OTHER AMERICAN COMPANIES

In this section, we provide a brief summary of the position of other American computer companies aligned more or less in accordance with the management paradigms we used in our discussion of IBM. We make no pretense that our list is comprehensive—there are many hundreds of computer companies in the United States—and our categorizations are often merely approximate.

To begin with, a number of companies have recent performance levels usually associated with American Rust Bowl industries, rather than with computer companies. Our Hall of Shame includes:

Company	1987 Fiscal Year Revenue	1991 Fiscal Year Revenue	Trailing Price/Earnings Ratio	Annual % Change in Revenue
Unisys	$9,732.00	$8,696.00	Loss	-2.7%
CDC	$3,366.50	$1,524.90	Loss	-13.7%
Prime	$960.90	$1,382.40	N/A	11.0%
Wang	$2,836.70	$2,091.50	Loss	-6.6%

Unisys is the spawn of a hostile takeover by Burroughs of Sperry Rand. Both companies were tired members of the old BUNCH, who were rapidly falling behind in the race with IBM. W. Michael Blumenthal, the Burroughs CEO who drove the takeover, was a former treasury secretary in the Carter administration and knew little or nothing about computers, including, apparently, the iron rule that computer companies cannot be leveraged. After running the merged companies into the ground, he was rewarded with a senior mergers and acquisitions position at Lazard Frères. Unisys has managed a recovery of sorts under new management, based mostly on niche bank back-office products, but has only limited prospects. CDC had the best high-performance scientific computers in the 1960s—Seymour Cray was their top designer—but went on a seemingly random diversification binge in the 1970s and stopped investing in technology. Prime was the victim of another leveraged buyout and is in the process of going bankrupt as we write. Wang wasted a powerful position on office desktops by trying to move upscale, of all things, into mini-computers. It is on the life-support system of Chapter 11 bankruptcy.

These companies were all megaproject-style companies, selling tightly bundled closed architectures, who failed to make the transition to a new generation of computing. Several other companies are in the process of struggling to make such a transition.

Company	1987 Fiscal Year Revenue	1991 Fiscal Year Revenue	Trailing Price/Earnings Ratio	Annual % Change in Revenue
DEC	$9,389.44	$13,911.00	Loss	12.0%
AT&T-NCR	$5,640.70	N/A	N/A	N/A
Data General	$1,274.35	$1,228.90	6.3	-0.9%

We have discussed DEC at some length elsewhere in the book, and we think it will do well in the UNIX-RISC world, although at a much lower level of sales and profits. NCR had also carved out an interesting position in UNIX-based multiprocessor architectures before AT&T bought them after a hard, and very hostile, fight. NCR has enjoyed a quiet success cannibalizing their mainframe product line with great élan. Thus far, at least, AT&T's management has adopted a hands-off attitude, but their ability to destroy a promising company will remain a continuing threat. With access to AT&T's capital and manufacturing capabilities, and appropriate management restraint, AT&T-NCR could become a successful company. Data General, a DEC look-alike, is a less hopeful case, but is also trying to recast itself as a parallel systems/UNIX company; its disk array technology has received favorable notices.

• • •

The next group of companies are not traditional American computer companies, but have enjoyed good success bringing a basically lean manufacturing approach to engineering and design-sensitive segments of the industry. With the occasional exception of Hewlett-Packard, and even more occasionally, Motorola, they have tended to eschew architectural contests.

Company	1987 Fiscal Year Revenue	1991 Fiscal Year Revenue	Trailing Price/Earnings Ratio	Annual % Change in Revenue
HP	$8,090.00	$14,494.00	20.5	19.8%
Motorola	$6,727.00	$11,341.00	20.9	17.2%
Compaq	$1,224.07	$3,271.40	18.4	41.8%
AMD	$997.08	$1,226.60	14.8	5.8%
LSI Logic	$262.13	$697.84	Loss	41.6%
Cypress	$77.25	$286.80	15.9	67.8%

Hewlett-Packard is known for its meticulous engineering, good cost control, and high quality. It has successfully gone head-to-head with the Japanese in the very tough printer market and dominates the low end. Because of its highly decentralized management organization, it has also enjoyed a good run of modest successes in RISC/UNIX minicomputers and workstations. All in all, its management deserves much credit. Motorola is similar; it is not a computer company, although semiconductors make up about a third of its sales. Motorola is a meticulous producer of very high-quality mass-produced products such as cellular phones and has proven it can beat the Japanese at their own game on their own turf. It will be a valuable resource in a computer-intensive consumer electronic industry. We should, however, like to see both Hewlett-Packard and Motorola adopt more architecturally oriented strategies.

Compaq is in the process of reestablishing itself as a high-quality, competitively priced clone-maker. The company competes on quality without controlling implementations; that is a difficult strategy, but one they have carried out successfully in the past. A recently introduced line of network printers is very impressive and suggests that the company is regaining its old product development touch. The fat profit margins Compaq enjoyed under IBM's pricing umbrella in the mid-1980s, however, will never be seen again.

AMD has lived a roller-coaster existence cloning the Intel architecture. It is currently enjoying its best sales and returns in years. Both LSI Logic and Cypress are struggling to keep up with process technology, although both have been very successful with short-run, high-intellectual-content chips, almost always designing to architectures controlled by other parties.

Next, there are a series of point product vendors with often profitable but always precarious existences within architectures controlled by other companies. Borland has a shot at breaking into an architectural position in data base software.

Company	1987 Fiscal Year Revenue	1991 Fiscal Year Revenue	Trailing Price/Earnings Ratio	Annual % Change in Revenue
Lotus	$395.60	$828.89	23.2	27.4%
WordPerfect	$100.00	$640.00	N/A	135.0%
Borland	$38.12	$226.75	Loss	123.7%
Chips & Tech.	$80.24	$225.09	Loss	45.1%

Finally, there are the companies who have managed to achieve, or are struggling to achieve, some proprietary architectural control over a significant competitive space.

Company	1987 Fiscal Year Revenue	1991 Fiscal Year Revenue	Trailing Price/Earnings Ratio	Annual % Change in Revenue
Apple	$2,661.07	$6,309.00	19.8	34.3%
Intel	$1,907.11	$4,779.00	12.9	37.7%
Sun	$537.54	$3,221.30	14.9	124.8%
Microsoft	$345.89	$1,843.40	36.9	108.2%
Novell	$221.80	$640.10	42.7	47.2%
Adobe	$39.32	$229.70	23.7	121.0%

Microsoft is the supreme architectural competitor. At the moment, its main competitive threats are OS/2, which is a long shot, and possibly more formidably over time, the Open Software Foundation's UNIX system. The Justice Department's apparent intention to proceed with an antitrust suit, however, may be more worrying. A more effective counterweight might be a combination between IBM's OS/2 or the OSF together with, say, Lotus, Novell, Borland, and Word-Perfect. Novell controls the network standard, although it is hotly contested by Microsoft, among others.

Intel dominates the American merchant semiconductor industry and controls almost 60 percent of the world microprocessor market. Widespread cloning of its 386/486 designs by AMD, Cyrix, and others is disciplining its pricing. But Intel is cash rich, is investing aggressively, and has one of the best management teams in the business. We expect them to maintain their position for the foreseeable future.

Apple appears to be successfully re-creating itself by finally recognizing that its great software and design skills are the source of its competitive advantage. Apple may also be the best-positioned large American company to move aggressively into consumer applications, like multimedia home computing and games; the company's friendliness toward the naïve user has always been one of its great strengths. But

the company has too little control of its key implementations. At the moment, Apple's implementation partners in
consumer-oriented computer applications are Sony and
Sharp. Japanese partners are always dangerous; the operating system in Sony's new palmtop computers is a Macintosh
clone. In our view, Apple has suffered from a lack of strategic clarity for a long time. It still has the ingredients for a
great success in two separate businesses—as a competitor to
Microsoft in open-systems software, and if it can get better
control over its implementations, as a major player in a future consumer computer market.

Sun is the Apple of the workstation world. Its success is
based on its systems software and its RISC SPARC architecture, and it is still the largest player in the very competitive
workstation market. But like Apple, it was late to separate its
software and bundled hardware-software businesses and it
has far too little control over its implementations and has been
suffering for it. Sun made the additional mistake of not rede-
signing its outstanding operating system software so it could
compete effectively at the lower end, thus restricting itself to a
smaller market than was necessary.

Adobe still largely controls the printer and type font software standard, although it faces fierce competition from Microsoft, Hewlett-Packard, and a host of PostScript clones.
Like Sun, Adobe has also resisted a move to the low end—
effective use of PostScript requires lots of processing power,
unnecessarily limiting its effective market.

JAPANESE COMPANIES

As we have suggested throughout this book, the computer
wars are essentially a two-party contest between the United
States and Japan. But Japanese *computer* companies are not
the primary threat to American firms. The Japanese industry's
computer hardware revenues are about the same as IBM's.
Japan's leading computer company, Fujitsu, with almost $14
billion in hardware revenues, is heavily oriented toward mainframes and minicomputers, much as IBM is. Hitachi has a
similar profile. Both NEC and Toshiba have strong positions

in personal systems, but largely as IBM-compatible clone-makers within the Intel and Microsoft architectures. NEC has its own personal computer architectural standard, which it has not been able to establish outside of Japan.

By themselves, Japanese computer hardware sales are not particularly imposing. The threat comes from Japanese component-makers, including the companies above—Toshiba is the world's leading merchant semiconductor-maker—but also many others including Sharp, Sanyo, Epson, Matsushita, and NMB. While the Japanese control less than a quarter of the computer industry, they make well over half of its components. The race over the next decade will be between the Japanese and American styles of industry development. The Japanese will drive to componentize and commoditize every sector of the industry so their great monolithic and lean manufacturing skills can define the industry's future. American companies must keep accelerating the pace of technological change to avoid giving the Japanese a stable target to shoot at, and at the same time develop their own manufacturing skills to the point where low-end market share is not conceded too easily. We will discuss these issues at greater length in Chapter 16.

The sharpest edge of the contest between American and Japanese companies will come as computers move into consumer markets. There is little precedent for attacking consumer industries with the kind of architectural, design-oriented strategies that are the American strength, while the Japanese have long demonstrated a brilliant understanding of consumer product manufacturing. The most formidable Japanese companies in a consumer/computing battle would not be the present Japanese computer companies, but probably Nintendo, Sega, and Sony. Neither Nintendo nor Sega are known as outstanding engineering or manufacturing companies, but they clearly understand software and architectural control. Sony is the most American of the Japanese consumer product companies and could probably create the most formidable combination of architectural and manufacturing skills. A Sony/Apple alliance could be extremely effective in a new era of architected consumer electronics, although Sony has not always been a trustworthy partner.

Other Countries

The other major Asian competitors in the computer industry are the Koreans and Taiwanese. The Koreans have adopted, even exaggerated, the Japanese industrial model. Their monolithic model semiconductor operations were a major factor in breaking the Japanese DRAM cartel of the late 1980s. Although long-standing ethnic mistrust militates against it, a Japanese-Korean DRAM cartel could be very dangerous.

The Taiwanese have developed in an entirely different direction and are well on their way toward creating the first non-American Silicon Valley. The Chinese entrepreneurial tradition, the predilection for small firms, ample government-funded venture capital, and close family and business ties with the California university and business system are all coming together to create possibly a major new center of computer innovation. It bears close watching.

Finally, there are the Europeans. The European national champions—Siemens-Nixdorf, Groupe Bull, ICL, and Olivetti—have about $20 billion in sales between them that, with the exception of Olivetti, are heavily weighted toward traditional systems. Some three quarters of their sales take place in Europe, mostly in their home countries. None of them has a 5 percent global market share in any product line, and none of them has a leadership position in any computer technology. The great portion of their sales is made up of relabeled American or Japanese equipment; ICL is now merely a Fujitsu marketing subsidiary. Instructively, the French taxpayers' subsidy to Bull in 1990 to cover operating losses was greater than the computer technology investments of America's venture industry. The Europeans are no longer a factor and show no signs of becoming one.

15

Government and Computers: Prologue to Policy

From its very inception, the computer industry has been the child of government in all industrial countries, including the United States. But the policies followed in Japan, Europe, and America have been quite different in their conception, execution, and consequences. Japanese policies are remarkable for the single-minded consistency and focus with which national industrial goals have been pursued over a period of more than thirty years, despite many setbacks and tactical shifts. Equally strenuous exertion by the governments of Europe, however, has produced only elaborate and expensive muddles. American policies evolved along quite different lines from those in Europe and Japan, and are remarkable both for their great, if sometimes inadvertent, successes as well as for the severe, if often equally inadvertent, damage they have wreaked upon native industry.

JAPAN

The Japanese ruling political establishment recognized clearly by the late 1950s that electronics and computers would be an essential "driver" in the quest to build Japan into a major industrial power. They created the legal framework and the political commitment to make Japan independent of imported electronic technology. The drive for industrial autarky had deep roots; as one senior policy-maker put it: "We were conscious of the fact that we were abhorred by the whole world because of World War II. We felt that if something bad happened to Japan, no one would help us." The specific objectives entrusted to the powerful Ministry of International Trade and Industry (MITI) were both broad and precise. Electronics was identified as the ideal industry for an island economy with limited natural resources. The broad objective was to establish a world-class presence in consumer and industrial electronics manufacturing—Japan was the only country without a significant military component in its electronics industry. In the computer industry the goal could be defined with laser-sharp precision: catch IBM.

In 1960, the Japanese electronics companies—Fujitsu, Hitachi, Nippon Electric (NEC), Mitsubishi Electric, Oki, and others—had only a small presence in computers, producing low-performance imitations of IBM's machines. Despite an explicit "Buy Japan" policy sponsored by the government and heavy-handed tariffs and import controls, IBM still dominated the Japanese industry, and was becoming increasingly assertive about widespread patent infringement by Japanese companies. Alone among foreign electronic firms, IBM had reentered Japan during the Occupation, before Japanese law required local joint-venture partners. But IBM badly wanted permission to manufacture in Japan to avoid import controls, and the right to repatriate its export earnings. American policy requiring IBM to license its patents to all comers strengthened Japan's hand in the patent negotiations. A bargain was finally struck at the end of 1960, whereby IBM made all its patents

available to Japanese firms at a low royalty rate, was allowed
to open a factory for its best-selling 1401 business computer,
and agreed to an aggressive program of exporting from Japan.

With the IBM patents in hand, the Japanese companies,
despite MITI's misgivings, formed a series of alliances with
second-tier American firms to produce a broad line of reasonably competitive computers. NEC allied with Honeywell,
Hitachi with RCA, Toshiba with General Electric, Oki with
Rand/UNIVAC, Mitsubishi with TRW. Only Fujitsu, the Japanese company most focused on computers, went it alone. At
about the same time, MITI also forced a shotgun marriage
between Texas Instruments and Sony in order to acquire TI's
semiconductor technology; when a foreign partner such as TI
entered into a joint venture, moreover, its licenses were made
available not just to its partner, but to the entire Japanese
industry. The Japanese patent system was turned into a formidable competitive weapon. Japan recognizes patents in order of filing, as do the Europeans, but requires that filings be
public. Actual approval of American patents, however, was
typically stretched out for decades, during which time American technology was freely available for local piracy. (In the
landmark case mentioned earlier, Texas Instruments won
Japanese recognition of infringement on its basic integrated
circuit technology after twenty-nine years of pursuing its
rights through the Japanese patent and legal system.) Overall,
the Japanese administered their tangle of licensing, partnership, and trade laws with remarkable skill, and the absolute
transfer of American technology to Japanese firms, particularly during the 1960s and 1970s, was very large.

In its early days, Japanese industry needed finance as
much as technology, and IBM's generous leasing terms were
still a major competitive advantage. Japanese computer-
makers did not have the capital to finance leases themselves,
and few of their customers could come up with the cash for
outright purchases. The government stepped in again, organizing the Japanese Electronic Computing Company (JECC),
a stock company owned by the computer companies that provided subsidized government financing for leases of Japanese-
made computers. (When IBM asked to join the consortium, it

was politely told that MITI had no objections, but since JECC was a private company, it was a decision for the shareholders.)

Although the actual subsidy delivered through JECC was not large, the cash flow provision may have been crucial to the industry's development. One scholar has estimated JECC's cash flow contribution at more than $260 million in the 1960s—an amount equivalent to the Japanese computer industry's investment in capital equipment and R&D in the decade—and almost twice that in the 1970s. The percentage of Japanese-made computers that were leased rose from almost nil in 1960 to more than 75 percent by the mid-1960s, or about the same percentage as IBM's. Not only did Japanese companies' local market share increase rapidly, from less than 10 percent to more than 50 percent in less than a decade, but the lease terms also facilitated the expansion of computing throughout Japanese industry. The JECC was also used to pressure companies MITI considered overreliant on their American partners. Local-content leasing requirements were gradually raised from 50 percent to 75 percent to 90 percent, even at the cost of excluding consortium members from financing privileges.

A critical feature of the JECC arrangement was that the government had only a limited voice in the actual production decisions of the participating companies. For the most part, they were free to compete fiercely with each other for market share and profits, as well as with continuing, if controlled, imports from the West. MITI's preferences, in fact, were to impose much greater "rationalization" on the industry; the original plans for JECC envisioned the kind of "national champion" company that was favored by European policymakers. But the Japanese companies would have none of it—Fujitsu and Hitachi, for instance, repeatedly resisted MITI's attempts to force them into a single mainframe consortium, but insisted instead on a uniquely Japanese, and very complex, mix of broad cooperative policy coordination and fierce intercompany competition at the product level, to the great benefit of the continued advance of Japanese technology.

For all the successes of the first rounds of MITI's computer-targeting policies, IBM relentlessly kept raising the stakes. The rest of Japanese industry was pleased to cooperate with MITI's computer program, but not at the cost of compromising its own drive to industrial supremacy. As soon as local computer technology slipped too far behind IBM's, the clamor would rise for more imports. The announcement of System/360 in 1964, with its hybrid integrated circuits, was a shock, and exposed the weaknesses of Japanese semiconductor technology. MITI responded by quadrupling computer research expenditure and organizing a massive cooperative venture— the Super High Performance Electronic Computer Program— consisting of the government communications monopoly, or NTT, the national laboratories, and all the computer companies to catch up. The project produced the first Japanese semiconductor memories and logic circuits, and by about 1968, Hitachi and Fujitsu were turning out machines that were at least reasonably competitive with the IBM standard.

But just as MITI may have been breathing easily again, IBM dropped its System/370 bombshell, embodying a long and formidable list of advances. It incorporated time-sharing, which the 360 series had lacked, much improved integrated circuit technology, the first use of semiconductor main memory, and a very complex and powerful new operating system, the MVS; the machine overall was much faster, with larger and faster memory, better file handling, and greater reliability. At the same time, the Nixon administration was pressing the Japanese to loosen its computer trade regimen and, over MITI's objections, the government was anxious to agree. The oil price shocks restricted Japanese financial flexibility, and to make matters worse, with the exception of Honeywell, Japan's American computer partners, who had been a critical technological resource in the struggle against the 360, gave up the ghost and dropped out of the mainframe race.

Yet again, however, MITI threw its formidable bureaucratic and financial resources into the breach and rallied the flagging Japanese companies. Although it could not prevent the prime minister from signing a trade pact with Nixon, it did everything in its power to frustrate its terms, enmeshing IBM in a web of official negotiations and unofficial delays to gain more breathing space. MITI also forced, finally, a measure of its long-sought industry rationalization. The companies resisted, but a sweeping price cut by IBM concentrated minds wonderfully, and for a brief period at least, they danced to MITI's tune. Fujitsu and Hitachi cooperated on architectural development, and Oki, Toshiba, and Mitsubishi left the mainframe industry. The Fujitsu-Hitachi alliance quickly dissolved, but only after they had devised an IBM-compatible Japanese standard mainframe, shared with NEC. MITI greatly increased computer research spending—the total Japanese computer R&D budget increased by 60 percent in 1973 alone, with a much larger share financed by the government. In 1971, virtually all computer research was conducted in Japanese companies; just three years later, 60 percent was carried out in government research institutions or in MITI-sponsored industry research consortia.

But perhaps the most important technological initiative of all was carried out against MITI's express wishes. One of IBM's leading designers, Gene Amdahl, who had made major contributions to the 360/370 system, left IBM in 1969 to manufacture his own line of plug-compatible computers. His idea was to build an IBM-compatible central processor and marry it with the large number of compatible peripheral devices that were by then available on the open market. Sophisticated customers, who did not need IBM's formidable service and support backup, could then buy a complete "IBM" package at substantial discounts over standard equipment. But Amdahl ran into financial difficulties and shopped for capital in Japan, finally entering into a deal with Fujitsu: Amdahl got an equity infusion, and Fujitsu manufactured his line of computers in Japan for sale in the United States. MITI was opposed to more American tie-ups, but the Amdahl deal may have been a critical factor in keeping the Japanese mainframe manufacturers competitive with IBM through the late 1970s. In the event, Japanese local market share, which had slipped to 48 percent after the 370 was introduced, quickly recovered to 60 percent, and by the end of the decade Japanese mainframes were gaining a world reputation as the equal of IBM's.

Although the Japanese had made remarkable progress, their position remained precarious. For one thing, Japanese companies had little experience, and less success, in producing advanced software; but by the late 1970s, software had come to represent about 50 percent of the value of a major mainframe installation. Repeated attempts to organize Japanese software consortia had failed, and one in particular, Japan Software, Inc., was a much publicized and expensive fiasco. And while Japanese hardware skills were now world-class, word of IBM's F/S initiative caused much anxiety. Finally, and most important, while Japanese companies had vastly improved their capabilities to match or even improve on IBM products, they were acutely aware that they were still playing IBM's game—they were making computers to fit within a set of rules that IBM wrote. In other words, the overall architecture of mainframe systems was still the IBM architecture, and IBM could, and often did, change it—as F/S threatened to do—forcing the Japanese into one wild catch-up scramble after another. The Japanese were also acutely aware that they were still living on borrowed American technology, and could hardly assume that American supineness in intellectual property enforcement would continue forever. (Even in 1992, in fact, the flow of intellectual property earnings from Japan to the United States was quite large, a net of more than $3 billion.)

MITI accordingly embarked on a series of initiatives to establish the independence of the Japanese industry and a greater equality with IBM. The VLSI (Very Large Scale Integration) program was probably the most successful. A major cooperative R&D program, it was started in the early 1970s in response to the F/S program, and aimed at vaulting a generation ahead in semiconductor technology, involving a broad range of process technologies, new equipment development, and new semiconductor designs. By the end of the decade, Japanese semiconductor process and manufacturing technology was the equal of anyone's in the world, and Japanese companies were poised for their massive, and successful, assault on world semiconductor markets.

Macroeconomic conditions in Japan in the 1980s were also ideally suited to a major semiconductor initiative. Throughout the 1960s and 1970s, the Japanese government ran massive budget deficits and industry was typically capital starved. But by the 1980s, after a decade of growing trade surpluses, Japan's capital position had reversed. The central bank then adopted an extremely expansive monetary policy, enlarging the money base at double digit annual rates through most of the decade. In Europe or America, such rapid money expansion would have touched off runaway inflation, but docile Japanese consumers plunked their new wealth into low-interest savings accounts. Over the long term, unrestrained monetary growth created the dangerous run-up in Japanese stock market and real estate prices currently hanging over world financial markets. But the immediate consequence was that in real terms investment capital was free in Japan throughout most of the 1980s, a colossal advantage in an industry as capital intensive as modern electronics. Even more important is the fact that the Japanese had the courage to seize the opportunity and create the extraordinarily aggressive investment pattern we call the Japanese monolithic style that has been so successful in the semiconductor industry.

Policy met with less success in other areas. Efforts to create new generations of Japanese computer designs, while they produced much useful technology, never achieved their main objectives. The position of Japan as technology follower was luridly, and humiliatingly, revealed by the 1982 IBM-FBI sting operation against Hitachi and Mitsubishi, and by Fujitsu's effective admission in the 1987 arbitration settlement of expropriating IBM operating system software.

Finally, the single-minded, thirty-year-long focus on IBM's position in mainframes has left the Japanese industry overcommitted to a commodity manufacturing and a mainframe strategy. Fujitsu and Hitachi are primarily IBM mainframe clone-makers in a shrinking mainframe market, while the other Japanese majors have been sliding into the position of commodity implementers of foreign architectures. The Japanese manufacturing strategy might still carry the field; more than half of all systems components can be characterized as commodities. But they also risk being squeezed into an unattractive high-investment, low-return industry, while architectural leaders in other countries reap the "sweet-spot" profits.

From Japan's standpoint, a far better strategy would be to continue to consolidate their great manufacturing advantage, but at the same time attempt a transition to the much more freewheeling competitive style in keeping with the open, radically decentralized systems environment that will dominate the industry for the next decade. At the moment, Nintendo, Sega, and Sony would appear to be the only Japanese firms in a position to make such a transition successfully.

That said, the accomplishments of Japanese industrial policy in computers have been formidable. Regardless of the outcome of the next round of the computer wars, MITI's policies have succeeded in making it a true two-party contest.

EUROPE

If the Japanese experience—indeed, that in almost every Asian country—confounds the standard warnings of neoclassical economists on the futility of industrial policy, the record in Europe resoundingly confirms them.

Policy initiatives differed from country to country, of course, as did the quality of national technologies. Great Britain emerged from the war with an advanced computer pure research capability that was at least the equal of America's, and in certain respects, still is. Germany also had some outstanding technology, but the capabilities in the rest of Europe were far less formidable. The major countries all have somewhat different political systems and assigned different importance to technological industrial policy at different times, but there are still certain common major themes in the Continent's overall approach, particularly the leading role accorded government policymakers in shaping the industry.

To begin with, every country, at one time or another, adopted roughly the same policy objectives and embraced very many of the same tools as MITI did. They identified computer technology as a major industrial driver for modern industry, became alarmed at the growing dominance of IBM in world computer markets, adopted more or less similar protectionist and government-purchasing policies for the home industry, embarked on large-scale "rationalization" schemes, created joint research consortia, and bestowed massive subsidies on their native companies. But there the similarities end.

No European country enjoyed the extraordinary stability of government and consistency of national purpose that characterized Japan's postwar era. As countries veered from conservative to socialist governments and back again, the favored approach to industrial policy would veer as well between extremes of nationalization, free trade, and varying subsidy regimes. In the late 1960s, for instance, the British Labour government, promising to revive British industry with the "white heat" of technology, created a government-backed semiconductor company, Inmos, that was repudiated, justly, as an expensive failure by the Thatcher government in the 1980s—at the very same time as the new French Socialist government under François Mitterrand was merging the French industry into a single nationalized computer company, CII-Bull.

Just as important, European companies were much more willing to roll over for bureaucratic rationalization schemes than Japanese companies were. Japanese *keiretsu* are organized vertically—a family of companies will include favored parts suppliers, financial services, and distribution arms—but interfamily competition is fierce. The European industrial tradition, on the other hand, as in chemicals and steel, encouraged market-sharing arrangements among nominally competitive companies. Whatever the explanation, companies raised little resistance to the convergence of computer policy in every European country on a "national champion" strategy—effectively merging each national industry into a single company that received the lion's share of subsidies and the favored position in government procurement. The designated champion in England was International Computers, Ltd. (ICL); in Germany, Siemens; Olivetti in Italy; and eventually CII-Bull in France.

What is remarkable is not the failure of each country's national champion, but—as if in a tale of Ricardian revenge—the astonishing speed and devastating extent of the failures. ICL, designated as Britain's computer flagship in the mid-

1970s, was ignominiously sold off to Fujitsu, essentially as a marketing and distribution arm, in 1991. Siemens's position in computers is virtually nonexistent outside the German government market, although it is competitive in the European office machinery market. In France, Bull is almost a parody of industrial policy gone awry. The annual taxpayer subsidy just to cover Bull's losses exceeds the entire American venture capital infusion into new computer start-ups. Most strikingly, despite the most explicit preferential purchasing policies, none of the national champion companies, by the mid-1980s, commanded a majority market share even in its home government market. Indeed, the only European computer success story over the past twenty years was Nixdorf, a German minicomputer company on the DEC model, the one company that received no government assistance. But Nixdorf's capital base was too thin to keep pace technologically and, on the brink of insolvency, it was merged into Siemens in 1989. The failed promise of Nixdorf also demonstrates the lack of flexibility of the European financial system. There has never been a European venture industry of any significance; with investment limited to rigid established channels, sclerotic national champions absorbed, and usually wasted, the available capital. (This should be an explicit warning to analysts, like Harvard's Michael Porter, who have been suggesting that America restructure its investment system along European lines.)

There were critical features of the European policy setting, besides the mercurial dispositions of its governments, that predisposed toward failure. For one thing, a national champion strategy in every country effectively foreclosed any company from pursuing a continentwide strategy, because of protectionist barriers against each other's champion on the one hand and excessive inward focus by the home champion on the other. But none of the home markets by itself was large enough to support the level of investment the modern computer industry demanded. In addition, partly because the nationalistic strategies were so ineffective, partly because European businessmen needed advanced Europe-wide computing solutions, and partly because the American companies like IBM were there so fast after the war, the national champions could never match up against the Europe-wide computer manufacturing and distribution networks put in place by American companies. Even now, DEC Europe is bigger than any European company and IBM Europe is bigger than the top three combined.

In the later 1980s, with the steadily increasing integration of the Common Market, European policies shifted from national to continentwide strategies, involving supranational research consortia like the Siemens-Philips MEGA project and the government-sponsored JESSI project for semiconductors. And in a marked shift of policy, prompted by joint fear of an unstoppable Japanese technological conquest, the Europeans grudgingly accepted IBM and DEC into their consortia. None of the consortia has enjoyed notable success, and all have been very expensive. By the end of the decade, arguably, no European computer company had a lead position in *any* computer technology. Increasingly, they are either, like ICL and Olivetti, simply distributors of Japanese or American equipment, or like Siemens and Bull, licensees and, occasionally, local manufacturing partners for IBM or the Japanese.

THE UNITED STATES

America is often criticized for lacking a high-technology industrial policy. Nothing could be further from the truth. During the postwar period, it has usually had two. One has been run by the military: its ambitions have been, if anything, even broader than MITI's, its financial commitments even more lavish, its objectives as consistently pursued, its successes at least as impressive. The other, more public policy is plied by the official national government. While it has been marked by the same abrupt zigs and zags as in Europe, it has been more often characterized by a marked hostility to large companies, usually in the context of a good deal of macroeconomic irresponsibility.

The first working computers were developed during the war for code-breaking and ballistic calculations. By the war's end, the American military had identified computers as a strategic industry; in a potential conflict with the Soviet Union,

American technology would have to balance the Soviet man-power and supply advantages. There was a sharp increase in military electronics spending at the time of the Korean war, an even sharper spike with the Sputnik hysteria in 1957, and yet another at the outset of the Kennedy administration. Through most of the 1950s, the American government paid for almost all computer R&D, until IBM's spending became an independent force in the last half of the decade.

Conventional caricatures notwithstanding, the military's management of the American electronics sector in the 1950s is extraordinary both for its results and for the remarkable *competence* displayed. The 1950s, indeed, were a golden age of weapons procurement, almost all of them electronics based. The Minuteman missile, the Polaris-class nuclear submarine, and the B-52 bomber—for thirty years the mainstays of the American nuclear triad—were all built in the 1950s. The first paper sketches of the Minuteman missile were made in 1955; it was ready for deployment only five years later, on schedule and under budget. The Polaris submarine's development was even faster. The U-2 spy plane was designed and built in just seventy days. In 1958, the SAGE early-warning and air inter-ception system launched two surface-to-air missiles from a lo-cation 1,500 miles from control that tracked and killed a pilotless drone 100 miles from the launch point, an altogether remarkable accomplishment for the technology of the day.

The military required high-reliability computing, exten-sive miniaturization, and complex systems skills. The quanti-ties required were small by commercial standards, and price was no object. Since technology was viewed as America's main advantage over the Russians, constant pushing against tech-nological frontiers was considered essential to national pres-ervation. A better greenhouse for technology advancement can hardly be imagined, and the American computer industry was prodded along in forced-march stages. IBM's entry into electronic computers was largely underwritten by military contracts—its work on just two projects, including building the computers for the SAGE system, supplied about half of its computer revenues throughout the 1950s. Military pressure for reliability and miniaturization was also the major driver for the semiconductor industry, and at various times, the military absorbed almost all the semiconductors America could produce. When the Minuteman program was accelerated in the early days of the Kennedy administration, by itself it consumed a fifth of the nation's integrated circuit output. Bell Lab's transistor and Intel's microprocessor may be the only major computer inventions of the postwar period that were not underwritten in some explicit way by the American military.

With the commercial computer boom of the late 1950s, private company computer R&D spending began to catch up to the military's, and by 1965, IBM's computer R&D budget alone exceeded that of the entire federal government. But the federal contribution has always been important; until the 1970s at least, it dwarfed that of MITI or of European governments on either a gross or a per capita basis. Even in the 1970s, at the height of MITI's research involvement in Japan and when the American technological commitment was flagging badly, direct government funding of computer research and development in the two countries was still about equal. Some analysts also include Bell Labs, before the 1982 consent decree, in the government spending total. With AT&T's communications monopoly, research funding at Bell Labs was effectively financed by a national tax on telephone calls.

The military emphasis of American technology has been much criticized, and deservedly so. Unlike MITI in Japan, the commercial position of American companies has never been a prime concern—in the late 1960s, in fact, Congress expressly forbade so-called dual-purpose funding. In industries such as machine tools, indeed, the military emphasis may have been disastrous. American companies lead the world in high-performance, high-complexity, handcrafted tools for, say, milling airplane wings, but have suffered catastrophic market share losses to the Germans and Japanese in more prosaic, mass-market equipment lines. To an extent, the same phenomenon appears in electronics. Handcrafted semiconductor or display technologies, and the lack of cost discipline characteristic of military procurement, served companies poorly, particularly in consumer electronics.

But the argument that military involvement damaged the

American *computer* industry is much harder to make. Military funding agencies, particularly the Defense Advanced Research Project Agency, or DARPA, have amassed a truly remarkable record of identifying and husbanding technologies of future importance, with a relatively small budget (just short of $2 billion in 1992, or only about 3 percent of the total military procurement budget). Parallel processing, networked computers, software-based design tools, and a host of other technologies that are critical to the decentralized computing environment of the 1990s were all nursed through their early development by the military. The extraordinary pace of technological change in computing places such a premium on high-intensity advanced research that it may overbalance any consequent inattention to refining and honing current products. Just as important, the formidable commercial skills of IBM were virtually an autonomous force in the American industry, constantly disciplining any company that allowed military procurement to dull its competitive skills.

The sheer adventurousness of the military's funding programs is also remarkable. We have seen how DARPA funded Bill Joy at Berkeley to create the Berkeley UNIX. Joy did not have a Ph.D., was not a student or a member of the faculty, and was not associated with any company; the fact that he was a genius was enough for DARPA. The military's willingness to experiment with unconventional approaches in small start-ups was the seedbed not only of the Silicon Valley model but of the American venture capital industry as well. The military broke the trail, and the financial industry followed.

The *overt* American industrial policy, however, is in stark contrast to the one pursued by the military in computers. For most of the past thirty years, American policy has been distinctly hostile to big companies of almost every variety. Intellectuals were already mocking organization men early in the 1950s; and from Eisenhower's warning against a military-industrial complex, through Kennedy's confrontation with the steel industry, to the war in Vietnam and the rise of the counterculture on American campuses, American policy focused primarily on curbing the power of American corporations, rather than worrying about international competitiveness.

In many industries, such as in the flaccid auto and steel businesses, the jaundiced view of big American companies was amply justified. But in high technology, a persistent, indiscriminate attack on bigness per se, whether or not success was fairly won, did serious damage. The Justice Department, for example, forced the Bell companies to make their technologies broadly available to all comers in 1956 at a very low charge and forced Bell Labs to give up its patent rights to the transistor, even though it had already licensed it broadly. The 1982 consent decree, from a national technology standpoint, was much more damaging, effectively ending the leading role Bell Labs had played in ensuring American postwar dominance in electronics and subjecting American telecommunications policy to a decade of highly idiosyncratic judicial mismanagement. Xerox and other companies were similarly hounded. The government's general hostility to proprietary technologies and muddled patent administration also contributed substantially to the American predisposition for generous patent cross-licensing and lax intellectual property enforcement, vulnerabilities that were enthusiastically exploited by the Japanese at every opportunity.

The thirteen-year-long antitrust action against IBM was probably most damaging of all, blunting IBM's traditional competitive instincts against both American start-ups and prowling foreign companies. Antitrust concerns were partly at the root of the company's reluctance to exploit fully its software and hardware technology in the PC contest and a major factor in IBM's unwillingness to act against Amdahl when he transferred so much IBM know-how to Fujitsu. Ironically, if the antitrust suit had been settled quickly and IBM divided into smaller companies, the company's shareholders might well have been better off—*intelligently* broken up, that is; the Justice Department's plan made no economic sense at all. As it was, the protracted war against the jewel of America's technology sector had no good consequences. The same Republican and Democratic administrations that hounded IBM also imposed sharp reductions in military research budgets and pursued national macroeconomic policies that virtually destroyed the possibility of reliable long-term industrial financing. All in all, it was a sorry performance.

16

Toward an American
Technology Policy

The struggle for control of the computer industry is now a two-party contest between the United States and Japan. Europe has long since dropped out of the running. The other important Asian high technology countries—Korea and Taiwan—chart a gingerly independent course between the two main players.

We think it extremely important that America maintain, or regain, its lead in computer technology. Electronics is now the biggest manufacturing industry in the world, poised to pass the trillion-dollar mark shortly. It is a high-growth, high-wage industry, with important technological spin-offs. A country with a strong vendor's position in computer technology enjoys an inherent advantage in almost every other technology-based, productivity-driven industry. We also believe that a strong technology infrastructure will have many noneconomic spin-off effects, such as in education. Finally, to the degree it is still a concern in the post–Cold War world, America's technology position has always been central to its national security.

For America to win in computer technology, it will be necessary, but not sufficient, for companies to adopt and execute the right strategies. But they will also need help from the government—although not handouts or protection. Government, including America's, has always been deeply involved in computer technology. Over the past few decades, however, American government policy has been more consistently hostile to technology businesses than supportive. Only government can create an environment that makes it possible for businesses to invest and succeed over the long term in high technology. Only government can remove the barriers to technological competitiveness that government has raised. Only government can support the precompetitive basic research capabilities that have fueled America's technological successes. And only government can act on the scale that may occasionally be necessary to counter national cartels controlling critical technology components. In this chapter, we lay out the realistic requirements for American success in high technology industries, the obstacles to achieving them, and what government can do to help.

The shift from mainframe computing to decentralized, componentized systems has been accompanied by a slow drift of manufacturing revenues and employment away from traditional American firms such as IBM and DEC toward Asian commodity component manufacturers. Over the past ten years, total American employment of U.S. computer hardware companies has dropped by almost a third, from 320,000 to 225,000; that's about the same size decrease as the employment cuts at just two companies, IBM and DEC, much of it in middle-level managerial ranks. The total world electronics industry, now about $800 billion, is growing at a rate of 8 percent a year; the American electronics industry is growing at a rate of 5 percent a year. On a gross basis, therefore, America has been slowly losing market share over an extended period of time. Slow share losses over an extended period become very significant. Over the past decade, for example, the American share of global computer exports has fallen from 39 percent to 24 percent, while Japan's has risen from 4 percent to 18 percent. In microelectronics, America had an 18 percent share of global exports in 1980 compared to Japan's 13 percent; now the two countries are in a standoff at 22 percent each.

But the loss of American market share has not turned into the rout that many feared only a few years ago; there has indeed been some recent stabilization in critical areas like semiconductors. The high technology contest between America and Japan, in fact, appears to have reached a highly unstable, quite unbalanced standoff. The Japanese are totally dominant in those segments of the industry, such as commodity semiconductors and flat panel displays, most suited to their monolithic manufacturing and investing style. American firms have equivalent dominance in those segments of the industry suited to the Silicon Valley architectural competitive model, such as microprocessors, systems design, and software, which are among the most profitable in the industry.

Neither country can be satisfied with its position. A bad, and quite plausible, outcome for the United States would be for its computer companies to be squeezed down to a small number of highly profitable architectural boutiques, selling designs into an almost totally commoditized industry, more or less like the Italian fashion industry. For Japan, being relegated to the position of the world's supplier of highly capital intensive, low-profit commodity products such as DRAMs—in effect, renting its vast accumulated savings at very low returns—would be an equally bad outcome, and not at all an implausible one. Thus the mortal danger to each is that the other will gain sufficient control to channel the industry in the direction most favorable to its own skill base.

The Japanese are certainly aware of the danger and have been investing heavily in architecturally related technologies, although only a small number of Japanese firms have yet shown signs of being architecturally sophisticated competitors. We think it is wise to assume, however, that the recent financial disturbances in Japan will hasten the transition of the Japanese into more balanced, and therefore even more formidable, competitors, since the distortions in past investing practices should now be clear. American firms tempted to relax their guard by the apparent hiccup in Japanese capital spending may be in for some very unpleasant surprises.

To win the computer wars of the next decade, America will need a much better balanced industry, particularly as the battleground shifts to more consumer-oriented and mass-produced products, where industry leaders will need to combine lean manufacturing and architectural skills. We expect, for instance, that there will be much tighter bundling of product implementations and architectural solutions in palmtop computers than in desktop systems. More precisely, to win, America must:

• Maintain its position as the industry's architectural standard-setter

• Achieve parity with Japanese lean manufacturers as implementors in architecturally important components and in products where architectures and implementations are tightly bundled

• Retain domestic capabilities in commodity semiconductors and other critical components sufficient to defeat foreign cartels, while conceding mainstream production to monolithic Asian, or government-supported European, suppliers

There is reason for concern in every area. Maintaining America's lead in innovative architectural, design, and software-based technologies will require a continued flow of resources to refresh the industry's rich basic research capabilities. Cutbacks in defense research spending after a decade of strong growth, a slowing of R&D spending by American firms, and an apparent upwelling of congressional hostility to university-based research programs are not good auguries.

Achieving parity with Asian lean manufacturers, however, is more possible than many analysts thought even a few years ago. IBM's OEM peripheral manufacturing operations, its new PC subsidiary (presumably shorn of old-style Armonk overhead), IBM-Lexmark, Hewlett-Packard, Motorola, and Compaq are the nucleus of a potentially formidable engineering and lean manufacturing competitive presence tightly integrated with the American architectural standard-setters. But it is still much too small compared to the Japanese consumer electronics giants and will need continued nourishment and expansion.

Finally, competing head-to-head with Japanese or Korean monolithic manufacturers in commodity products like DRAMs or flat-panel displays would be a foolish waste of investment resources. The absence of *any* domestic commodity manufacturing base, however, would be very dangerous, given the behavior of the Japanese DRAM cartel in the late 1980s. We believe that the reorganization of IBM inevitably places its high-cost commodity semiconductor operations at risk. When decentralized lean manufacturing IBM divisions start buying their semiconductors on the open market, as sooner or later they must, the captive semiconductor operations will be exposed to harsh price competition and, we expect, large financial losses. Loss of a semiconductor manufacturing base of that scale would leave America dangerously exposed to a resurgent DRAM cartel, possibly organized jointly by the Japanese and Koreans. (There have been more unlikely industrial alliances in pursuit of windfall profits.)

None of these challenges is beyond the skills and capabilities of the best American companies, but all will require a very healthy pace of investment. We are concerned, however, that the political behavior of both ruling parties may make such a stream of investment impossible. Specific government policies in support of high technology will be useless unless the government reduces the powerful policy bias toward current consumption over investment that pervades American policy.

PREEMPTING INVESTMENT

American macroeconomic policy has been characterized by chronic government budget deficits since the mid-1960s, typically running between 1 percent and 3 percent of GNP. In the early years of the Reagan administration, large tax cuts coupled with a sharp increase in defense spending pushed deficits to more than 5 percent of GNP. Deficits returned to approximately normal levels by 1989, but soared again with the savings and loan bailout. In principle, the defense spending spike and the bank bailout were onetime events. But, as of mid-1992, it appears that deficits will not be reduced as savings and loan spending drops. Long-term trends built into the federal domestic budget portend deficit levels at the 5 percent to 6 percent level of GNP, and possibly much higher, for the foreseeable future.

Health care is a good example. Some 40 percent of all health-care spending is funded by various levels of government, and government policies on coverage, benefits, payment programs, and mandated private insurer programs are the most important force determining the direction of the industry. In 1987, health care consumed about 9 percent of GNP, the highest rate in any country; by 1992, health care's share of GNP had risen to 14 percent. The increase in hospital workers in 1991 alone was about the same as total employment in the computer hardware industry. The Commerce Department forecasts that health-care expenditures will continue to grow by 12 to 13 percent; at that rate of increase, health care will be near 20 percent of GNP by the end of the decade.

Technically, the budget deficits themselves are not the issue; what counts is a chronic federal policy tilt toward consumption over investment, which is no longer sustainable. American business investment was relatively healthy through the 1980s, but was heavily supported by inflows of foreign capital—Japan and Germany supplied most of the world's surplus investment capital. By the middle of 1992, the American economy and much of the rest of the industrialized world have slipped into a prolonged period of economic stagnation. Japan is now repatriating capital to deal with its own looming savings-and-loan-scale banking crisis, while Germany is struggling to fund its very expensive unification/welfare program for the East.

In a sagging economy, in other words, America will have to fund its budget deficits and investment requirements from its own pocket; without a drastic reordering of federal fiscal policy and spending priorities, investment will necessarily get short shrift. If America allocates 20 percent of its GNP to health care while our competitors allocate only half that much, other countries will necessarily have a major industrial investment advantage—and, of course, health care is only the most obvious example of the government's anti-investment tilt. In the 1992 presidential campaign the candidates of both parties dutifully paid lip service to the need for more industrial investment, but at the same time both proposed to expand federal health-care coverage and both promised not to reduce benefits. Neither candidate, that is, was really serious about investment. Grandiose visions of a government-led renaissance of industrial investment are a chimera unless both political parties agree to address the current proentitlement, proconsumption, and anti-investment biases that pervade government policy-making. That said, we turn now to the specific policies that will be appropriate for an investment-friendly administration.

A PROTECHNOLOGY POLICY AGENDA

The essential requirement is to recognize, first, that government has always had a prominent role in the development of American high technology, whether in computers, biotechnology, or aerospace, and second, that policies have been most successful when they have been limited and facilitative rather than overreaching and prescriptive.

Free-enterprise zealots in the Bush administration, particularly in its early years, attempted to destroy the government's leading technological development role. The policymaking nadir came with the firing of DARPA's Craig Fields in 1990; Fields had been closely involved with almost every major DARPA technology initiative of the previous decade. Also during the Bush administration, there was a flattening out of federal technology R&D spending after a period of strong growth during the defense buildup of the Reagan years.

While the policy preferences of a Clinton administration are not clear as this is written, we are concerned that the statements of his advisers (or people claiming to be advisers) betray an indiscriminate taste for the kind of subsidized, cartelized *dirigisme* that has been the downfall of the European industry.

(There are Clinton advisers, such as Robert Kuttner, who inexplicably view Europe as a model for technology policy.) Some campaign puffery sounded depressingly like the "white heat of technology" speeches so relished by Harold Wilson's failed British Labour government of the 1960s.

We believe there is a realistic path for government policy between the virginal free-marketism of the Republican Right and the Fabian impulses of the Democratic Left. We organize our suggested agenda by the three priorities identified above—maintaining architectural leadership; expanding lean manufacturing capabilities; and creating a defense capability against commodity cartels.

BASIC RESEARCH

America's architectural leadership rests on its unmatched basic research capabilities and institutions. Such a national resource takes a long time to create, and fortunately, takes a long time to decay. We have serious concerns about the continuing health of America's basic research establishment. At the same time, however, we find the tendency toward self-interested shrillness on the part of the computer industry and science establishment when comparing Japanese and American technologies occasionally reminiscent of the American military's annual compendia of Soviet military prowess, and equally damaging to credibility. American research spending slipped in the 1970s, grew strongly in the first part of the 1980s before slowing and finally flattening out for the past several years. That is not a crisis, but there are still ample grounds for concern, since we believe that industrial R&D is due to slow down sharply even as the government is pulling back. The effects of a double withdrawal could be quite serious indeed.

A leading government role in basic research is essential on purely economic grounds. There are ample data to demonstrate that the social returns of basic research exceed those to the firm. That is to say, the actual products that will eventually emerge from good basic research are quite unpredictable, and even when good product opportunities appear, they may not be suitable for the firm that sponsored the research. The normal course for a firm is to focus its resources where returns are surer—on product development rather than on basic research. In fact, in Japan, where the government funds a much lower portion of the R&D budget, the portion of R&D devoted to product development is much higher than in America.

The major exceptions to typical private firm research behavior in America are Bell Labs, IBM, and on a much smaller scale, Xerox PARC. Until the breakup of AT&T in 1982, Bell Labs was a kind of quasi-public research facility funded by a small tax on telephones; since 1982, however, Bell Labs has been shrinking and becoming much more commercially focused. For its part, IBM was a kind of world institution that transcended economic rules of any kind. While IBM has not yet cut its R&D spending significantly, Akers has already announced that it will shift away from its traditional basic research emphasis. Based on our analysis of IBM's future prospects, we think it possible, if misguided, that IBM's R&D budget could be cut very sharply. Those are two huge holes to fill, and there will be many other smaller ones, as traditional firms cut overhead. Xerox's new chief executive, Paul Allaire, however, seems committed to maintaining the PARC investment tradition.

The federal government has amply demonstrated that it knows how to run a good basic research establishment. The records of DARPA, the National Science Foundation, and the National Institutes of Health are outstanding. Just as the American computer industry has been nourished with government research dollars, in a directly parallel case the world position of American pharmaceuticals has been dependent on federal funding of basic research and early-stage technology development, primarily through peer-reviewed research grants to university laboratories. The common characteristic in both instances is that the research is funded through elite bodies of experts, pursuing autonomous long-term objectives, with little political oversight, an uncommon arrangement for American institutions, but one that has clearly worked well. Finally, the American interventions in both the computer and pharmaceutical cases were in keeping with political tradition by concentrating much more on fundamental technologies than did the company-focused initiatives of Europe and Japan.

In the near term, we believe there are ample funds that could be made available for basic research simply by canceling high-visibility engineering projects such as the Space Shuttle—probably as good an example as any of the consequences of politically directed technology spending. We are also concerned by an antiresearch bias that has recently been evinced at a series of well-publicized congressional investigations of university spending abuses and alleged scientific fraud. While there is no excusing fraud and abuse, we are concerned that the consequences will be reduced funding and increased political oversight, to the great detriment of the country. Finally, we should like to see serious attention paid to the rules by which government and university-funded research becomes commercialized. We offer no specific proposals, except to note that it is an area fraught with confusion and conflicts of interest.

In the last analysis, there is no escaping the reality that, to maintain American architectural leadership in electronics and computers, a substantial and predictable flow of federal research funds is a necessity. Moreover, funding levels will have to increase steadily to make up for the partial withdrawals of IBM and Bell Labs from their traditional basic research commitments.

TECHNOLOGICAL PUMP-PRIMING

The United States needs the information age equivalent of the interstate highway system, a digitally switched, very high bandwidth information network, using fiber optic, microwave, infrared, satellite, and other relevant technologies. Communication and cable television companies are creating improved networks as fast as they can afford to, but at a pace much slower than would be ideal. The total cost of an adequate system is unknown, but is usually estimated to be in the range of $200 billion; ten years is a realistic construction schedule. We believe that the federal government should play the leading role in getting such a network installed, and we believe it can do so without doing violence to traditional American government-industry spheres of responsibility. Undertaking such a project would be a major boost, not only to the American electronic manufacturing industry, but to the productivity and competitiveness of American industry in general.

There are two major obstacles to building a world-class national fiber optic information network. The first is money. Funding could be made instantly available, however, by changing utility depreciation schedules to create greater cash flow for new construction. There are ample regulatory mechanisms already in place to assure that funds are properly spent. While the cost, again, is unknown, the range of estimates centers around an average $10/month per telephone rate increase for businesses and $5/month for residences—in effect, a tax on telephone service consumption directed to new electronic investment. The inflationary or depressive effects of such a tax would depend entirely on what else was happening in the economy. If health-care costs were spiraling toward 20 percent of national income, any new tax would be a strain; if they could be brought under control, there would be plenty of room.

The second obstacle is in sorting out the politics of the winners and losers from a national information network. Telephone companies, newspapers, cable television companies, broadcasters, print advertisers, and many others have major stakes in accelerating or delaying a modern electronic information transmission capability. Hewing a sensible policy line between legitimate transition concerns, naked self-interest, and the national interest will be very difficult, but that's what a government is supposed to be for.

Finally, the federal government could give a helpful regulatory boost even to present network-building efforts by adopting standards to ensure the compatibility and appropriate interconnectivity of public and private networks. Some of the recent initiatives of the regional Bell operating companies presage possibly incompatible regional communication networks, which would be a great waste of resources. Any such standards-setting exercise, of course, must walk the fine line between "good" standards and bad ones. Standardization of railroad gauges, for instance, was a powerful impulse to growth and connectivity. But standards such as the CCITT fax standard has locked an important technology into a lowest common denominator solution. Some standards, that is, create opportunity while others limit it.

These are all very hard issues that can be solved only by government. The patchwork web of regulatory obstacles and subsidies was created by government, and can be cleared away only by effective government action. There are, we concede, severe doubts that consistent, clear-sighted, and courageous policy-making is still within the capabilities of the "oozing behemoth" that our federal government has become. But if the new administration is concerned about national technology policy, these issues should be front and center on the policy agenda.

If a national information network initiative could actually get under way, it would be a great spur to American computer and industrial electronic manufacturing. The digital switches required are actually very powerful stand-alone computers. The use of advanced decentralized computing applications would be greatly accelerated, very much to the benefit of American industrial competitiveness; consumer computing applications should increase apace. We believe that an advanced information network is sufficiently important that it should be the best in the world and use the best products and devices regardless of where they are made. But we also believe that communication technology is an area of great American strength, and that the national industry will fare extremely well in a nonprotectionist procurement environment. An important but transitory benefit is that during the ten-year construction period, probably half of the new jobs created would be in construction and other blue-collar industries.

ANTICARTEL INSURANCE

The dangers of cartelization exist in a few critical components where investment requirements are very high and free-market competitive profits are very low. DRAMs are the quintessential case; there are only a small number of high-volume manufacturers of advanced DRAMs in the world; if one country can control the DRAM industry, there is a real risk that it will control advanced semiconductor process technologies generally and manufacturing equipment to boot. We do not believe that the dangers of cartelization can be legislated away. Trade vigilance, of course, is a necessity, but other steps can be taken.

In general, we have little confidence in industry-government syndicalist planning exercises, and we don't think the government should go into the DRAM business. But the monolithic management style that fits commodity semiconductor production makes it one of the few electronic industries that actually lends itself to such long-term, top-down national-level planning. The question will require immediate attention if IBM's commodity semiconductor divisions begin to run very large losses, which we consider likely.

We make only the most general proposals, in the interest of limning the range of possibilities rather than making specific recommendations. We see three alternative, or possibly complementary, courses of action:

• Direct government subvention of a strategic semiconductor process and manufacturing equipment research and development capability, freely licensed to all American companies. (Two or three competitive institutions roughly the size of Sematech—$100 million annually—would probably be sufficient.)

• Standby authorization for national semiconductor purchasing cartels, when circumstances warrant

• Least intrusively, vigilance to ensure that new transnational partnerships in commodity semiconductor production locate enough facilities in the United States under control of the American partner to forestall foreign cartelization. (Standby legislation might be required to prevent an American partner from cooperating with a cartel for contractual reasons.)

We should be very cautious about extending the DRAM model to other commodities, like flat panel displays, although we don't deny the possibility of its applicability. Anticartel provisions such as the ones suggested above will feed directly into the well-entrenched political instinct for logrolling or shoveling taxpayer funds at losing industries. We make even the DRAM recommendation with the greatest caution and would hesitate greatly before expanding the argument in any way.

Finally, we make no specific proposals for trade agreements. We believe, however, that a commitment to open markets is far more productive in the long run than protectionism; antidumping provisions, especially in the electronics industry, create bizarre unintended consequences and run counter to the basic economics of the industry. It is essential, however, to maintain pressure on the Japanese government and industry to continue to open its markets equally with America's. We do not believe that Japanese electronic markets are truly open, but we also note that American firms like Intel that have invested aggressively in local Japanese-style distribution and servicing networks have been far more successful in increasing Japanese sales than firms relying solely on trade negotiations.

None of the measures we have discussed, from basic research through anticartel insurance, is heroic, requires the creation of huge new government bureaucracies, or violates existing norms of the American structure of political and economic institutions. All are well within the realm of American political possibility, given intelligent and committed political leadership. Finally, none of them will be as important for the future industrial health of the country or as difficult to execute as the reordering of federal allocation priorities, such as reducing health-care spending, that will make a healthy industrial investment regime possible in the first place. If investment capital is available and federal allocation mechanisms are not excessively distorting, good consequences will inevitably flow. If investment capital is not available, no amount of microeconomic tinkering can produce useful results.

OTHER POLICIES

We close with some brief comments on other policy areas relevant to American technological leadership. In setting out our primary recommendations above, we attempted to confine ourselves to policy changes where the mechanisms for action were relatively clear-cut. In this section, we list other policy or statutory changes we feel would be desirable, but where we recognize that the possibilities for change and the mechanisms for effecting it are not at all clear.

ANTITRUST.

As this book goes to press, we expect the Justice Department to file an antitrust suit against Microsoft. There is at least a legitimate argument, although it is obviously yet to be proven, that Microsoft has used its control over systems software to disadvantage its applications software competitors. We do not quarrel, therefore, with the principle of the anticipated action. On the basis of history, however, the Justice Department will harass Microsoft for the next decade without ever reaching a conclusion in the case, to the detriment of everyone except lawyers. (The fact that the original 1990 case papers accuse Microsoft of conspiring with *IBM* to monopolize PC software betrays fundamental misunderstandings.) We would plead for a better mechanism than the law courts for such actions, perhaps a statutory arbitration proceeding with expert fact-finding.

IMMIGRATION.

Foreigners are drawn to America's basic research institutions and high-technology companies. Fairly or not, America has long benefited from a "brain drain" of other countries' best and brightest seeking a world-class educational and working environment. Worries occasionally surface that other countries will benefit disproportionately from America's open-armed policy toward foreign students. The reality is often the reverse. Because these students usually stay in the United States if at all possible, it is actually America who benefits. However, the Immigration Service frequently forces highly qualifed foreigners doing important work to leave the country when their visas expire. From the admittedly narrow perspective of America's technological self-interest, there would be great dividends from a broad policy of skill-based waivers of standard policies and quotas.

INTELLECTUAL PROPERTY.

Intellectual property enforcement and company vigilance are much improved in recent years, but there are still glaring deficiencies. Recent proposals on law reform by the Advisory Commission on Patent Law Reform seem to us to go in the right direction. But even with a well-crafted legal structure, patent disputes are far too lengthy and resource consuming; as in antitrust, courts of law, even specialized ones as in patent practice, may simply be the wrong type of forum for resolving such issues.

CORPORATE GOVERNANCE.

In general, we believe the record of large American technology companies in the 1970s and 1980s suggests that existing corporate governance mechanisms have served shareholders and employees abysmally. We applaud the recent trend among institutional shareholders to monitor more closely their holdings and suggest that director responsibility issues may be an area for substantial legal or regulatory reform. Although markets regularly punish shareholders for management failings, managers and directors not only escape unscathed, but are often also paid large sums to cushion their failures.

MONITORING JAPAN.

Despite the much greater economic diversification in Japan in recent years, just six companies control some 25 percent of the Japanese economy. While it is harder for them to act in concert, they have a long tradition of doing so. The penchant for quasi-militarized, win-at-all-costs business strategies, while perhaps reduced, is still evident. We make no recommendations aside from noting the importance of careful monitoring, particularly of the flow of Japanese funds to public institutions, to campaigns for public office, to families of public officials, and to former public officials in a position to influence American policy.

CONTAINING BILL GATES.

We would be remiss not to comment on the degree of personal sway that Bill Gates is beginning to exercise over the computer industry. Although Microsoft's sales are much smaller than those of big hardware companies, it stands, or soon may stand, athwart most of the industry's critical architectural control points. Outside of Microsoft, Gates himself is investing personally, and heavily, in a striking number of new company start-ups and initial stock offerings. Gates's strategy is very ambitious, and he may well stumble in the next few years, but for the moment he has a uniquely powerful personal influence over the industry's future, not far from, say, J. P. Morgan's in the turn-of-the-century steel industry. We raise this point with great ambivalence, for Gates is a singular national competitive asset. In theory, intelligent antitrust policy could, and should, prevent Gates's, or Microsoft's, exercising excessive power; in practice, our government tends to destroy its antitrust targets, not reform them. The best policy, we feel, is first, not to discourage the countervailing combinations that may be necessary to keep the industry competitive; and second—and far more important—to maintain a research and investment climate that ensures such a rapid generation of new technologies and new competitive entrants that no stakeholder, even one as powerful as Bill Gates, can stifle the industry's progress.

EUROPEAN TECHNOLOGY.

We are concerned by the headlong technological decline of Europe; we do not believe that a moribund European technology sector is in the best interests of the United States, but we have no specific proposals to offer. We recommend the issue, however, as a possible field of inquiry for others. At the very least, Europe may represent an opportunity for component partnerships to maintain a balance between Asian and Western electronic commodity production capacity. To some extent, such partnerships are already forming, largely under the impetus of IBM and DEC.

GRADUATE EDUCATION.

We have commented extensively on the need for a greater flow of funds into basic technology research. Here we merely add that an appropriate portion of such funding should be earmarked directly or indirectly for the support of graduate students. Our observation is that the most fecund research institutions spawn many generations of new graduate students who are a critical refreshing resource to the country's technological talent pool; other institutions produce far fewer graduate students for comparable amounts of spending. It is the talent that is important to the country, not bricks-and-mortar laboratories.

Public Education.
The poor quality of American education is much commented on. For perspective, however, it is important to realize that the computer industry itself is very small. About 225,000 people are employed in America by computer manufacturers and about 130,000 by software companies. The output of America's elite universities is more than adequate to refresh a work force of that size; indeed, it is not widely understood that newly minted physics and math Ph.D.s have a hard time finding jobs. The necessity for improved education in primary and secondary schools is not for the sake of American technological leadership, but for the students' own sake—so they can live happy and productive lives in an increasingly technological society. In an information-oriented society, the unskilled will be at a painful disadvantage, even more so than at the present. A good education is the least we owe our children.

The computer wars are a two-party contest between America and Japan, with Europe and the rest of Asia as supporting players. It is the most competitive, swiftest-moving, and hardest-fought industrial battle in history. With sound strategies, good execution, continued investment, and wise public policy, it is also a battle that America can win.

FURTHER READING

The historical analysis and strategic synthesis that we have set forth in this book are for the most part not based on secondary sources. We set out below, however, a select list of works that we found helpful and could recommend to readers seeking further information on particular topics.

Anchordoguy, Marie. *Computers, Inc.: Japan's Challenge to IBM.* Cambridge, Mass.: Harvard University Press, 1989. A comprehensive and balanced analysis of Japanese industrial policy toward the computer industry.

Braun, Ernest, and Stuart MacDonald. *Revolution in Miniature.* 2d ed. New York: Cambridge University Press, 1982. The best available general history of the development of semiconductor and computer technology.

Brooks, Frederick P., Jr. *The Mythical Man-Month: Essays in Software Engineering.* Reading, Mass.: Addison-Wesley,

1975. Mainframe-oriented, but an enduring classic, full of wisdom and insight.

Chposky, James, and Ted Leonsis. *Blue Magic: The People, Power, and Politics Behind the IBM Personal Computer.* New York: Facts on File, 1988. A sourcebook for the early history of the IBM PC.

Clark, Kim B., and Takahiro Fujimoto. *Product Development Performance: Strategy, Organization, and Management in the World Auto Industry.* Cambridge, Mass.: Harvard Business School Press, 1992. An exploration of the success requirements for global competitiveness in the automobile industry; many insights into Japanese competitive methods, particularly the relation between product design and manufacturing.

Comerford, Richard. "How DEC Developed Alpha." *IEEE Spectrum* (July 1992): 26–31. Case history of the development of today's fastest microprocessor, including many false starts.

Cringeley, Robert X. *Accidental Empires.* Reading, Mass.: Addison-Wesley, 1992. A gossipy but insightful account of Silicon Valley's sudden millionaires.

Ferguson, Charles H. "Computers and the Coming of the U.S. Keiretsu." *Harvard Business Review* (July–August 1990): 55–72. The case for pessimism for American computer-makers; superseded by the discussion here.

Fisher, Franklin M., John J. McGowan, and Joan E. Greenwood. *Folded, Spindled, and Mutilated: Economic Analysis and U.S. vs. IBM.* Cambridge, Mass.: MIT Press, 1985. Economists dissect the Justice Department's antitrust suit against IBM. Fisher was IBM's chief witness for the defense, but the case for the wrongheadedness of the government's suit is overwhelming.

Flamm, Kenneth H. *Creating the Computer.* Washington, D.C.: The Brookings Institution, 1987. And Flamm, Kenneth H. *Targeting the Computer.* Washington, D.C.: The Brookings Institution, 1987. Companion volumes that taken together are solid histories of the computer industry with particular emphasis on the interaction between the industry and governments in America, Europe, and Japan.

Ichbiah, Daniel, and Susan L. Knepper. *The Making of Microsoft.* Rockland, Calif.: Prima, 1991. A sourcebook on Microsoft, particularly for its earlier period.

National Advisory Committee on Semiconductors. *Annual Reports to the President and the Congress.* Washington, D.C.: USGPO, 1990–1992. Compendia of basic data on critical semiconductor technologies, and many recommendations for government policy, including much wheat with the chaff.

National Science Board, Committee for Industrial Support for R&D. *The Competitive Strength of U.S. Industrial Science and Technology: Strategic Issues.* Washington, D.C.: National Science Foundation, August 1992. An R&D sourcebook.

National Science Foundation, National Research Council, and National Academy of Engineering. *Science and Engineering Indicators.* Washington, D.C.: USGPO, various years. The state of the world and of America in science and engineering.

Rappaport, Andrew S., and Shmuel Halevi. "The Computerless Computer Company." *Harvard Business Review* (July–August 1991): 69–80. The optimists' rebuttal to the Ferguson article cited above. Also superseded by the discussion here.

Rose, Frank. *West of Eden: The End of Innocence at Apple Computer.* New York: Viking, 1989. The rise, fall, and recovery of Apple.

Smith, Douglas K., and Robert C. Alexander. *Fumbling the Future: How Xerox Invented, Then Ignored the First Personal Computer.* New York: William Morrow, 1988. An extraordinary tale of big business incompetence.

Tanenbaum, Andrew S. *Structured Computer Organization.* 3d ed. Englewood Cliffs, N.J.: Prentice-Hall, 1990. An unusually lucid text on the basics of modern computer technology. Contains clear discussions of recent topics such as RISC and parallel processing. See also the same author's *Computer Networks* (Englewood Cliffs, N.J.: Prentice-Hall, 1991).

Wallace, James, and Jim Erickson. *Hard Drive: Bill Gates and the Making of the Microsoft Empire.* New York: John Wiley &

Sons, 1992. Relies heavily on *The Making of Microsoft*, by Ichbiah and Knepper, but contains some more recent material.

Watson, Thomas J., Jr., and Peter Petre. *Father, Son & Co.: My Life at IBM and Beyond.* New York: Bantam, 1990. The glory days at IBM.

Womack, James P., Daniel T. Jones, and Daniel Roos. *The Machine That Changed the World.* New York: Rawson Associates, 1990. The basic text on the Japanese lean production system.

INDEX